TOTALLY
UNINHIBITED

Books by Lawrence J. Quirk

Robert Francis Kennedy
The Films of Joan Crawford
The Films of Ingrid Bergman
The Films of Paul Newman
The Films of Fredric March
Foreword: *Photoplay* Magazine Anthology
The Films of William Holden
The Great Romantic Films
The Films of Robert Taylor
The Films of Ronald Colman
The Films of Warren Beatty
The Films of Myrna Loy
The Films of Gloria Swanson
The Complete Films of Bette Davis
(Update from 1965)
The Complete Films of Katharine Hepburn
(Update from 1970)
Claudette Colbert: An Illustrated Biography
Lauren Bacall: Her Films and Career
Jane Wyman: The Actress and the Woman
The Complete Films of William Powell
Margaret Sullavan: Child of Fate
Norma: The Story of Norma Shearer
Some Lovely Image (*A novel*)
Fasten Your Seat Belts: The Passionate Life of Bette Davis
Totally Uninhibited: The Life and Wild Times of Cher

TOTALLY UNINHIBITED

THE LIFE
AND WILD TIMES
OF CHER

Lawrence J. Quirk

WILLIAM MORROW AND COMPANY, INC.
NEW YORK

It is the policy of William Morrow and Company, Inc., and its imprints and affiliates, recognizing the importance of preserving what has been written, to print the books we publish on acid-free paper, and we exert our best efforts to that end.

Library of Congress Cataloging-in-Publication Data

Quirk, Lawrence J.
    Totally uninhibited: the life and wild times of Cher / by Lawrence J. Quirk.
        p.   cm.
    Includes bibliographical references and index.
    ISBN 0-688-09822-3
    1. Cher, 1946–   .   2. Motion picture actors and actresses—United States—Biography.   3. Singers—United States—Biography.
    I. Title.
    PN2287.C534Q85   1991
    782.42164'092—dc20
    [B]   91-4385
                                                                                        CIP

Printed in the United States of America

First Edition

1 2 3 4 5 6 7 8 9 10

BOOK DESIGN BY M & M DESIGNS

For
William Schoell

ACKNOWLEDGMENTS

With thanks, above all, to my agent, Daniel A. Strone. Special thanks to William Schoell, who helped greatly with the research and general detail work and shared with me his insights into that phenomenon of phenomena Cher. He deserves, and receives, the dedication to him of this book. And with sincere appreciation to my editor, Doug Stumpf, and to Erik Palma.

Also, thanks to the many who knew and worked with Cher, a number of whom did not wish to be named and others of whom are mentioned throughout this book. Special thanks to Robert Heide and John Gilman, who knew Cher back in the 1960's and shared their memories with me; to Richard Dysart, her co-worker; to Kyle Baxter Utley, who discoed and partied with Chastity Bono; to Robert Dahdah, who knew Cher professionally; and to Barbara Barondess MacLean and Curtis Roberts, who often crossed paths with Cher over the years and gave me fine insights into her.

And thanks to Douglas Whitney for the many wonderful

pictures he has lent over the years. And to Doug McClelland, always helpful with research and tips.

Also, my appreciation to Mike Ritzer, Arthur Tower, John Cocchi, Don Koll, the James R. Quirk Memorial Film Symposium and Research Center, New York; Mary Corliss and the Museum of Modern Art's Department of Film Photo Archives; the staff of the Margaret Herrick Library of the Academy of Motion Picture Arts and Sciences, Hollywood; British Film Institute, London; Dorothy Swerdlove, Rod Bladel, and their associates at the Billy Rose Theater and Film Collection, New York Public Library at Lincoln Center; Ernest D. Burns and the former Cinemabilia, New York; Mark Ricci and the Memory Shop, New York; Jerry Ohlinger's Movie Material Store, New York; and Photofest.

Thanks, too, to Barry Paris, John Gallagher, James E. Runyan, John A. Guzman, Mike Snell, Jim McGowan; Frank Rowley of the Biograph Cinema, New York; Howard Otway of Theatre 80, New York.

CONTENTS

CONTENTS

TOTALLY
UNINHIBITED

Sonny and Cher as a "married couple" when they weren't actually married until they were nearly half a decade into their career.

Now on her own as a major star, Cher continues to perpetrate a sham, creating the illusion of a wild, promiscuous slut and zany lady when she has never really indulged in dope, booze, or sleazy one-night stands to any extent. The image of her in rock videos —parading around, showing off the tattoo on her butt—is that of a much younger, more vulgar, more exotic woman. Yet there is no denying that Cher *is* a touch hedonistic, is a definite exhibitionist, and has had a succession of highly publicized affairs with a variety of handsome, much younger men (even if she takes on only one at a time). Part of her image is illusion; part is real. Perhaps finding out which is which is the clue to finding out what makes the woman tick.

During the preparation of this volume one thing became clear. People *like* Cher. Well, maybe not everybody. Maybe not some of her costars and former or would-be boyfriends; maybe not certain members of the press with whom she's crossed swords. But the public and most of her colleagues like and admire, maybe even respect Cherilyn Sarkisian. Even people who are dubious of her abilities seem to like her. One TV critic, Kay Gardella, savaged her show back in the seventies, criticizing every aspect of it and practically labeling Cher a glitzy, zero-talent performer, yet wound up her review by saying how much she *liked* Cher in spite of it all. As Cher has proved she has acting talent, garnering an Oscar, that "like" has turned to respect in many cases.

People love to talk about Cher. There's an almost inexplicable good cheer and admiration in the air when people discuss her. And not just hard-core fans but most people.

Perhaps it's not so inexplicable. Cher is considered a success story. She's a survivor of the sixties when many others fell by the wayside. Many women see her as a champion who has slain the twin dragons of an oppressive man and marriage to emerge as a triumphant single who lives by her own rules. Both women and men admire the power that she denies she has. Perhaps she's a little girl who never quite grew up, who has remained childlike and vulnerable in some ways, yet seems in full control of her enviable life and career.

But like all little girls running free, Cher can make mistakes, bad choices, wrong turns, enemies. . . .

Cher has said that she doesn't keep a diary but keeps it all up in her head. "I would be sued up the ass if I wrote what was really happening to me. I'm always truthful, but truth is such a weapon," she told *Interview* magazine. "Someday I'm going to write a book that's going to make *everybody* crazy. . . ." She added, "Everybody in the world thinks they know everything about me—nobody knows anything."

As biographer Katherine Ramsland has pointed out, "A biography is a *perspective* based on a biographer's vision." And no biographer can ever be omniscient. This "vision" of Cher's life, her triumphs and disappointments, career highs and lows, romantic attachments and devastations, is a fair one, giving the lady her due without glossing over or whitewashing any facet of her life. Her story is a study of celebrity in America, of image versus reality, of the glorious, seedy, unreal, and very often *too* real world of pop music and Hollywood and the strange, heady corner where they meet.

It is, of course, not true that "nobody knows anything" about Cher. The deepest recesses of any human being's heart may always be out of reach to other mortals, but details, facts, times, and places are another story. Many people know quite a bit about Cher, and some of them have shared their knowledge. It will suffice until such time as Cher opens up her mental diary and writes that book that will "make everybody crazy."

ONE

SVENGALI

When I was little, I wanted to be famous. I didn't know what it was going to be, I just wanted to be famous. And when I was famous, I just wanted to be good at something.
—CHER

At sixteen years of age Cherilyn Sarkisian was no prize.

She was like a walking lump of defiance and low self-esteem. The defiance and underlying toughness covered up the insecurity that came with being not quite attractive enough. The girl who one day became the glamour puss Cher had a large nose, crooked teeth, and poor posture, not to mention slightly bowed legs. She had bad skin and wore too much makeup. She affected a harsh fuck-you attitude that was meant to lacerate others before they had a chance to hurt her.

For a girl who wanted someday to be famous, she seemed to lack any kind of ambition. She'd come from a troubled home, was out on her own at an early age, and was looking for a surrogate father, someone to take care of her, watch over her—someone like Sonny Bono.

Although years after the fact both Sonny and Cher like to suggest that theirs was "love at first sight" when they met at a Hollywood Boulevard coffee shop in November 1962, in retrospect it is not very likely that Cher could have felt any kind of truly mature love or passion. For one thing, Sonny Bono was no prize. "I didn't even like him that much," Cher said years later. "I just thought, That is the weirdest-looking man I've ever seen. I mean, he was ugly." He was also, at age twenty-seven, eleven years Cher's senior. With his whiny, hesitant, nasal voice, long nose, silly haircut, and short stature, Sonny was not exactly a dreamboat in an era of Troy Donahues, Rock Hudsons, and Tab Hunters. For his part, he was certainly not instantly smitten with Cher. Although they went out on a group date that very night and dated a few times after being introduced by mutual friends at the coffee shop, Sonny was more interested in Cher's roommate than in Cher.

But Sonny had one facet that did attract Cher: He was in *show business*. Those were the magic words to an unpolished Hollywood hopeful who devoured fan mags and fancied herself living the glamorous life of a movie star. Suddenly Sonny Bono seemed six feet tall. To immature girls of sixteen even people on the fringes of show business seem instantly fascinating, and Sonny by that time had been a recording artist and record promoter and knew many people in the industry. Cher was starstruck, and those stars blinded her to certain realities about this man. Perhaps at first she thought of him only as someone to use, but it must also be remembered that Cher was a young girl estranged from both mother and father; Sonny must have seemed kindly, concerned, protective, fatherly. He was not entirely unattractive. He had a boyish charm, even a ragged, limited sex appeal. Cher might well have thought an older man in show business was a good catch for a gawky sixteen-year-old with pimples and no boyfriend.

For his part, Sonny might have been annoyed by certain slothful, gross habits of Cher's, but he also would have noticed that the girl with the winning smile and long black hair had some nice qualities. For one thing, she had a voice. In retrospect, Sonny and Cher used *each other* to grab just a piece of the dreams that were obsessing them: for Sonny, ascendancy in the rock world, for Cher, an opportunity to become "somebody."

For the most part, Cher did all the pursuing. "I was crazy about him in the beginning," she has recalled, throwing jealous rages when she'd go over to his apartment and realize he was with another woman. Sonny treated her with a certain amount of respect and made her feel pretty. Netting him had become important to her. It was as if he or, rather, his approval of, or desire for, her had become the symbol of a newfound self-respect, and without him her sense of self-worth would disintegrate.

When her roommate moved out, Cher realized with dismay that her occasional part-time jobs wouldn't pay the rent. She was reluctant to go back home to her mother. She wanted to be with Sonny. His spirit weakened from her pleading, perhaps responding to an inner feeling he didn't even realize he had Sonny told Cher she could move in with him rent-free as long as she did the cleaning. For months they led a completely chaste existence. Sonny not only didn't get (or necessarily want) sex in return for his generosity but didn't even get cleaning. The Cherilyn of that period stayed out all night and slept in most of the day when she wasn't affixed to the TV set or raiding the refrigerator.

It was a good thing the girl could sing, or she probably would have been booted out onto the Sunset Strip before she could say, "The beat goes on."

Sonny was born in Detroit (on February 16, 1935). Sonny was the nickname given to Salvatore Philip Bono by his mother. He had two older sisters. When Sonny was seven, the family moved to Los Angeles, where he was bitten by the show biz bug. He dropped out of high school and fell into a series of odd jobs, got married, and had a daughter, all the time planning and hoping for the day his ambitions would be realized. He wanted to be, of all things, a songwriter. Rock and roll was sweeping the country, planting a kiss of death on more sedate forms of music and changing the face of the whole music industry. Sonny was itching to be part of this.

Sonny Bono at twenty-one was working as a trucker when he stopped at Specialty Records in Hollywood and tried to sell some mediocre songs he'd written to Harold Battiste, who was in charge of artist relations and promotions for the firm. Battiste didn't think much of Bono's music but did admire the young man's enthusiasm. He made Bono his partner in his division, and soon Bono was screening song submissions. Eventually Bono improved his own work enough so that Battiste felt it was usable. Before long Sonny was writing and producing records and recording under pseudonyms. Meanwhile, his marriage (to Donna Rankin) was taking a backseat to his career aspirations. Still and all his efforts seemed to go for naught. None of his records took off. He started his own recording labels, and they failed. He was great at promotion but couldn't accept that the basic product—his voice, his derivative songs—was second-rate and the public wasn't buying. He went back into the promotional end of the business.

This was when Sonny met a man who was to have a major influence on his life and career, Phil Spector, who owned Philles Records. Spector was a white New Yorker transplanted to Hollywood, where he took charge of an empire based on a number of mostly black recording artists whose careers he'd guided successfully.

Bono wanted to emulate his idol, Spector, in every way possible, but this was not always a healthy thing to do. The music industry at that time seemed to contain a number of powerful male individuals who played Svengali to lovely young Trilbys. There was Berry Gordy in Detroit, who romanced and advanced the career of Diana Ross, who later broke away from him. Ike Turner performed with his wife, Tina, in the early years, but she later left him and emerged as a single superstar. Ironically, in their first stage engagement Sonny and Cher opened for Ike and Tina Turner.

Phil Spector's Trilby was his wife, Ronnie, lead singer of the Ronettes (whose one big hit was the sexy "Be My Baby"). If Cher had it bad in later years, Ronnie had it worse. She blames Phil's insecurity for his inability "to accept a wife or girlfriend being even bigger than him." As she put it in a *Good Morning America* interview, Spector aborted his wife's promising career with the

Ronettes and made her a prisoner in their home, complete with, as Ronnie puts it, "gates and barbed wire and security guards." He subjected her to psychological abuse, screamed at her, and ran her life to a ridiculous degree, even telling her what she should eat and when she could go to bed. "I was a servant—maid, butler, and wife," Ronnie says. "I couldn't get out unless I asked a servant to take me out. The servant had to ask Phil. . . . My mother and I schemed to get out; I walked out literally with no shoes on."

Cher has expressed her admiration for Spector's production abilities but has categorized him as somebody you would be crazy to want to live with.

This, then, was the man that Sonny Bono was so anxious to imitate. And Cher—the messy, pimply, lazy girl who slept for endless hours back in his apartment and rarely changed her underwear—was going to be his Diana, Tina, Ronnie, Sonny's Trilby.

Sonny's failure to take the recording world by storm was due to one basic, inalienable fact: He had hardly any talent. True, Bob Dylan's voice was hardly any better, but Dylan was a true product of his time, writing lasting songs like "Blowin' in the Wind," songs *about* something.

That didn't stop Bono from being influenced by Dylan in what has to be a macabre musical irony or cosmic jest. "I Got You, Babe" has been called reminiscent of Dylan's "Catch the Wind"; so has "Where Do You Go?" "The Beat Goes On" was similar to Dylan's "The Trip." In fact, a large majority of Sonny's compositions were heavily "influenced" by other songs. Sonny "borrowed" from such tunes as "We'll Sing in the Sunshine," "Happy Together," and even "Hava Nagila"! Writer J. Randy Taraborrelli states that "You Better Sit Down, Kids" is Sonny's "first truly *original* composition."

If Bono had problems as a songwriter, he wasn't much better off as a performer. Early reviews of their stage act suggests that Cher was the act's main, if not only, focus of appeal. Sonny "is mainly a distraction," wrote *Variety* in its review of a 1964 engagement at Ciro's Le Disque in Hollywood. "His shoulder-length coiffure and frantic contortions detract from his far more reward-ing spouse," it deemed. The act was "ragged and not very profes-sional. Success for the team looms as a question of maintaining a slicker presentation for Cher's talents, and either toning Sonny down or consigning him to an unseen, creative role."

Poor Sonny. Always the bridesmaid, never the bride. A later *Variety* review of an act at the Elmwood Casino claimed that "Cher dominates the stage, even during husband Sonny's solos." Time has already proved the theory that without Cher, as a singer and lounge act Sonny would have been washed up before he started.

Ironically, Sonny's greatest musical triumph might also be considered his nadir. In 1965 he managed to achieve a *solo* hit record entitled "Laugh at Me." The song was his reaction to failing to achieve respectability among his show business peers even after Sonny and Cher had made an impact on the charts; he was also reacting to humiliating encounters with a not-so-adoring public in a restaurant whose manager blamed Sonny and Cher for at-tracting trouble with their outré outfits. The song was taken as an outcry of disaffected "youth" (Sonny was thirty at the time) and sold nearly three quarters of a million copies. But although the song was successful, it still represents a low as well as a high point because it must be classified with such dreadful songs as "Muskrat Love," "They're Coming to Take Me Away, Ha Ha" and other weird comical atrocities.

Sonny was basically a man of limited ability who got some-place, as do many people like him, through chutzpah and persis-tence. More talented people who lack these qualities often go unnoticed. Sonny did not go unnoticed. And to hedge his bets, there was the statuesque Cher to help him every step of the way.

It all started, according to Cher, at a recording session at Phil Spector's Gold Star studios; Sonny occasionally did percussion for some numbers and brought Cher along to the studio where she could mingle with all the singers and musicians. One day a backup singer didn't show up. Spector looked at Cher and said, "Sonny said you can sing." Before she had a chance to explain her qualifications, Spector snapped, "I just want noise. Get out there!" It was not a particularly auspicious debut—hardly comparable to the understudy's going on to stardom when the star breaks her leg backstage—but for Cher it began a long-standing association with the recording industry. She sang backup on a number of songs for the next few months.

Circa 1962 Elizabeth Taylor and Richard Burton had gotten tremendous publicity via their on-screen and offscreen romancings in the mammoth overblown film *Cleopatra*. In 1964 Sonny came up with a bone-brained inspiration: He and Cher would form a singing duet called Caesar and Cleo. Their first record, "The Letter," was a less than inspired bomb that laid a big fat egg. Still, the powers that were felt there was still life left in the Caesar and Cleo gimmick, and the two cut another record. "Love Is Strange." At about this time, still hedging his bets, Sonny got himself and Cher, under their own names, signed up with manager Brian Stone and cut "Baby, Don't Go" as Sonny and Cher. "Baby, Don't Go" and Caesar and Cleo's "Love Is Strange" both were released on the exact same day in September 1964. Obviously the former record was the more successful of the two, or Sonny and Cher would have gone on to fame as Caesar and Cleo.

Their first big hit, which went solid gold in 1965, was, of course, "I Got You, Babe," the simple story of two young lovers who remind each other that although they're poor when it comes to material goods, they still have each other when times are hard. The arrangement basically makes something out of nothing, and even today the song is immediately recognizable. In 1966 Cher was on her own, performing Bono's song "Bang Bang (My Baby Shot Me Down)," which was the first big solo record she ever had. "The Beat Goes On" hit the top ten in 1967, and a new phrase entered American culture. Another simple song celebrating the joys of rhythm and music, it is probably familiar even to people who have never heard the record.

During this period, Cher has admitted, "I wasn't in control of anything. I was delighted for [Sonny] to take care of everything," and he did. By this time Cher's infatuation with, or dependence on, Sonny had become complete. "I thought he was the tower, the pillar, of strength and maturity and intelligence." It was just as well Cher felt this way. According to Cher's mother, "Sonny had to be the boss."

Having risen to the top of the recording industry, Cher did stage shows and made TV appearances. She occasionally wore her trademark long black hair in braids. Sonny, with a haircut that made him look like one of the Puritans at the Salem witch trials, affected hideous mod clothing that made him resemble a slumming sheepherder: sweater, dungarees, boots, all dominated by a shaggy fur vest that looked like a pelt that had been shedded by a peeling werewolf. He eventually grew a mustache that did little for him. Clad in bell-bottoms and blouse, looking out of it, Cher stood a few feet behind Sonny during TV appearances. Sometimes Sonny did odd bits of shtick, such as staring down at the floor while singing, ignoring Cher, and waving his finger up and down as if trying to make a point of remembering where he was and what he was doing there. Half the time the two of them at least *looked* stoned, although they weren't.

"We were America's hippies," Sonny says. "I don't think there were any longhairs back then except for us. We were shock-ing the world."

Well, "making it giggle" would be more like it. Sonny looks ludicrous in some of the old tapes of the two performing. Cher began developing her arsenal of tics and nervous habits that she seems only recently to have shed: licking her lips too frequently (in a furtive way that is not sexy); shaking her head back and forth after finishing a verse. They were hardly what could ever be called riveting performers.

And they were not hippies either. For one thing, Sonny had already become the "older generation." Although he tried for years to pretend he was still a youth, he was into his thirties by the time Sonny and Cher had become successful. For another, Sonny was politically conservative, particularly considering the times: the Vietnam War, the sexual revolution, Students for a Democratic Society. Sonny and Cher had not dropped out but had fervently embraced the establishment. Hippies sat in marijuana smoke–filled basements in Haight-Ashbury and talked of fighting the system, protesting the war, and "dropping out" of straight society. Hippies did not make fistfuls of dollars and antidrug government films or buy tons of material possessions, clothes, and knickknacks, as Sonny and Cher did. They were patently phony. Their clothes and basic demeanor, the whole hippie shtick, were just a publicity ploy. But it worked. Kids believed that this pair was representative of the kinky, dropped-out, turned-on generation. Instead, Sonny and Cher were like their parents.

Sonny and Cher had little to do with the idealism of the hippie movement. They were not out to change America; they wanted to advance their careers (at least Sonny did) and make money. Not only was Sonny conservative, believing that demonstrations and picket lines were unproductive and that one must effect change by working through the system (which he had tapped into, and milked, successfully), but in all likelihood Cher in those days had no opinion on anything of a political nature. Vietnam? Where was that? She was a girl—not a woman—in thrall to her Svengali, and she did what she was told, no matter how much she resented it. Sonny had made her "somebody" after all. What was happening all around her in the country was of small import in her scheme of things. If she had opinions, she kept them to herself.

Meanwhile, the reaction to Sonny and Cher as performers was decidedly mixed. Teenagers saw them as holy messengers of peace, love, and youthful rebellion and were eager to buy their records and go to their concerts. However, the mob scenes that ensued whenever they went out left Cher more depressed than exhilarated. Acquiring fame meant that she lost something just as, or even more, precious: freedom of movement. Sonny tried to be as accommodating as possible, arranging special screenings so that she could avoid crowded movie houses and booking her on special sight-seeing tours when they went to foreign countries.

Variety noted that Sonny and Cher had appeal for adults as well and that the couple demonstrated "respect and admiration for each other in their songs," adding, "If anyone can help to close the gap between generations these two should help do it." It was as if grown-ups could see through the facade that fooled their children and could recognize that Sonny and Cher were more like them than they admitted. Also, many adult fans secretly admired the couple's so-called rebellious quality, which made them feel a little less dull and conventional.

But acceptance by the public did not necessarily add up to acceptance by one's peers. Nancy Sinatra first met Sonny and Cher when they did *Hullabaloo* together in September 1965. Ol' Blue Eyes's daughter, who'd just had a big hit with "These Boots Are Made for Walkin'," thought the couple looked ridiculous, and she couldn't take them seriously at all. She thought they should more properly be exhibited in a circus sideshow.

This Hollywood snubbing reached epic proportions the night Sonny and Cher appeared as guests at a World Adoption International Fund charity ball. They wore clothes of a more conservative cast—for them—but it didn't help any. Such luminaries as Jane Russell, Bob Hope, Doris Day, Danny Kaye, and Rock Hudson were on the stage or in the audience, making both halves of the duo exceedingly nervous. They could impress teenage boys and girls well enough, even get a charitable review from time to time in the daily and weekly trades, but this was the "big time." Stacked up against all that "major talent," Sonny and Cher felt small.

Princess Margaret had requested their participation, but when they started singing, even she looked stricken. Apparently Cher was singing too loud, or the microphone was malfunctioning. Attempting to correct the technical glitch, the sound man inadvertently cut off the microphone altogether. Later Sonny attempted a bit of stand-up comedy and succeeded only in offending people. When he sang his solo number, he was heckled by a drunk whose comments inspired the entire star-studded audience to burst into laughter.

Hollywood had made it clear: Sonny and Cher were not equals. They were a joke complete with fur vests, long hair, and off-key voices.

Cher found experiences like that bad enough, but what she really hated were the concert tours. They had to travel on crowded, dirty buses where music blared from radios for hours. Sonny didn't allow Cher to mingle with the other performers, who he was afraid might corrupt her with their nasty habits, so she had no social life. Cher suffered acutely from stage fright and almost had to be shoved out in front of an audience. "I don't believe she would have gotten up on the stage without Sonny," Cher's sister has said. "He was a major, motivating force" and the only reason why Cher endured it all. The yowling fans were bad enough when Sonny and Cher were just the openers for better-known groups, but as they themselves got bigger and bigger, the fans really began to scare her. Afraid they might pursue her, she refused to hang around after the performances. Once an overzealous security guard confused Cher with one of her multitude of look-alike fans (many of whom deliberately modeled themselves after her in their dress and hairdo) and slammed her against a wall.

In 1965 I was the editorial director of a group of fan magazines (*Screen Stars, Movie World, TV Movie Album, Screen Stars Album*, et al.), and I can attest to the fan response (and fan mail) Cher elicited, with Sonny pulling even more often than not. There was tremendous curiosity about their private lives that they were in no mood to gratify. Once, when they were in the New York area, I cadged an interview with them, most of it conducted with Sonny, who tended to jump in and speak for Cher whenever she started to open her mouth. "We are really grateful that our fans love us," he told me. "Cher feels the pressure more than I do, but at times it *can* be nerve-racking, admittedly!" Laughing, Sonny added, "I'll start to worry only when they don't show up." I braved Sonny's interference running to ask Cher directly what she thought of it all. She looked first to him for corroboration, reassurance, permission, or whatever, then replied in a low voice that people who didn't appreciate fan devotion or curiosity "ought to have their heads examined."

That afternoon in 1965 I got a clear impression that Sonny did all the talking and all the planning and had all the ideas. Cher was quiet and withdrawn. I wouldn't have described her as "cowed," but she did look to Sonny, obviously, for answers and kept her eyes on him at least half the time.

The next time I saw them, in 1966, I saw little change in the Sonny-Cher juxtaposition. She seemed more composed, more self-assured, but obviously he was her main-man source of all sustenance—in spades. "We are very happy," Sonny said. "We feel we are making the most of our abilities, and we work wonderfully well together, and who could ask for more?" Cher on that occasion surprised me by interjecting (Sonny, too, seemed surprised) the point that two people, personally and in their career teaming, had to "like each other—really like each other—to make it all work," and Sonny, for once at a loss for words, nodded vigorously in agreement, as if he couldn't have said it better himself. Usually, though, when I directed a question at Cher, Sonny jumped in and answered it, in the best PR man style.

In 1965 and 1966 I carried away an impression that theirs was a contented, solid, well-balanced relationship, obviously because Cher let Sonny take the lead in all matters and make the decisions. From what I saw and knew of her at the time, it was probably just as well because the Cher of that period (just turning twenty) did not seem overloaded with self-confidence or quickness on the uptake. "But then why should she?" I wrote. "She has Sonny there—always there—always 'in charge.' "

Sonny proved particularly helpful in shielding Cher from even more importunate fans when they made a European tour in 1966. "They really scared her that time out," I wrote for *TV-Movie Album.* "Cher probably expected European audiences and fans to be more 'conservative' or 'restrained' or 'low-key' or whatever; she found they were even wilder in their reactions!" Someone else who wrote about Sonny and Cher's adventures in Europe was Nora Ephron, whose piece about the tour for the New York *Post* was breezy and insouciant—and uncritical, surprisingly enough. Many years later Ephron cowrote the screenplay for Cher's movie *Silkwood.*

I, for one, found the snobbery directed at Cher and Sonny

by more "established" Hollywood performers meanspirited and unwarranted, especially since the fan mail and requests for articles about the pair drew five and even ten times more than the requests about some of the very people who looked down on them. Write it off as the jealousy of the "arrived" of the "arriving."

Sonny and Cher might not have been accepted by the traditional Hollywood of the mid-sixties, but there were always other venues where they felt at home. They found themselves invited to parties given by members of the Andy Warhol troupe, for instance. Sonny and Cher never became close friends with Andy or any of his company, though. Too many of Andy's friends were druggies and weirdos for that to happen. Robert Heide, co-author (with John Gilman) of well-received show-business books and one of the more stable, talented, and respected people around Warhol, recalled his first meeting with Cher at the Silver Factory, about 1966. At the time Warhol was promoting an experimental rock band called the Plastic Exploding Inevitable for a road tour with fourteen members, including Lou Reed. According to Heide, Cher, who to Warhol represented a high priestess of rock music, commented on the performance of the new musical group thusly: "This group will replace nothing currently happening in the world except maybe suicide!"

Heide saw Cher as "a kind of arrogant, defensive bitchy type, who was intent on hiding the insecurity and low self-esteem she felt about herself which were nevertheless lurking just under the surface of her show business persona.

"She didn't feel herself to be attractive," Heide continued, "and was jealous of the more glamorous Warhol superstars like Edie Sedgwick, Baby Jane Holzer, and Nico. She seemed to be attracted, certainly at that time, at age twenty or so, to men who could take control of her life but resented the control at the same time." To Robert Heide, "this was her basic problem with Sonny in that period."

Cher, commenting on Andy Warhol's stinginess, once referred to him as a five-and-dime guru. Heide recalled that Warhol once asked Cher to pay for a container of coffee and a hamburger he had ordered from a White Tower restaurant. She claimed that she had no change and, when pressed, simply ignored his request. "Andy looked at her almost crushed." Heide laughed, then added, "Yet Cher was attracted to what she conceived to be the power emanating out of Warhol and at the same time was afraid of him. At one point she began calling him a prince of darkness." Heide recalled the 1966 Cher, age twenty: "Her manner of dress was not as outlandish as it later became. She wore loud show business versions of the hippie look with Gypsy and Indian influences, often sporting bright orange sashes and favoring reds, fuchsias combined with earth colors of green or brown. She tended to favor slacks over skirts, giving her a mannish aura. There was a naïveté about Cher then which she also covered with a mask of hardness and cynicism. Though she laughed a good deal and in a loud manner, it was usually at someone else's expense, and to me she appeared to have no real sense of humor, particularly when the joke landed on her. She used her rock stardom and position to look down at those around her in dismay as if she wondered why they dared to be standing in the same space as she was." Heide's summation of the Cher of 1966: "A real prima donna!"

Andy interviewed Cher for his magazine *Interview* at that time and became annoyed with her for repeating somewhat obsessively the story of the woman who had passed out and "peed all over herself" at one of Jane Holzer's parties. She also told the story of how Sonny nearly got sick from looking at a *moving* picture of the ocean that Holzer had on her wall. Although the crowd around Warhol was racy for Cher's speed, she liked their parties because "they made good conversation for a year."

Like most rock stars, Sonny and Cher sought to expand their repertoire. Sonny, whom people seemed to regard as a clown, reasoned: Why not get them to laugh *with* him instead of *at* him? That way he could get even with "those Hollywood snobs" by beating them at their own game in movies and on TV shows. More than anything, Sonny wanted people to take him seriously.

The TV show they chose to appear on was *The Man from U.N.C.L.E.* with Robert Vaughn and David McCallum. The series was then in its third season and slipping. What had started out as a mostly serious, if slightly tongue-in-cheek, spy program was rapidly turning into an out-and-out comedy, and the sagging ratings reflected the public's disapproval. If people wanted comic spy shows, they could have watched Don Adams in *Get Smart*. Don was doing comedy in far more seasoned, professional terms than could be found in the archly self-conscious *Man from U.N.C.L.E.* Some of the third-season episodes of *U.N.C.L.E.* were as silly, if oddly less professional, as anything on Adams's show, such as one with an exploding stink bomb that is regarded as one of the all-time worst.

Sonny and Cher's episode, "The Hot Number Affair," was not much better. The singing duo might have been out of place on the show in its first two years, but by the third season, they seemed to have the requisite silliness to fit right in. Sonny Bono specifically asked producer Boris Ingster if they could appear on the show, and a script by Joseph and Carol Cavanaugh was written specifically for them (the original title was "The Fashion House Affair").

In the story Cher is Ramona, a model who works for two designers who have seen better days. Sonny is Jerry, the cutter who is infatuated with Ramona. The main plot has the evil group THRUSH hiding a code in a dress pattern, which both THRUSH and U.N.C.L.E. agents try to retrieve, while Ramona keeps misplacing it, in her scatterbrained way. To judge from their performances, one would not have imagined that an acting career was in the offing for either Sonny or Cher. Background music included "I Got You, Babe" and "The Beat Goes On," but the duo did not sing on the show.

Nonetheless, Sonny enjoyed being on it and was, if nothing else, enthusiastic in his role as Jerry, even appealing in a gawky sort of way. Cher played the mannequin in convincingly stiff fashion. But although he could handle his dialogue in adequate fashion and stay in camera range, Sonny wasn't so swift in the fight scenes. Despite meticulous rehearsals and careful guidance, he didn't get out of the path of David McCallum's fist in time and wound up with a punch in the nose. From the blood that resulted, Sonny feared his nose might have gotten broken, but what was eventually to hurt far more was the knowledge that the silly episode, which was aired on March 10, 1967, did nothing to enhance the prestige of Sonny and Cher. Since *The Man from U.N.C.L.E.* was swiftly losing popularity, an appearance on the show was no longer anything to brag about, let alone take pride in, especially considering the dopey story line of "The Hot Number Affair."

Undaunted, Sonny decided to try the movies next; *here*, he reasoned, he might get more control over everything. His inspiration this time was the success of the Beatles' feature *A Hard Day's Night*. The mistake Bono made at this point was perhaps to overestimate Sonny and Cher's national popularity and their ability to bring the public into movie theaters.

Sonny's added mistake was to assume, without asking her in advance, that Cher would want to do a picture. As it turned out, it was the farthest thing from her mind. She knew that she'd have no input and that it would be hard and tedious work (like concert tours) and would allow her little time to be alone with business-minded Sonny. Their relationship seemed *all* business now, and she didn't like it. She had discovered the down side of show business. Being "somebody" wasn't all it was cracked up to be. Cher felt increasingly that she had no control over her life. In retrospect it seems that her biggest objection to the movie was that it would only offer Sonny another opportunity to humiliate them in public. Those humiliations made her shrivel inside. She had not forgotten the fiasco at the Hollywood charity affair.

But Sonny was on a roll, and he was not to be dissuaded. He proceeded to make a deal with Columbia Pictures. The television sale alone would pay for the production costs; Sonny and Cher would get a third of the profits. It seemed like a risk-free enterprise.

Bono picked documentarian William Friedkin to direct the picture, his first. Although Friedkin has said that he liked Sonny personally and admired the man's music, *Good Times*, his picture with Sonny and Cher, is probably not underlined and capitalized on his résumé. Friedkin, of course, went on to enormous fame and success as the director of *The Exorcist;* he has been trying ever since to make it back to the top.

Friedkin was determined not to make *Good Times* a mere "camera exercise," as he thought the Beatles film *A Hard Day's Night* had been. He expected to make a film that would not just dazzle with tricky editing, effects, and cinematography but would actually tell people what Sonny and Cher were all about. He felt that the film would make a point about integrity and the right of the artist to portray himself and his emotions with honesty. It is debatable whether or not the film succeeds in doing this. On one level it seems like a rehearsal—or audition—for all those sketches that Sonny and Cher were to do on their TV shows in the seventies.

In the film Cher and Sonny play themselves. A film producer (George Sanders) wants to star them in a film, but they have problems with the script. It doesn't portray them as they really are and gives them personalities that are alien to their natures. Sonny tries to come up with some better ideas, and most of the film consists of vignettes that illustrate these ideas as fantasies: Sonny as a sheriff or detective or jungle lord, with Cher as a moll or suspect or jungle queen. Most of the vignettes were parodies of old movies or specific movie genres and were silly. Visually the picture is perhaps more mod-looking than Friedkin suggested it would be. Cher did a reprise of "Bang Bang" in the movie, among other numbers. A sound track album was released, but it did not do well.

Good Times is a pleasant enough little movie, and considering that this was their first stint before the cameras, Cher and Sonny summon more aplomb than one would expect. There is a forced, heavy-handed feel to some of the escapist fantasizing, however, and the Sonny-Cher acting "styles" do not blend felicitously with the style of the far more experienced George Sanders, who is amusing but also dour in the ineptly written role of the producer. Nor can his occasional impatience, quite apparent even on-camera, be faulted; there is an amateurish, jerry-built feel to the proceedings, which an archprofessional like Sanders caught.

Behind the scenes the situation was almost as bad as in the movie. Cher objected to the script's portrayal of her real-life self just as the movie Cher did in the screenplay. She really wanted no part of the project and whined and carried on like a spoiled brat for hours, even in front of interviewers like me, then editor of a film publication called *Screen Life* and on hand to take note of Sonny's and Cher's offscreen reactions to their advent into movie "acting."

Cher seemed to me nervous and preoccupied. She obviously hated every second of it and reacted to Sonny's desperate offscreen sallies with a mammoth sullenness. She fussed with her hair endlessly and kept applying makeup, courtesy of a small hand mirror, though Friedkin reminded her that this was the province of the makeup woman, who, when she did appear, seemed mightily in terror of both Sonny and Cher. When I ventured to ask Cher how she felt about this, her first movie, she pointed over to Sonny, who was busy with what seemed to be an argument with Friedkin, and said, "I refer all questions to Sonny this time around; just keeping the lines in my head exhausts me!"

Sonny's rejoinder to my question about Cher was: "She's nervous, naturally. This is *new* to her!" Then he added, "Wait till she sees herself on the screen; she'll feel much better then. The camera is kind to her."

Friedkin agreed. "All she has to do is be her natural self," he said. "That'll carry her through splendidly."

George Sanders, whom I had interviewed many times, was looking (for him) discombobulated when I seated myself next to him, a yard or so back from the set. He made no bones about the fact that he had taken this film for the money. "Money—the root of all evil," he purred-snarled, "but a highly necessary commodity." His opinion of Sonny and Cher was, for him, charitable and restrained but nonetheless condescending in the best Sanders manner. "They are new to all this and must be treated with tolerance and understanding," he purred, then snarled, "I'll be bloody glad to have it all over with. Then I'll take the money and scoot off to Europe!"

Did Sanders think this first film would create a cinematic Sonny and Cher vogue? "You'll have to ask whoever the publicity people are about *that*," Sanders said. "*They* are being paid to pump up material of *that* kind." It was apparent that the talented and notoriously temperamental and unpredictable Mr. Sanders was aware that neither his role nor *Good Times* was within shouting distance of the *All About Eve* that in 1950 had won him a supporting Oscar. Then he had been forty-three; now it was 1966, and he was a few months short of sixty. The look on his face that day could be called "cynically resigned" for lack of a better term.

Good Times did better than its principals expected when it came to overall quality, but it did poor business. Almost as if Bob Dylan were getting revenge for all these Bono tunes that reminded listeners of Dylan's music, a documentary on Dylan's life and career did much, much better at the box office and was, for that matter, more pointedly timely. In 1967, the year of *Good Times*'s release, there was political and social upheaval. The music of Dylan, Joan Baez, and others was more socially relevant, the 1967 audience decided, than a foolish hodgepodge featuring Sonny and Cher spoofing Hollywood and each other. The fact of the matter in 1967 was that Sonny and Cher, at least in their current incarnation, were already becoming passé. The image was tarnished, dulled. People were "on" to them. If they were hippies, then so were John Wayne and Ginger Rogers.

Several critics were surprisingly merciful to *Good Times*, and the film got a lot of attention from the media. Part of the reason for this may have been a longing—of a sort, confused and misdirected though it may have been—to return to escapist Hollywood glamour and "old-fashioned, square" values instead of the now-grating angry questioning of Dylan and "Hanoi Jane" Fonda. It appeared, on balance, that Sonny and Cher were treated kindly in 1967 simply because they were so "out of it."

For instance, Richard F. Shepard wrote a review for *The New York Times* that practically reads like a press release—to wit: "There are lovely little bits of fun sprinkled throughout the reels. [*Good Times*] is part tongue-in-cheek, part-time beguiling foot-in-mouth. It's a tasty tidbit of entertainment to lure you off the street on a sticky afternoon." He praised Sonny's comic skills and admired the film's visual quality, calling it "a splashy pool of pop art in itself, fooling around with brilliant colors and what seem to be experiments in reversing the negative." Shepard's prose reads like something sent off by a professional publicist, and the review lacks critical acuity.

The *Christian Science Monitor* was more reserved. "In one of those Hollywood coincidences worthy of Maupassant, the Sonny and Cher *in* the movie are signed up to *make* a movie." The critic thought Cher disclosed a "nice wifely smile to go with the low bangs and made-up eyes familiar in her singing partner role" but added, "It is hard to imagine what this long-haired boy and longer-haired girl could play except themselves. . . ."

The Bonos were supposed to star in a follow-up movie, the oddly titled *Ignatz*, but the production was later canceled, to Sonny's consternation and dismay. The favorable notices that *Good Times* had received had filled him with overconfidence. Defiant before the world and its press, he boldly predicted that he and Cher would be doing two film projects a year. But alas for his sanguine hopes, *Good Times* didn't rake in enough box-office moolah to rate a sequel, and the production company pulled the rug out from under Sonny and *Ignatz*, sinking Bono into depression. The Beatles, the harder-edged Rolling Stones, the peacenik poets, and drug culture prophets were, on balance, the big thing in the music of the time. Sonny and Cher were beginning to resemble dinosaurs. If the act folded, if the record deals dried up, if they failed to make the grade in films, what would happen to Sonny and Cher? Where would they go? What would they do?

Not that things were *that* bad in 1967. The movie was released in June. Cher had a top ten record in November with "You'd Better Sit Down, Kids." And Sonny proceeded to spend a cool million dollars on a Tudor-style mansion that he bought from Tony Curtis. Maybe Sonny's real problem was that Cher had had another big hit as a solo, while the Sonny and Cher single "Plastic Man" (in which he rebutted Timothy Leary and urged people to think for themselves and not be pressured or taken in), released in July 1967, went nowhere. Sonny hadn't been taken seriously as a singer, but his comedic playing in *Good Times* had been favorably received. Now his acting career was practically over before it had started, and Cher's singing career was nearly as strong as ever. This, Sonny told himself, fuming inwardly, was *not* the way things were supposed to work out.

His problem was that no one—but no one—would bankroll another comic spoof like *Good Times*, to Sonny the very sort of thing in which *he* could excel. Also, to his chagrin, he had to accept that *Good Times* had been a financial failure. In Hollywood success was measured in only one way: *money*. The favorable reviews he had gotten for *Good Times* were, he realized, simply not enough to win him the respectability he craved.

For Sonny, there was but *one* answer: another picture. Produced and written by himself. Cher as star. Damn it, if he couldn't be up there with her on the screen, as he knew he could not, he *would* have control, *total* control, *final* control, *behind* the scenes. Sonny Bono was preparing himself for the ultimate day when his performing career would be over and he would be moving on— onward and upward, ever upward—into the production end of pictures just as he had started out in the promotional end of the recording industry. Things were full circle for him, he felt.

It was of crucial importance to Sonny that this new film project succeed, *big*. A year after he had spent close to a million for that beautiful new mansion, the Sonny and Cher act was on its last legs, and they simply weren't making enough money to cover their expenses. Even Cher's solo singing career had, for the time, dried up. The fickle public of the late 1960's just seemed to have gotten tired of both of them, and new recordings were unsuccessful. Sonny tried everything he could think of as a prospect—a Broadway show, a TV spectacular, film scripts—but nothing ever panned out. He decided to bankroll the proposed new film, which he called *Chastity*, by mortgaging their doted-upon mansion, their "Hollywood home to beat all Hollywood homes." Movie biz insiders couldn't believe it, shook their heads

ominously when they heard the news. Cher couldn't believe it
either.

Sonny was banking on the support of the country's flower
children and disaffected youth when he wrote the story of *Chastity*.
He was in a cynical mood at the time. The public, their former
fans, didn't want "fun" movies anymore, as he perceived it. They
wanted "relevance" and sexiness and a downbeat atmosphere,
something dark, stark, and gritty. So he proceeded, after much
cogitation, to fashion a screenplay about a victim of childhood
incest, one Chastity, who goes on a "soul search," a search for
innocence and purity, as she hitchhikes across the country. The
film was a series of moody encounters with a truck driver, a college
student, a cabdriver, and the madam of a brothel with whom
Chastity has a brief lesbian encounter. Interspersed with these
activities were speeches about love, life, and morality, with the
viewpoint being basically liberal (or even radical) for 1969.

The screenplay had something for everyone—straight sex,
lesbianism, prostitution (Chastity becomes a hooker at one
point)—and it was obviously geared by Bono for a target audience:
the kind of people who had labeled him and Cher a couple of
squares. The trouble was that Sonny's heart wasn't in it, and when
filming actually began, with the inexperienced Alessio de Paolo
directing, he began to alter the screenplay, watering it down until
it came across as a very different, and much less controversial,
product. What was left, unfortunately, was a lot of talk and aimless
meandering. The picture looked good but said little.

Cher had actually wanted to do the picture. She liked the
screenplay when she read it, and she identified with the heroine,
who may have been somewhat modeled after her. So when Sonny
began chickening out and changing and watering down the script
and taking, in her view, all the guts and relevancy out of it, she
quarreled bitterly with him. *This*, she declared, was *not* going to
be a silly Sonny and Cher costume spoof like *Good Times*; *this* was
going to be a *serious* motion picture and a major change for *her*,
Cher (clearly she still had ambitions), and she would be damned
if she would let Sonny's squeamishness and conventionality fuck

it up. Cher, it emerged, was as anxious to prove herself as Sonny was, but in this instance it turned out to be a losing battle.

Cher's whining, complaining, and reluctance to perform in earlier years were now put into context. She had been *embarrassed* to perform with Sonny; she knew she outweighed him in talent. She knew she was the act's true strength and draw. As of 1968 she knew, for chrissake, that she towered over him. In *Chastity* she could be "on her own" at last. When she recorded her solo records, there was no real audience, and when she sang alone onstage, she always knew that Sonny was right there standing ahead, beside, or behind her and that he was always a pervasive presence. But when she appeared on that big screen in *Chastity*, despite Sonny's behind-the-scenes involvement, she would be, at last, alone, alone, *alone*! Up there on that high mountain, in the bright, clean air, all by herself! She wasn't scared of that (she couldn't see the audience, true, but *they* could see *her*!); she was exhilarated!

But after all the script changes, arguing, and marital hysteria, *Chastity*, in the long run, did nothing for Cher or for Sonny. It got some nice write-ups but made no money. *Time* magazine praised Cher's performance but thought the film bore "the mark of first effort. It tries, awkwardly, to innovate: the heroine has several thought-through soliloquies that are slangy, pretentious mini-sermons on God, man and morals. The final frames, which flash back to reveal a troubled upbringing, are too late and too pat—merely a neat way to leave things and go home. The film is arch and inconclusive." *Time* added, "Sonny Bono's screenplay and production are flawed. But the acting debut of Cher, his marital and folk-singing partner, is creditable."

Motion Picture Daily wrote that "Cher makes an impressive debut as an actress" and also praised Barbara London, "who sensitively and with restraint underplays her role as bordello madame with a lesbian interest in Cher." The reviewer added that "the entire production is marked by good taste, restraint, and, for the most part, technical competence. Although technically rated 'R,' not even the bordello scenes carry any suggestion of pornographic intent." Of course the R rating meant that many of the youths at whom the picture was aimed couldn't get in to see it. Not that they would have been all that shocked, riveted, or turned on if they had. Cher, incidentally, got to sing in the film a number called "Band of Thieves."

In *Current Screen*, one of my early film newsletter-review sheets, I wrote of *Chastity*: "Its good intentions stand out strongly. Its heart is in the right place. The problem emerges not in intent but in execution. One gets the feeling that too much has been re-thought, re-appraised, that there has been a holding back, a 'chick-ening out' if you will. Unquestionably the original concept was far stronger than what emerges as the final product. But Cher promises well for the future, so far as films are concerned, if this is any indication. *Chastity* gets an A for good intentions and a B for execution, or perhaps a B-minus."

Not long after *Chastity* was released, the Hollywood com-munity was rocked by one of the most ghastly multiple murders of all time, the deaths of Sharon Tate and others at the hands of cultists unleashed by the maniac Charles Manson. Manson had wanted a singing career and begged Doris Day's son, Terry Melcher, a record producer, to get him an audition. When Manson proved impossible, Melcher knew he could do nothing more for him. Manson went out to Melcher's house on Cielo Drive, in a remote hilly area near Benedict Canyon, and confronted him. Melcher rebuffed Manson, who left shaking his fists and vowing revenge. Shortly afterward Melcher moved out of the house, and Tate, and her husband, Roman Polanski, the film director, moved in. Manson came back to settle accounts with Melcher and found the new tenants instead. They rebuffed him, and he vowed to get even with them, too. While Polanski was in London, Manson, who did not actually participate in the slaughter, sent Charles Watson, Susan Atkins, Patricia Krenwinkle, and Linda Kasabian to execute them.

Sharon Tate was unbelievably mutilated. A rope was tied around her neck and around the neck of her former lover Jay Sebring, who was shot and stabbed. The cultists also killed Wojtek

Grykowski, a narcotics dealer, and the coffee heiress Abigail Folger. The pregnant Tate was bayonetted in the stomach by Watkins, and Susan Atkins tried to cut the baby out with a knife in order to offer it to Manson as a trophy. They wrote "PIG" on the white front door. Manson also sent disciples out to commit similar atrocities on others in the area.

All Hollywood was in terror, and stars began to realize how exposed and vulnerable they were. Like others, Sonny and Cher were horrified. They bought a pit bullterrier (years before they became popular) to protect themselves and their baby, Chastity (named after the film). They put in new locks and alarms and turned their Hollywood mansion into a fortress. Cher would lie awake at night and think of how open to assault stardom could make you, how easy a target. First it took your freedom; would it also take her *life*?

Sonny and Cher gave an interview to Earl Wilson of the New York *Post* at that time. (Stars are never publicity-shy when their careers are on the wane, only when they're riding high. Thus it was with the Cher-Sonny duo at this time.) Cher's comments were surprisingly callous. "We don't run in that set," she said. "We went to dinner there and I never liked Sharon. She was always making passes at Sonny. I'll say this for her, she was very female."

Perhaps Cher—who'd starred in her own movie but was at that point facing bankruptcy with her by then not so beloved Sonny—was in a particularly bitter, sad, and cynical mood when she added, "We have a strange feeling the murderer is going to be someone we know."

Sonny and Cher did not know Charles Manson, eventually uncovered as the mastermind of the massacre at the Polanski house. But he could be taken as a symbol of the fury of those-who-fail, a personification of the rage of the also-ran and never-was. He had tried to be a rock star and hadn't succeeded and he was now making everybody pay for it. How many more like him were out there? Cher and Sonny wondered as they checked, for the tenth time, their locks in the million-dollar Tudor mansion, that ultimate symbol of whatever success they had garnered to that point.

But by that time Sonny and Cher had other, crucial troubles to occupy them. With *Chastity* a total failure, they were in danger of losing everything. Cher had vowed she would never allow herself to be poor again. She recalled only too well, only too clearly, how it had all begun. . . .

TWO

MOTHERS AND DAUGHTERS

*I'm scared to death of being poor. It's like a fat girl who loses
500 pounds but is always fat inside. I grew up poor and will
always feel poor inside. It's my pet paranoia.*
—CHER (*People*, January 1982)

Although she was not told
until many years later, Cher spent time in an orphanage and with
foster parents from infancy until the age of three. She had never
understood why waking up in a strange hotel room while she was
on a tour was always so unsettling. Life on the road was difficult
for everyone, of course, but Cher had found it unnervingly lone-
some and haunted and evocative of things that were deeply buried
in her subconscious—like waking up and not remembering where
she was. When she finally found out what her first three years had
been like, she understood her feelings a little better. It was another
bone of contention between her and her mother.

Her mother, Georgia Holt, born Jackie Jean Crouch in Arkansas in 1927, spent her early life traveling the country with an
alcoholic father, whom she supported by singing in local bars. She
got a job as a vocalist with a country and western band by day,
and at night she and her father would sleep in filthy, depressing
shelters, until finally they made their way to a tenement in L.A.,
where they became public charges. A job as a maid in a wealthy

home when she was thirteen filled Jackie with resolve. She wanted a house like that someday. No more saloons or tacky bands or tenements. She wanted to be successful and have all the good things that life had to offer. She figured she'd certainly paid her dues.

But at eighteen she fell in love with an Armenian farmer named John Sarkisian, and her dreams nearly disappeared. Her life turned into a sadly predictable nightmare. The day after her Reno wedding to John, she wanted to leave him, as he proved more Toad than Prince Charming. Before she could get a divorce, though, she got pregnant. She originally planned to get an abortion, but the trip to the clinic, which seemed hardly cleaner than the shelters and slums she had spent so many nights in, quickly put an end to that idea. She stuck it out with the drunken, perpetually unemployed Sarkisian, before getting her divorce and fleeing with her child.

This, then, was the situation into which Cher was born, in El Centro, California, on May 20, 1946.

Her mother was a struggling single parent (in the days before single parenthood became common) who was desperate to get a break in show business. Baby Cher was dumped on people while Mother went off to auditions and to a succession of sleazy bars where she actually sang for her supper. In fairness to Jackie, who around this time changed her name to the more striking Georgia Holt, she always managed to pay the bills and feed the child. She might have been more practical, might have accepted steadier work that would have ensured little Cherilyn's upbringing in more pleasant and stable surroundings, but Georgia was still a teenager, spinning incessant dreams of becoming "somebody." She hung on to those dreams, and she did the best she could. It was years before her daughter could see it that way. All that Cher could remember was her mother's occasionally hinting that she'd had lousy luck as a wife and entertainer because she'd been saddled with children. Even so, Cher later dubbed the mother of her childhood and early youth "a combination of Auntie Mame and Florence Nightingale." That's a rather charitable assessment, but then Cher, like her mother, is a prisoner of escapist notions and did a little reinventing of her sad and harried parent as the years passed.

Georgia's other child was Georgeanne La Piere, the daughter of her third husband, John Southall, another marriage that had only a brief existence. Cher doesn't even remember her mother's *second* husband; she was only two at the time. Husband number four, Gilbert La Pierre, adopted both sisters, and for a time Cher used his last name. Her sister retained it until her recent marriage.

These frequent marriages and rotating stepfathers were hardly a stabilizing influence for Cher. What made it worse was that Georgia took Cher's biological father back *twice*. Sarkisian's behavior, if anything, had deteriorated since her birth: He was arrested on drug charges and for passing bad checks, did time in a penitentiary, and was a morphine addict. Despite Cher's love for him, he always let her down. Both mother and daughter had been smitten with Sarkisian's good looks and charming, charismatic manner. Cher conceded later that she got her looks and much of her own temperament and magnetism from him, but when his drunken, selfish, and irresponsible behavior undermined and nearly destroyed their lives, Cher wrote him off. Not so her mother, who divorced him a second time, then remarried him later.

Oddly enough, one part of Cher positively throve on the chaos; perhaps it was in her blood, part of a basically bohemian and unconventional nature. She recalled: "When I was little, my mother used to say, 'Oh, I wish I could find someone nice, so we could settle down and have a normal, everyday life.' And I used to think, 'Boy, I hope that doesn't happen!' Because the way we lived seemed like so much more fun. Maybe it was crazy. But it seemed like fun."

Cher for a time thought of her half sister's father, John Southall, as her father, too. "He was the only one I spent any time with until Gilbert." Gilbert La Piere also had, for the most part, a good relationship with both his stepchildren. About her biological father, Cher later said: "He didn't have any features that I think are

45

important; he had no character. So even though he could be cute and adorable, he had no backbone. I didn't find him respectable."

Years later some of her printed comments about her father so angered him that he sued her and the magazine that published them in a sleazy attempt to get money. John Sarkisian died in the mid-1980's, the lifetime conflicts between father and daughter unresolved. "I'm sorry, I guess, but it is difficult to miss someone you didn't know," she said later. What Cher remembers of that early period is her being at the mercy of her mother, her mother's marriages, and the demands of her mother's "career."

She was to tell the *Ladies' Home Journal*: "My mother was working in an all-night diner and had nowhere to put me. It was tough. She moved me from place to place while she was doing these kinds of jobs. I think that's why I have a hard time staying with anything for too long a time now."

For long stretches Georgia and her daughters were three women on their own. Georgia had plenty of dates, but a strong, viable male presence in the home was usually lacking. And at times Georgia's ambitions were sharply narrowed by fate and circumstance. She was always to recall, ruefully, the time Cher was graduating and wanted a pair of attractive brown sandals she'd had her eye on. Georgia couldn't afford to buy them: "I've heard about it ever since. I will hear about those sandals for the rest of my life."

With such a chaotic homelife, Cher found herself with fewer restrictions than many children her age. She had inherited show biz leanings from her mother and a kind of wild streak from her father. Her first sexual experience was at age fourteen: "I was really in love with him. He was too old for me. He kept bothering me and bothering me. . . ." Cher sensed he was interested in just one thing, and one day—or night, rather—decided what the hell, she'd give it to him. "Okay, let's do this thing that you're always wanting to do," she announced to her importunate swain. So they had sex. She remembered it as "nothing special"—at least with this person—and dismissed her "first love" from her life without a backward glance. She always remembered the encounter with the guy ("whose brain was in his crotch") as not so much disillusioning as just plain disappointing.

Cher's next experience with men was a little more on the sinister side. She has maintained that when her mother dreamed up her name, she did a variation on Cheryl Crane, Lana Turner's daughter. Cheryl, who had murdered Lana's lover Johnny Stompanato in order, she maintained, to protect Lana from abuse, later wrote a book in which she claimed, among other sensational revelations, that one of her mother's later husbands, actor Lex "Tarzan" Barker, had molested her behind her mother's back. One of Georgia's boyfriends, then a ripe, potent thirty-five, did the same thing to Cher; only Cher was a willing victim. Nevertheless, she was only fourteen and a half at the time—it was late in 1960—and the horny thirty-five-year-old was technically committing statutory rape. This despite the fact Cher of her own volition had jumped into his bed after he gave her a "stimulating" grab and kiss as they passed on a stairway.

The man, was one of her mother's best friends and a romantic interest, it appears. She didn't tell her mother what had happened until long after. "She would have killed him," she said.

Cher recalled being very much in love with this man, but not necessarily in the passionate, all-out way she was to be in love with young superstuds like Rob Camilletti in later years. Curiosity and emotional hunger seem to have hung her on *this* peg: "I just wanted to be close to him. I would have really enjoyed just kissing him as much as having sex." Many years later, she was, she indicated, to appreciate fully what good sex he *had* been. "He was pretty weird, but I was crazy about him." Their affair lasted for about a year. Cher today is blasé about it all. Although she was hardly a total innocent at fourteen and a half and wanted the relationship as much as, if not more than, the man did, she *was* below the age of consent. The man clearly took advantage of her interest in him.

At age sixteen (1962) she went to bed, she told *Playboy*, with another notorious—in this case, famous—lover boy, the actor Warren Beatty. At the time he was twenty-five, an acclaimed new star after *Splendor in the Grass* and *The Roman Spring of Mrs. Stone* the year before. His 1962 film was *All Fall Down*. Beatty then, as now, was the narcissist supreme, in love with his own sexuality and the reaction it produced in others. All of Cher's friends, and even her mother, were attracted to Warren. She and her family were at the time living between Hollywood and North Hollywood, and Warren, at the height of his manly charms and everlastingly conscious of same, was busily proving himself with all comers. As she told it, she made herself available to Beatty, he responded with alacrity to the bait held out, and they repaired forthwith to his private quarters, where Beatty set forth to unveil, display, and demonstrate the secrets of his manhood. But for Cher the interlude was a dud. "*What* a disappointment!" she said later. "Not that [Warren] wasn't technically good, or couldn't be good, but I didn't *feel* anything!" That decided her that one night in Warren's bed was enough—*more* than enough. Considering the Beatty peregrinative capacities, one night's stand was probably, in fact almost certainly, enough for *him* with this sixteen-year-old nobody. She indicated that she had done it only so she could tease her friends with the news of her night in the sack with Beatty.

While her daughter was satisfying her curiosity with assorted males, Georgia Holt was still trying to establish herself conclusively in show business. Ever the eternal optimist, she worked for a time as a fashion model under the name Georgia Pelham. Jobs in movies were scarce for the gals who didn't put out for producers and directors. (Georgia was in top company when she said later that she got married so often because she was born in an era where sex was supposed to come *after* the legal hitching; Bette Davis said the same thing, adding that had she been born fifty years later, she'd have taken her guys to bed without benefit of clergy.)

Many years later Georgia seethed over "those events of 1949," when John Huston cast her in a small but pivotal role in *The Asphalt Jungle*, in which he was directing Sterling Hayden. Georgia, in full womanly bloom at twenty-three, felt that this MGM A picture could really do it for her, but at the last minute a woman a year older, Marilyn Monroe, was rushed into the role while

Georgia got the heave-ho. Saucy, sexy, wiggly, la Monroe used the part to advance her Hollywood fortune dramatically. There have been many stories that more than one male associated with *The Asphalt Jungle* got Monroe to "put out" in exchange. Since both Huston and Hayden were guys given to compulsive comparisons of their penis sizes, it is easy to see who led the list of the men Marilyn had to service. "She gave her all to the part, and it did a lot for her; but she was probably sore down there for weeks afterward," was how one wag put it. Meanwhile, Georgia Holt, neglected, downgraded, and ejected, beat the walls with anger and frustration. The money, as ever, was tight, and she had the girls to worry about. With each successive marriage she hoped she'd land herself a *"true* good provider" in the ever more likely event that her movie dreams didn't pan out.

That *"true* good provider" came along in the person of Georgia's third husband, Gilbert La Piere. Presto chango, the three orphans of the storm found themselves living in the lap of comparative luxury. It was vacations in Palm Springs, nice clothes, servants, snappy cars, handsome dwellings. But by this time Cher was man-wise and street-hardened, and she found she did not fit in with the more prim and proper girls she went to school with. These silly, innocent, but catty and snobbish girls bored Cher silly and aroused her contempt; the chaotic circumstances of her upbringing had also not prepared her for the disciplines of study, and she was a conkout in that department, not that she gave a damn.

Those who knew Cher during this relatively short period of prosperity always found it difficult to give full credence to the proliferation of hard-luck stories she tells about her early life; they just remember (at least for that time) a spoiled rich kid with a very wealthy daddy. But the daddy who provided Georgia and her children with that "new car, champagne, caviar" (as the song lyrics go) turned out to be just another of the endlessly fleeting fathers of the era. Georgia's marriage to the fat cat lasted only a couple of years.

As Cher matured, her belligerent attitude, understandable

confusion, and disorientation brought her into sharp conflict with her mother again and again. At sixteen she moved out; she made it plain to Mama Georgia that she was on her own, wanted to be left to her own devices, such as they were. Her mother tried to retain control. She was particularly upset over Cher's relationship with Sonny. As Georgia recalled it, "She told me she was going to live with a girl friend, and I went over to the house one day without calling. 'Oh, honey, I'm here,' [Georgia called]. 'Oh, wait a minute,' [Cher replied], 'the apartment's a mess, I've got to fix, wait a minute—' She took all of Sonny's clothes and threw them out the back window of the apartment."

When Georgia found out whom Cher was really living with, she hit the ceiling. Sonny reminded her unpleasantly of Cher's father and even looked like him; Sonny was still married (his wife divorced him in late 1963) and had a child; Sonny, at twenty-eight, was much too old for her daughter. Sonny, in short, was not up to snuff for Georgia's style or scene. Scared that Cher would repeat her own pattern of mistakes, she insisted that she move out. At sixteen Cher was two years short of being her own woman legally, and she so hated her mother at the time for infringing on what she saw as her rightful and hard-won independence that she announced she would rather move to a girls' residence (one step above a reform school) than back into Maison Georgia of the Many Husbands and Myriad Boyfriends. When the Sonny-Cher "romance" continued in spite of this, Georgia packed her two daughters and herself back to her home state of Arkansas. The doings were so dull, though, that she was more than happy to head back to L.A. after her brief homecoming. Cher made a beeline back to Sonny as soon as they hit town.

Georgia's animosity toward Sonny abated somewhat, when, in 1964, Cher, at last a legal eighteen, informed her that they had been married in Tijuana that year. What Georgia didn't know was that there was no minister or justice of the peace at the ceremony. Rather, it took place in a hotel bathroom, just Sonny and Cher pledging their private troth complete with rings and vows of their own authorship. To this day why a tiny bathroom was the scene

50

of the informal hitching is a mystery. They did not marry legally until 1969, when Cher was a ripe twenty-three and Sonny a mature thirty-four, before the birth of their daughter, Chastity.

Back in 1964, however, after the *fake* wedding Sonny and Cher moved in with Georgia and stepfather La Piere in his elegant home in the exclusive Truesdale Estates. The two were broke and, in retrospect, shrewdly manipulative. Now that she was of age and ostensibly a "married woman, Cher could handle her mother differently; now the power was distributed on more equal terms. Georgia still had plenty of clout, however, and she still didn't care for Sonny. To her, compared with La Piere—or anyone—he was just a long-haired bum. Sonny, no shrinking violet when it came to seizing an opportunity, got after La Piere to bankroll his and Cher's first recording act as Caesar and Cleo. However, Gilbert had his reservations, which were reinforced by his distrusting and sullenly hostile wife, Georgia.

Yet Georgia was not the Wicked Witch of the West when it came to her daughter's tales of woe. Years later, through her friendship with the wife of director Robert Altman, she added her two cents' worth in getting Cher cast in Altman's Broadway production of *Come Back to the Five and Dime, Jimmy Dean, Jimmy Dean*. And in the early days, as a number of friends insist, Georgia did her best to advance Cher's professional interests. For instance, she had come to know Ahmet Ertegun, the president of Atlantic Records, and on one social occasion happened to mention that she had a daughter who could sing. Supposedly Ertegun did not even know who Cher was when he signed Sonny and Cher up a few years later; he claimed to be surprised when he found out who Cher's mother was. There was no question but that in this period the combination of La Piere's dough and Georgia's brassy push helped make the difference in the advent of Cher on the road to show biz success.

None of this, however, seems to have prevented Cher from fighting the usual pitched battles with Supermom. "My mother and I haven't gotten along for almost my entire life," Cher has said. "We've always fought; we've always not talked; we've always argued. My mother is crazy, and so am I, but my mother is very special."

Cher has come to accept her mother's flaws and has worked hard to forgive her for her earlier years. She knows that her mother did her best to provide for her children and keep her family together. This is not to say that there hasn't been, and won't always be, a certain strain, a mutual wariness between them, a perennial difficulty in living together or getting along.

As late as the 1970's, when she was on the point of giving Sonny the heave-ho via the divorce courts, Cher was reported as saying, "I felt like going home to Mother, but I'm not that crazy about my mother!"

There is no denying that in its own way Georgia's life has been as colorful as Cher's. Mother can match daughter in sophisticated awareness of men, in variegated experiences. Whatever understandable jealousy Georgia might have nursed concerning her daughter's spectacular ongoing success has given way to a backhanded pride and to the realization that to be the mother of a national phenomenon like Cher is something of celebrity accomplishment in itself. Certainly Georgia Holt has capitalized on that celebrity; she still, yes, at sixty-three, has her own personal and professional ambitions, and she revels in the spotlight as much as Zsa-Zsa Gabor.

Back in 1978, at age fifty-one, Georgia opened an act at Studio One in West Hollywood; her two daughters were on hand to cheer her loudly and applaud her singing. There was talk of her and Georgeanne La Piere's hosting their own late-night talk show (both, to be fair, are personable enough to do just that, more at ease during televised interviews and more animated than Cher herself seems to be). Even the tabloids have found fodder in the particulars, real or imagined, of Georgia Holt's life. One story had Georgia falling for eighty-two-year-old "Mr. Television" Milton Berle. Milton liked to crack that he was older than Henny Youngman's jokes but that down under he felt younger than springtime. Georgia said Uncle Miltie made her laugh all the time, and reportedly Uncle Miltie was pleased that Georgia wasn't after his money. Cher was said to be delighted with the match and wanted them to get married. Whether Uncle Miltie was in actuality one of Georgia's heavy romances is debatable.

Cher, however, has confirmed that Georgia for a decade had a red-hot affair with a man who was a year younger than Cher herself, hence twenty years Georgia's junior (like mother, like daughter) and that this gentleman was "devastated" when Georgia broke it off. Reportedly *Playboy* magazine even offered Georgia fifty thousand smackers to pose for it. Georgia was reportedly "ecstatic" over the idea; she's kept her body fit like Cher's (to this day she looks remarkable young for her age, sixty-three), and thought it would be refreshing to demonstrate that senior citizens could have sex appeal. But the deal fell through when Georgia asked for twice the money the magazine was offering.

Georgia is said to be close friends with Sylvester Stallone's colorfully vulgar and outrageously publicity-hogging mother, Jackie, but to the wonderment of many, the two women have *not* conspired to create a romance between their two movie star off-spring (and Cher does like Italian stallions!). Maybe what is nearer to the truth is that both moms tried to do just that—and failed. Sexy and well endowed as Stallone is, he has, if Georgia thought about it circa 1990, just one major drawback: He is a bit long in the tooth these days for a lady who likes her men *young* and early-twenties virile.

Georgia, always full of ideas, some hot, some cold, tried to gain a little financial security back in the 1970's by opening up a store, fetchingly, if ill-advisedly, entitled Granny's Cabbage Patch in the elegant Brentwood section of L.A. The store sold expensive quilts, and Cher did her daughterly, and young Chastity her grand-daughterly, duty by rising and shining for the garish opening.

Today, with senior citizenship approaching, Georgia Holt of the many amorous adventures and the myriad spouses is somewhat hard-looking but attractive. On television she comes off as plenty personable and feisty. She speaks proudly and affectionately of the cute little girl who grew up to become that superstar of superstars Cher.

★ ★ ★

There was some apprehension when Cher got pregnant in late 1968, because she had already sustained two miscarriages. But in March 1969 a healthy baby girl was born, and they named her, in temporary euphoric ecstasy, after the picture they had just completed and were entertaining such hopes for. Some years later Cher got custody of Chastity when she and Sonny finally split up.

Cher has always made every effort to be a good mother and avoid the mistakes her own mother had made. But whereas her own mother had to run off to part-time jobs and auditions, scrounging around for every buck, every negligible, pathetic career "advancement," Cher was, by the time of Chastity's birth and to an increasing degree as the years went on, a *star* with responsibilities. She had money, lots of it, but she also had places to go, meetings to attend, things to do. She had her own life to lead, romances to further, satisfactions to sop up. It often seemed to her that there just wasn't enough time for it all, her supposition being dead right.

"It's hard," she has said. "Being a mother, you have to remember that you *are* a mother, even when you want to do something that's not exactly 'motherly.' I felt kind of guilty splitting and saying, 'I'll see you in three weeks,' but I knew she would be with her dad, and I wanted to do it, I wanted to go away. If [Chastity] hadn't accepted it the way she did, I don't know if I would have done it, but she was real cool about it."

It wasn't always so easy. Occasionally Chastity felt abandoned and insisted on going with her mother, such as one time that Cher and David Geffen, her lover after Sonny, were going to New York. "[Chastity] absolutely got hysterical. She was sobbing, 'I want to go with you!' " Cher gave in and helped her pack her bags so she could join them. "She had the most terrific time. She was out all day long every day with this Pinkerton guard having the time of her life."

Cher tried to make Chastity part of her professional life as well. In various TV shows in the seventies Chastity came on at the end with her parents (and later just her mother). She became a backstage fixture during that period, and her face was familiar to millions of TV viewers. In 1977 Cher had even contemplated doing a movie costarring Chastity and her half sister, Georgeanne La Piere, but it never materialized.

Cher thinks a lot of her daughter: "Chas is much more responsible, more mature than I am. I have all the confidence in the world in her judgment, so I don't really worry about her." She added, "My daughter feels that excess in anything is kinda stupid. . . . I just hope she doesn't have to go through too much to find out it really works as well in fact as it does in theory."

Cher and her daughter are very different people. Chastity has said that when she's with her mother, it's "never just a quiet day at home with nobody around." Being with her father, however, has "always been really calm and normal. That serenity is one thing he gave me that's really important."

Chastity Bono is not all-out bedazzled by her formidable mom, however. She has let it be known that she doesn't always approve of Cher's flashy style of dress. Cher has dismissed this airily as a "phase" that she hopes Chastity would hurry up and get out of and at times has even publicly accused her daughter of dressing like a bum. Chastity countered that she was into jeans and T-shirts (as her mother had been when she was young) and not into being a fashion plate.

Certainly Chastity Bono has not had an easy time of it, having been shunted back and forth between her parents when they were separating, divorcing, etc. Over the years she learned that the only way she could adjust to their different life-styles was to keep them separate from her own. Her parents could do whatever they pleased so long as they granted her the same freedom. It hasn't always been easy, but it says something for Chastity's balance and good sense that she has managed to maintain, to this date, good relationships with both her mother and her father.

Chastity's career ambitions began to surface as a teenager. She wanted to be known as something other than the cute little girl from the Sonny and Cher show. "It was a lot of fun," she remembers, "but as I look back, it's not like it was some accomplishment to be proud of. I was just a little kid pushed out onstage. It took no skill or talent, and it's the only thing I've done that's been seen." She is anxious to change that.

First she appeared in an act with her father at the Palm Springs Convention Center on New Year's Eve in 1987 on an "oldies but goodies" night. She admitted to having mixed feelings about it; she has always wanted to do things on her own. But the evening didn't really lead to bigger things. For one thing, her father's voice, on the sour, ragged side to begin with, had, if possible, worsened with age.

Meanwhile, Chastity studied singing and acting at the Lee Strasberg Institute and at New York's High School of Performing Arts. Covering all the bases, she then became a student at the NYU Film School. She is a much quieter and less flashy person than either parent, in more ways than one a shell-shocked victim of the Hollywood "star wars."

More recently Chastity Bono has formed a band with her friend Heidi Shink; they had a showcase concert at New York's Cat Club in March 1990. As would-be rock stars, Heidi and Chastity dress a little more flashily than Chastity does offstage, a sort of nineties twist on her mother's old mod sixties outfits. David Geffen, Cher's old boyfriend and recent record producer, has signed the two young women to a developmental deal. Perhaps Chastity, having tried first with her father, has decided to take advantage of her mother's more powerful recording contacts.

When her mother and father were briefly reunited on the David Letterman show in 1988, Chastity admitted she was shocked. "They've led pretty separate lives. But it was really touching to see them together."

Kyle Baxter Utley, a twenty-three-year-old and sophisticated disco scene onlooker and commentator, travels in the same circles as Chastity Bono and has met her on a number of occasions.

"I wouldn't call us intimates," Kyle says, "but I feel I know and understand her, what makes her tick. We talk movies. She loves Wim Wenders: *Wings of Desire*; *Paris, Texas*. She very much wants to make it on her own, be accepted for what she is, a product of her own efforts, her own self-development. She doesn't want to be tabbed as Cher's daughter."

According to Utley, "Chastity doesn't like it when her mother, or either parent, for that matter, comes up in the conversation. She turns off immediately. She'll just walk away."

Like Chastity, Kyle and his friends have hung out at spots like the underground downtown disco 113 Horatio, where Heidi Shink also goes. "Of course, we all move around. There are so many places to choose from," Kyle reports. "Each has its own distinctive atmosphere and somehow a different crowd. New York people represent a greater variety, especially at the discos, than is known. People think disco crowds are all cut from the same cookie cutter. Well, they're not."

To him, Chastity is essentially aloof, cautious, on guard, and more than a little defensive. "Not that she doesn't have reason to be," Kyle says. "So many people are out to use her to get to her mother."

Kyle recalls Chastity sweeping in with an entourage of twelve at 113 Horatio. "She flits amidst the crowd, never gives anyone that much time, and if she sees someone more interesting or more worth meeting or knowing, she drops whoever she is with and goes right on to him or her like a homing pigeon." Kyle's analysis of Chastity: "She is trying to find some meaning in life, some center for her being. I think she is very intent on this."

Cher has always wanted her daughter to have a boyfriend, even at the age of twelve. She told off an interviewer who suggested Chastity might be too young. "Young for *what*? I don't want her to go out and fuck her brains out. It's friendship. I can't think of anything more fun for her than to have a boy she can have a good time with, go to the movies with, tell everything to. . . ."

Years later Chastity's friendship with bandmate Heidi Shink—which their publicists insist is entirely platonic—was exploited by the tabloid press. The *Star* ran a big cover story that alleged Chastity was in love with another woman and that Cher was furious with her. The story told of alleged lesbian love-ins at the (then) all-woman bar the Cubby Hole, on Manhattan's Hudson Street.

Shortly before the story ran, one of the hot subjects in the media was the controversy over outing, the practice of dragging public people out of the closet whether they wanted to come out or not. The gay community was divided on the issue. Outing advocates maintained that it was time people, and the press, stopped treating homosexuality like a dirty little secret; if homosexuals were just as good as heterosexuals, why should there be such a fuss about naming names?

The supermarket tabloids, with their own agendas, joined in and pretty soon were doing outings on many celebrities and children of celebrities who they alleged were gay.

This resulted in a battle of the tabloids. While the *Star* ran further pieces on Chastity's love life, the *Globe* and the *Enquirer* got into the act. The *Globe* claimed that Sonny Bono blamed Cher for the whole mess, that her dallying with one boy toy after another had probably turned Chastity off men, that Cher's wild, wicked ways had turned Chastity into a spoiled, rebellious child who wished to embarrass her mother. The *Star* then proceeded to uncover a supposed "lesbian movie shocker" that Chastity had filmed at NYU, along with other gay-themed movies. Chastity's alleged movie featured two lesbians throwing a man down a flight of stairs and then castrating him. Another film of two women making love was said to be practically pornographic.

Still another *Star* piece was totally prompted by an incident in which *Star* photographer James Edstrom tried to take pictures of Chastity and Heidi at their Cat Club concert. Considering that this was after the *Star* had run the outing story, it was understandable that there was a reluctance to let the man take pictures. In a piece in The New York *Post* Edstrom charged that the Geffen Records director of publicity Lisa Barbaris had gone so far as to have a roll of film removed from his camera even after he had agreed to turn it in at the door. He took pictures of the two women afterward out on the street, and Cher's lawyer, Fred Davis, according to Edstrom, chased him down the block, demanding that he turn over the film. Instead, Edstrom handed it over to the *Star*.

"I couldn't believe it," Edstrom told the *Post*. "Here's Chastity with her Mommy's bus, her Mommy's amplifiers, and even her Mommy's record people and she's acting like Madonna. I have an easier time shooting Cher." He claimed, "They did not want to be shot together because they were just singing love songs to each other. It was Sonny and Cher a la the '90's.''

Meanwhile, the *National Enquirer* came out with a major story, "The Truth About Cher, Men, and Me," supposedly an exclusive interview with Chastity Bono. Chastity never came right out and denied that she was a lesbian in so many words but insisted that she shared a Greenwich Village apartment with two other women friends purely as a matter of economics (considering the high prices of rentals in New York, this explanation doesn't seem mendacious) and that she dated men, although she admitted she didn't have a steady boyfriend. She also denied rumors that she and her mother had a strained relationship and that her mother was pregnant. Most incredibly Cher had also granted the *Enquirer* an interview, according to the story, and expressed her belief that her daughter had what it takes to make it in show business. "I never thought she would have the roughness to go into this business . . . it eats its young," she was quoted as saying. As of that point, Cher remained silent about Chastity's lesbianism.

It was up to Michelangelo Signorile, columnist for the gay newsweekly *Outweek* and the man who started the outing trend, to put it all into perspective, as he saw it. In the February 18, 1990, issue he wrote:

> Chastity Bono is . . . being victimized by powerful forces. Making her decisions, pushing her around are: a homophobic record company, a manipulative, powerful, internationally-recognized public relations firm where gay is a dirty word (even if half the staff is queer, of course), a mother, who, at worst, wants her daughter to

be depicted as a heterosexual because she's worried about both their careers, and who, at best, doesn't care one way or the other, even while her daughter is being victimized by so many people; and a slimy, sensationalist, money-hungry media which loves to feed a homophobic society.

Signorile felt that the original *Star* piece was not homophobic and even ran a sidebar with helpful information for parents of gays. He claimed that the most egregious inaccuracies in the story may have been in the way it depicted Cher's reactions. According to Signorile's sources, Cher would not have any problem with any life-style her daughter chose, and if she had any worries they would only concern possible damage to Chastity's career.

He also claimed that according to his sources, publicist Lois Smith orchestrated the *Enquirer* rebuttal because she knew it had the same (low) credibility level of the *Star* and would therefore not bring the controversy into the mainstream press.

Whatever Chastity's sexual preferences, Cher herself has proved to be pro-gay in the past, such as in 1978 when California introduced the controversial Proposition 6, which would have denied homosexual teachers the right to practice their profession in the state. When Cher found out that the Beverly Hills Chamber of Commerce had actually endorsed Proposition 6, she decided to use her influence to convince it to do otherwise. Cher knew that people could be motivated by money, if not by their consciences. First she phoned the high-class Right Bank Shoe Company—where she was supposed to have spent tens of thousands a year on shoes—and strongly suggested that it protest the Chamber of Commerce's decision and build a movement among other merchants to do the same. According to *People*, "Cher's efforts—combined with those of other irate conspicuous consumers who threatened to immolate their credit cards on Rodeo Drive—worked, sort of. After receiving 200 phone calls in 24 hours, the Chamber voted to take no position on the amendment."

Cher didn't stop there. To help raise money to defeat the

proposition, she went to the Beverly Hilton's grand ballroom in late August 1978 to attend a fifty-dollar-a-plate luncheon. Although many celebrities had promised to appear, Cher was one of the few who actually showed up. On this occasion Cher said, "I think [the proposition] is a total invasion of privacy. I think it's against your constitutional rights, and I think it's an incredible issue that you have to prove your sexuality . . . it's an invasion of your rights as an American."

About her children Cher has said, "I don't believe so much in interfering or making decisions about your children's lives. It's none of my business. My children are very bright, very resourceful. I don't care what they decide to do, as long as it's not destructive. I really don't care, even if they decide to do nothing on an island somewhere. That's fine. It's none of my business." She hasn't forgotten how her mother tried to control her life even after she had left home and gone out on her own and how she forced Cher to leave Sonny for a time when she didn't want to. In retrospect, she may now think that wasn't such a bad idea.)

As far as her children go, Cher knows that *whatever* she does, she'll be damned. She tried to keep Chastity close to her at all times, to keep her career from interfering with their time together, and look what happened. When she took her to the opening-night party of her Broadway show, *Come Back to the Five and Dime, Jimmy Dean, Jimmy Dean*, a newspaper bashed her for daring to keep the child up so late. "Should 13-year-old Chastity Bono really be partying until dawn on a school night? The dear child and Mama didn't even arrive at a disco until 2:30 the morning after Cher's Broadway debut."

Cher's younger child is her son with second husband Gregg Allman. Elijah Blue Allman is now fourteen. Cher is very proud of her boy: "He's going to be the greatest singer of all time. He's got his father's voice, only better. He's like a little reincarnation of his father—only better."

Cher has always had a good relationship with her half sister, Georgeanne La Piere, a pretty blue-eyed blonde, and loved Georgeanne's father, John Southall, much more than her own: "[South-all] was the person I loved most in my childhood. I thought he was fabulous. But I didn't understand him. I was crazy about him, but I didn't *get* him. My mother kind of lived a rodeo life-style with him. I used to hear about how charming my real father could be, but he couldn't hold a candle to my stepfather."

Since her mother was working, and Southall out gallivant-ing, Cher found herself taking care of her younger sister for much of the time. Not that she always did a great job. Once Georgeanne devoured the wheels of a toy car when Cher was supposed to be watching her. When her mother found out, she gave Cher a beating.

The two played practical jokes on each other as children. After Cher saw Alfred Hitchcock's masterful shocker *Psycho*, Georgeanne sneaked into the bathroom holding a big butcher knife while Cher was taking a shower. Cher screamed as loud as Janet Leigh did.

After appearing on commercials and on such shows as *Ozzie's Girls* and *Police Woman*, Georgeanne read for a part on the tele-vision soap opera *General Hospital*—without telling anyone who her big sister was. On her own merit she got the plum role of Heather Grant. This was in the mid-1970's. No one found out about her relationship with Cher until the *Hollywood Reporter* let it slip. *TV Guide* had this to say of Georgeanne: "She looks like a pretty, neighboring teenager, with none of the smoky, sexual quality that pours from Cher." Georgeanne never appeared as a guest on any of Cher's three TV series with or without Sonny, but she did appear in the chorus on Cher's solo series. Cher bristles at any suggestion that it was her idea to cut her sister out. She says that she doesn't know why her sister wasn't included more, that she didn't always have a say in those matters.

Georgeanne has said, "I don't feel like my life's been a soap opera. I know it's been unusual, but my life isn't nearly as dramatic as it might seem. I never take drugs. I don't smoke, and I hate parties. I was a *very* good kid for someone growing up in the sixties." She has always been one of her sister's biggest boosters and has said that she wants to be just like her, that "she always made me part of everything." She had problems with Sonny, however. He tried to act more like her father than her brother-in-law, and she resented it.

Georgeanne La Piere wouldn't be human if she didn't feel a certain measure of envy at her half sister's amazing success. With a key role in a top soap opera in the seventies, it looked as if G —Cher's pet name for her sister—might also be on her way to the top. But major, even minor, success never really materialized. Still, the sisters were and are too close for it to become a problem.

In September 1990 Georgeanne got married for the second time in Aspen, Colorado, with Cher as her matron of honor. The private ceremony took place at the Prince of Peace Church. There was some confusion in the press on the true identity of the groom, the trouble stemming from the mystery man's work in "securities." One paper, assuming this meant investments, named the groom as the investment adviser Edward Bartalat. The groom was Ed Bartylak, one of Cher's security men and the director of special field services for Gavin de Becker's Hollywood security firm. Cher's date at the wedding was Richie Sambora, former flame and rock star. Nowadays Georgeanne's career ambitions are taking a backseat to wedded bliss.

Today the three women—Cher, Georgia, Georgeanne—have a basically warm and stable, if a trifle guarded, relationship. Her mother would love Cher (at forty-four?)—or someone—to have a baby. "At home, we're really just like any family," Georgia says. "We just hang out." She told of how after the Oscar ceremony that feted her as best actress, Cher got into "little pink baby bunting things with feet" and relaxed. Georgeanne insists her sister is "just a regular person."

Interviewed just after winning her Oscar, Cher referred to her family—mother, sister, two children—thusly: "We talked about this all day: what'll we do if you win; what'll we do if you lose. I said we'll probably have pizza either way."

People ask Cher all the time if she'd like to add a husband to that mother-sister-two-children equation, but she doesn't think she'll ever marry again. There *was* that disaster with Gregg Allman.

And before that her "star wars" with Sonny. She'll *never* forget that. . . .

Cher and Sonny at the
beginning of their career

Cher and Sonny make with the
guns in an early publicity shot.
Notice that Cher is wearing a
ring with "Sonny" engraved
on it.

ABOVE: Sporting their ATCO gold record, "I Got You Babe"

Sonny and Cher belt one out for the home audience.

A composite of the show

On the surface, it seemed as if they had it all.

An early appearance on *The Mike Douglas Show*

ABOVE: With David McCallum and Robert Vaughn on *The Man from U.N.C.L.E.*

Meet the Bonos.

ABOVE: Ronald Reagan made a guest appearance on the show.

Sonny and Cher looking very lord and ladyish

REDD FOXX AND TOM JONES TONIGHT!
Sassy Redd jokes. Sexy Tom sings. And a good time is had by all!

SONNY & CHER 8PM

KOJAK TAKES ON THE CASE OF AN ICE SKATER CONVICTED OF HER MOTHER'S MURDER
Someone high up is trying to silence Kojak! Just as he's about to uncover the truth behind a sensational killing. Telly Savalas stars. Special guest: Geraldine Page.

A SPECIAL 2-HOUR MOVIE

KOJAK 9PM CBS◉2

A full-page ad in *TV Guide* for CBS's stars, Sonny, Cher, and Telly

Cher took to billing herself as "Cher Allman" during her days with Gregg.

Gregg seems more interested in his lighter than he does in Cher.

THREE
STAR WARS

I was never so alone as the eleven years I was married [to Sonny.]
—CHER

"Sonny and Cher should have been brother and sister," Cher said after the divorce from her husband Sonny Bono. But by the time she realized how bad a mistake the marriage had been, she and Sonny were top television performers with a hit show and many major commitments. There was a business empire, dozens of cast, crew, and other employees to consider. Cher could consider only one thing: "We have a number five television show, and I hate my life."

The Bonos' years on television offered the American public a long-running soap opera as their private lives were played out in front of millions of viewers. Before the big split, there was *The Sonny and Cher Comedy Hour*. After the divorce Sonny tried his luck with *The Sonny Comedy Revue*; then Cher had *her* turn with simply *Cher*. After minimal success with their solo series they got back together to do *The Sonny and Cher Show* in spite of their having been divorced and gotten new lovers. As one critic put it, "With the collapse of Liz and Dick, they have to pass as our First Family of Show Business. They are the ultimate entertainment couple because they squeeze all of life's misfortunes into their act—marriage, fights, divorce, more fights. They understand that a good scandal is worth three seasons on TV."

In fact, Cher thought of making the last show of their first series a special divorce show, but "the network wasn't eager to, uh, get into that kind of stuff."

Sonny and Cher were in a pretty bad way—comparatively—before the show started. The emergence of acid rock music heavily influenced by the drug culture had all but obliterated the youthful interest in their kind of work. That meant that the recording contracts dried up; it was the kids, after all, who bought records. Meanwhile, the twosome continued their nightclub work, entertaining the parents of the kids who wouldn't buy their records. The *Chastity* debacle had left them stone broke—to their way of thinking, at least—and somehow they had to pay off all the back taxes they owed. The only good thing they got out of that movie was a beautiful baby daughter, and they would have had her in any case.

Fred Silverman, a powerful man in the television industry at the time, caught their act at the Americana in New York. He saw potential in the duo, particularly in their comedic abilities. TV people are not exactly known for their good taste. That is probably why Silverman likened Sonny and Cher to Mickey Rooney and Judy Garland, an overstatement if ever there was one. A new George and Gracie, possibly, but the Bonos were never in the same league as the immortal combination of the delightful and ultratalented Rooney and Garland.

Silverman parlayed his enthusiasm for the duo into a guest host shot on *The Merv Griffin Show*. Inspired by their work on that, he decided to build a show around them, *The Sonny and Cher Comedy Hour*. The year was 1971, and Cher was almost twenty-five years old. At first the show had a seventy-five-thousand-dollar-an-episode budget, and it was produced by Allan Blye and Chris Bearde, who took stock of the couple's shortcomings and figured it would be wise to surround them with as much distraction as was humanly possible. A number of supporting cast members were hired: Ted Zeigler, Billy Van, Peter Cullen, the talented black comic Freeman King, and his partner Murray Langston (infamous as *The Gong Show*'s "Unknown Comic").

The show also began the long association between Cher and dress designer Bob Mackie, who was told to clothe the lady in outfits that might imbue her with the glamour, confidence, and personality that she was, circa 1971, lacking.

No one had high hopes for the show. Sonny and Cher were practically has-beens, one step above dinner theater and summer stock. People associated with the show could hardly see it as career advancement for themselves. Only Fred Silverman had any real faith in the project. Whatever doubts he had had to be put to rest as the pilot was made; it was too late to back out now. Jimmy Durante, a sure crowd pleaser with his lovable schnoz, was the guest star on the pilot. Silverman wasn't taking any chances.

To help publicize the upcoming show, Sonny and Cher gave interviews, with Sonny doing most, if not all, of the talking. Since their young fans had deserted them, he felt free to say exactly what was on his mind. He said he admired the Smothers brothers—"their timing was good and their comedy fresh" (their show was the one Sonny and Cher were replacing)—but criticized them for getting "political" and "shoving things down our throat." He attacked Jane Fonda ("she gives me a pain right in my ass") and Adam Clayton Powell, Jr. (Ironically, years later Cher said that Fonda was one of the women she most admired.) "If I had one criticism to make of young people," Sonny said, "it is the fact that they have no humor. They can't laugh at themselves or anyone else. The things they don't hear, but should be hearing, nobody has the courage to tell them." He gave the usual Kate "God Bless America" Smith spiel, telling how he and Cher started out poor and now owned "a 28-room home," adding, "And how dare anyone criticize America!" Although Sonny had campaigned for Robert Kennedy, he was about as liberal as the Duke or Bob Hope, his true progenitors. Now that the hippie act had worn thin, it was time to show his true colors.

Cher wasn't much better. "Our big dream was to walk into

a store dressed in blue jeans and buy a Rolls-Royce. All we cared about was spending. We're both compulsive buyers. Sonny owns seven cars, and I buy clothes constantly."

If ever there was a period in their lives when the Bonos seemed worthy of intense dislike, it was the seventies. They had pretended to be hippies just to make millions of dollars, had lost most of it on lousy business decisions (*Chastity* was a case in point), and were practically slaves to the IRS. Not only were they not humbled or repentant, but they were rubbing everyone's face in the deception. They had already lost their fans, so they had nothing to lose. Now they courted the conservative older people as ruthlessly as they had gone after the youngsters. Instead of being vilified, they were awarded their own program. What did the kids care? They weren't paying attention any longer. The parents, of course, mightily approved of their conservative statements, seeing Sonny and Cher as rebels who'd grown up and developed mature attitudes; they did not take into account the fact that the old act had always been phony-baloney. "The news may come as a complete shock to the teen world, but Sonny and Cher are going straight. That's right, straight!" wrote TV critic Kay Gardella in the New York *Daily News*. She wasn't the only one who was fooled.

Sonny laid it on thick: "At one point in our careers the establishment was the big ogre, our enemy, so to speak. It isn't anymore. You might say I've established a rapport with the establishment." What he actually meant had nothing to do with politics. He just saw the new TV show, the new image, as a way of finally gaining the respectability he had always been craving from his Hollywood peers.

The pilot of *The Sonny and Cher Comedy Hour* aired on CBS-TV on Sunday, August 1, 1971, at 8:30 P.M. Wrote *Variety*: "Their approach is basically a variation of the former Louis Prima–Keely Smith lounge act, with the male braggadocio being deflated by the deadpan femme's putdowns. . . ." After describing the musical numbers, the review continued: "All of this sound and fury is not without its rewards, which include an irreverent approach and a certain degree of contagious boisterousness . . . but essentially the comedic approach reflects saloon humor that seems always on the verge of sliding into double entendre, with some Italian ethnic stand-up routines of questionable value for the living room. . . . The feeling persists that cabaret humor is not exactly what today's viewers are looking for."

John J. O'Connor in *The New York Times* commented on the tailored new image, which was still mod but "sleeker": "Sonny's hair is long, but not too long, and it's arranged nicely to set off his moustache, the absence of which would probably spell social and artistic suicide. Cher strikes notes of far-off kookiness while slinking about in an expensive and extensive array of costumes." O'Connor had trouble with the alleged comedy aspect of the hour, but he thought overall it wasn't bad. Jimmy Durante was an unqualified success in all the reviews even if no one else was.

The ratings for the initial summer run of the show were strong enough to warrant its return as a mid-season replacement on Monday, December 27, 1971. Producers Bearde and Blye did everything they could to make the show as ratings-grabbing as possible. Guest stars included very popular TV personalities like Carroll O'Connor (*All in the Family*) and Harvey Korman, the wonderfully gifted "second banana" on *The Carol Burnett Show*. Even actor Glenn Ford made an appearance. Opera singer Robert Merrill was drafted to bring the hour some class and culture, although he, too, participated in the silly spoofs, including a well-received comic operetta entitled *All in the Familius* with Merrill as "Archibald Bunker." Korman played a German to Cher's Lili Marlene and an alcoholic in need of redemption to Cher's Sadie Thompson and Sonny's hypocritical preacher. There were lots of song numbers and dazzling costume changes.

Another angle Bearde and Blye adopted to try to keep the viewers interested—and their minds off the fact that the stars of the program were *not* exactly Mickey and Judy—was to add a lot of visual flash: superimpositions used to segue from one number to another; special animation sequences; as many clever tricks as a video camera would allow. Often standard introductions were dropped in favor of visually arresting bridges from number to sketch to number.

The reactions were mixed. Not everyone was so dazzled that he or she didn't see the essential problems. Cher, as usual, came off a lot better than Sonny. *Variety* opined:

> As for the headliners, they have problems that could inhibit the show's future. Cher's singing and skit playing is different and arresting . . . with an earthy, almost vulgar quality that will not hurt her appeal. Sonny, on the other hand, is a stagewait [*sic*] every time he talks—a liability it's going to be hard to disguise with less loaded episodes than the preem show. Blye and Bearde have labored effectively in devising all kinds of imaginative bridges and frameworks to give the stars a lustre they don't naturally possess. Cher seems capable of growing in stature as a skit performer, but her deadpan delivery in husband-and-wife exchanges is monotonous. Sonny, however, is upstaged by everybody on the show in timing and delivery.

Said Kay Gardella in the New York *Daily News*: "What Sonny and Cher lack in personality and animation they make up for in ingenuity and style." She noted, however, that their personalities were not "big league."

Perhaps proving the maxim attributed to H. L. Mencken about never underestimating the taste or intelligence of the American public, *The Sonny and Cher Comedy Hour* was a hit. Audiences loved her playing her saucy Laverne character and her sitting atop a piano warbling in a sexy way about "vamps" (she played a different famous vamp in history each week). Gradually Cher got more at ease in the sketches and dialogue, but she was never a polished performer. Standing with her hand on hip, slightly leaning to the side, she affected a bored, blasé manner and delivered

put-downs in a somewhat liquidy, mushmouthed voice that became her "style." She talked very fast, slurring words together,
as if hoping to get them over with to find out if the audience
would laugh or not. The fur vests and dungarees of yesteryear
were traded in for glamorous outfits of the sort she would never
have worn at home—another example of her moving from one
phony image to another. Sonny for his part dressed in tuxedos
and god-awful mod clothes that did little to enhance his limited
talents and atrocious "singing."

The show lasted three seasons, during which Sonny and Cher
opened each installment by doing a stand-up routine on a set
decorated with balloonlike ornaments featuring drawings of their
faces. Audiences thought the put-downs Cher visited on Sonny
—his height, his ethnicity, his mother, his bedmanship—all in
good fun, but at that time the glamorized Cher was beginning to
feel like Galatea with a troll-like Pygmalion squatting at her side.
The marriage did not last much longer. Sonny had a habit of
constantly pointing with his finger to accentuate his remarks; Cher
even took to imitating that onstage, ridiculing him inside the
boundaries of the script. At times like this the audience laughed
uneasily. Now that she was a glamour puss, accepted in show biz,
and a genuine television queen, Sonny's presence at her side was
more embarrassing than ever.

Not that she hadn't been grateful. He had promised her that
they wouldn't lose the Hollywood mansion to the IRS, and they
hadn't. He had promised they'd wind up back on top again, and
they had. And yes, at the time she had loved him for it. But Cher
was beginning to realize that maybe she didn't need Sonny anymore. Now that she had achieved a kind of legitimacy, maybe
she could—was it possible?—become an actress, a real actress, in
a respected, serious kind of picture, not one of Sonny's watered-
down nightmares or comic book fantasies. Also, as a toast of
television she was being introduced to many good-looking men
and handsome actors. How could Sonny stack up against the likes
of them? There were other problems as well.

While these rumblings were sounding in Cher's mind and heart, the show continued. So did the act. They appeared at the Westbury Music Fair in 1972. According to *The New York Times*:

> Every husband and wife in the audience can identify with Sonny and Cher; the interchanges are witty but not caustic; the remarks are the sort everyone thinks of making after the fact. The tunes are melodious, familiar and uncomplicated, and Sonny wisely allows Cher to handle most of the singing. Since neither performer moves with even a modicum of rhythmic feeling, they compensate for the lack of action by turning themselves into animated clotheshorses. . . . These two are spiritually as old as Jack Benny and Mary Livingstone and professionally as glossy as a Las Vegas revue. Perfect, as I say, for the suburbs, but they sure aren't going to steal any fans away from Carly Simon and James Taylor.

The story was always the same. People got a kick out of Sonny and Cher and their glitziness, but the more astute members of the critical establishment weren't fooled for even one minute.

For the beginning of another season of *The Sonny and Cher Comedy Hour*, an ad in *Variety* featured a large, brooding two-shot of their heads and shoulders—Cher facing sideways, Sonny forward, their naked shoulders making them appear nude. It was kind of erotic, if not especially "warm," and daring for the time. The photograph later turned up on the cover of *Sonny and Cher's Greatest Hits*, a record album release in 1974, which included revamped versions of "You'd Better Sit Down, Kids" (with Sonny as vocal this time) and new, live versions of "I Got You, Babe" and "The Beat Goes On."

Sexy pictures or not, the strain was beginning to show on *The Sonny and Cher Comedy Hour*. As usual, an astute *Variety* tolled the death knoll, though perhaps prematurely in 1973. "Could this couple once have been considered too hip for television? . . . The opening stand up turn of the preem featured a half-dozen references to Sonny's height and a couple or three about Cher's shapeless tallness. Once such would be stretching the gag. This highly personalized comedy . . . can be amusing only to video addicts who through some sort of bleak masochism wish to suffer TV's overexposed coterie of 'name' talent again and again and again. No wonder the tube is short on variety series. If this keeps up, vaudeville really will be dead."

The critic need not have feared. *The Sonny and Cher Comedy Hour* was nearly over (although, phoenixlike, it rose from the ashes three years later).

Cher Bono had just about had it.

Cher had thought about leaving Sonny long before the end of the first TV series. In fact, she claims she and Sonny went to the network and asked if they could continue the series under such auspices. "It would have been the same show," she said, "except that it would be a divorced couple. . . . The network didn't like it." They separated but remained married and did the show for two more years, with Sonny continuing to hope for a reconciliation. This isn't as strange as it sounds. "Work is not where our large problems ever came from," she said later. "Sonny and I get along really well when we just work together. I trust him completely when it comes to work."

But she felt she couldn't trust him in much else. "He was dictatorial, unfaithful, demanding." He pulled a page out of his mentor Phil Spector's book and intensified his control over every aspect of Cher's existence. He made her a prisoner in her own house. She couldn't play tennis or go to see a movie when *he* wanted her *home*.

"I didn't object to him running things," Cher said in 1974. "He was better at it than I was. But I think people, including women, should have more freedom about how your life is run than just saying yes."

She insisted Sonny was not a bad person as such, characterizing him rather as "a male chauvinist. He thinks women are beautiful but should stay in their place, wherever that is." In short, she was sick and tired of playing Eliza Doolittle to his Professor Higgins. Her anger at Sonny grew over the years as she gradually came to realize how much of a controlling influence he really was.

The beginning of the end occurred in October 1972, when they were doing their act at the Sahara in Las Vegas. Cher was bored with the city; she wasn't into gambling; she had seen the "sights" a hundred times and really felt that when the gig was over, she and Sonny deserved a rest. But Sonny refused to take her on vacation to Europe, although he certainly could afford it. Cher was livid.

Something had been building up inside her for quite some time, something ever more fierce and urgent. She had achieved the American dream, yes, but she was utterly miserable. She worked herself up into fits of guilt about feeling so unhappy when she had the things other people would give their right arms for. She even wondered at times if something was wrong with *her*, if *she* was the problem. The problem was simple: She was *lonely*.

Cher, like many celebrities, learned the bitter lesson that success isn't much fun without friends. She and Sonny weren't into the dope-smoking party crowd of Hollywood or part of the old guard. For that matter, they rarely went out, and people who worked on the comedy show said the duo never socialized with the cast or crew. It was enough for Sonny just to have Cher around when he needed her—that is, when he wasn't preoccupied with business and making money. This wasn't enough for Cher. She wanted to enjoy her money, to go out and *enjoy her life*.

A normal person, a normal wife, could have just walked out of the house, driven to a local bar, and made some new friends. But Cher wasn't a normal person. She was a highly recognizable queen of television. She knew that wherever she went she'd be mobbed, that people would want to meet, touch, ogle at the glamour puss they knew from TV, but they wouldn't be meeting the real Cher, and they wouldn't be real friends; they wouldn't see her as a real, down-to-earth person. There would always be a distance between her and everyone she met, a distance that would make her feel lonely even in a crowd. She also felt that Sonny loved the *act*, the show, the fame, and the money they generated more than he loved *her*.

Most celebrities handled the loneliness problem by becoming friends with other celebrities, at whose houses they could party without being bothered by starstruck fans and grasping groupies. But Sonny and Cher did not have those kinds of friends; Sonny kept Cher trapped in amber like a prized butterfly.

When Sonny refused to take Cher on vacation, something snapped. She had tried to make him understand her unhappiness, and he wasn't buying it. Talking to him didn't do any good. She would have to *show* him. Demanding money from Sonny—he still controlled all their finances—she left the Sahara Hotel, in Las Vegas, with two shows to go and fled to San Francisco. Sonny was stunned. He raged about how she was screwing things up.

Yet the relationship continued, only with a new, emancipated Cher. Even though she didn't let Sonny tell her what to do anymore, she was reluctant to give up her reign as queen of television just yet. Cher didn't want to lose her bread and butter. The couple continued to live in the same house but were decidedly separated. They pretended otherwise to fans and the press, but close associates on the show could see the difference. To underline her emancipation, Cher even started dating, but hardly in any serious fashion. She still had ties to Sonny whether she liked it or not.

They didn't fool all the press during this period. Columnist Liz Smith traveled around with them for days during a concert tour and thought them "a better advertisement for marriage than the Richard Burtons" (who at the moment were models of marital bliss—a highly temporary state, it developed). Liz announced that she planned to write an article about Sonny and Cher's "perfect marriage." But she later reported in her column that she just wasn't able to do the piece: "Something kept nagging at me. . . . Why? Because deep down I felt sure this perfect couple was going to divorce any minute. Sure enough, they did, and everyone was thus saved from large helpings of egg-on-face, even though their then-press agent (who shall be nameless) was so infuriated that he tried to have me fired from Cosmopolitan for not writing the romantic story of Sonny and Cher.''

The ultimate breakup, which led not to separation but to divorce, also occurred in Las Vegas, again at the Sahara, exactly a year after the first fight, and was basically a variation on the first time. Cher was tired of living a lie. Sonny would never change his ways. As far as she was concerned, nothing could be worse than the life she was leading.

"The night I left Sonny I was literally going to jump off a balcony,'' Cher remembered. "Sonny and I had been everyone's darling couple. I was afraid of what everyone would think. And when I left Sonny, he said, 'America will hate you.' I said, 'I don't care.' It had gotten to a terrible point. I weighed ninety pounds and I was literally going to jump. I thought: Cher, why don't you just leave him instead? I don't know why you don't think of things like that sooner. I guess it's why battered wives don't think, just pick up and go. It took a long time to pick up after that.''

When Cher split, there was no way to salvage the rest of the Sahara engagement, and they were sued by the hotel. The people they worked with on *The Sonny and Cher Comedy Hour* started counting the hours toward unemployment, although there were a few shows left in the season. Sonny and Cher managed to muddle through those remaining episodes, but the atmosphere was distinctly somber and icy. Everyone was riding a dying beast and knew it.

Except the network. As the New York *Daily News* reported, "The CBS puzzlement over whether Sonny and Cher Bono, either one or both, can be counted on for TV work next season, is a major factor in the network's delay in completing plans for its '74–'75 schedule.'' Cher could have told them that if Sonny went on, it would be without her, and that is exactly what happened.

The "star wars" were beginning in earnest.

Sonny fired the first salvo, his macho need for vengeance perhaps overcoming his common sense (would there, after all, have been a Sonny without Cher?) by filing for a legal separation in February 1974. In spite of this, Cher was legally bound to honor her commitments—the last show of their series, a concert engagement in Texas—when all she wanted was to be *free*. A little over a week after Sonny filed for separation, she filed for divorce. If she had needed any further impetus, Sonny had provided it. She was particularly angry that he hadn't waited at least until the season was over.

Cher wanted Sonny to move out of their Hollywood mansion, but the man wouldn't budge. She moved into a house in Malibu, while Sonny's new girl friend, Connie Foreman, took up residence chez Sonny. Cher had always let Sonny take care of the business side of their careers and discovered she had reason to regret it. Attorneys told her the bitter truth: She was just an employee of a firm owned solely by Sonny Bono (ironically, it was called Cher Enterprises). Because of this, she couldn't star in her own series even if she wanted to! Cher charged Bono with breaking the Thirteenth Amendment and putting her into "involuntary servitude." Sonny countered that Cher had never done anything she hadn't wanted to do. He bitterly resented being cast as villain.

Meanwhile, Cher did everything she could to get back into that magnificent mansion filled with elegant and expensive appointments and antique furniture. If Sonny didn't vacate, she'd move in anyway. When legal avenues and threats didn't work, Cher brought two armed guards she'd hired to the mansion one night while Sonny was at a studio and proceeded to remove every one of Bono's and Foreman's possessions. Connie made a hysterical phone call to Sonny while clothes and suitcases were busily being dispatched onto the lawn. The guards wouldn't let an intimidated but raging Connie anywhere near Cher, but when she poured out her emotions into Sonny's disbelieving ears, he nearly keeled over. Cher then moved back into the house with her daughter, new flame David Geffen, and a secretary. Sonny was informed that if he showed up at the house, a guard would forcibly evict him. Connie capped the proceedings by running screaming into the night.

That was not to be Sonny's only defeat. When the court battles were over—Sonny and Cher still feigning lovey-doveyness in public at the trials—Cher was awarded twenty-five thousand dollars a month and custody of Chastity.

The name of David Geffen, Cher's new boyfriend, came up at the custody hearings because of his relationship with Cher. (He lived with Cher and Chastity in the house at Malibu before he moved into the Hollywood mansion.) Geffen was the new man in Cher's life, personally and professionally, and quickly he became the object of Sonny's enmity.

Geffen's first brush with show business was in the film *The Explosive Generation* (1961), featuring him in a small bit and a pre-*Star Trek* William Shatner as a teacher expelled after talking about sex in school. Ironically, David later worked for Phil Spector, as Sonny did, and also became one of the man's protégés; after that his mentor was Ahmet Ertegun, who'd signed up Sonny and Cher at Atlantic Records way back when. Geffen eventually became a manager (Crosby, Stills and Nash; Bob Dylan, Sonny's big "inspiration"; Linda Ronstadt, among others) and created Asylum Records before becoming president of a record company with his own name. He was young, rich, and powerful, had undergone many of the same influences as Sonny Bono, and in some ways was the same kind of self-made go-getter, but nothing in his experience could have prepared him for stepping into Sonny's shoes with Cher. He, of course, had stepped not only into Sonny's shoes but into his bed, where, according to reports, he had proved his manhood to Cher's satisfaction far more than Sonny had been doing recently.

Some people, however, speculated that Cher's and David Geffen's relationship was a *marriage blanc*—that is, one based on emotional needs, with little or no sex. Cher has publicly stated that she occasionally sleeps in the same bed with male friends, just to cuddle, not to make love. Geffen's admission to being bisexual, in a recent *Vanity Fair* profile, has lent some credibility to this rumor.

Whatever the case, Geffen and Cher had first met backstage at a Bette Midler concert. In September 1973 Cher had gone, sans escort, to a Neil Young concert at the Roxy nightclub (which

Geffen cofounded) in Hollywood and asked to join Geffen's group when she spotted it. Dinner later that evening led to a two-year affair and a much longer professional relationship. Geffen was two years older than Cher and not a whole lot handsomer than Sonny. "I've traded one short, ugly man for another," Cher told Paul Simon (who couldn't have been thrilled by her blunt phraseology) at a gathering. Rumor, however, had it that down between his legs Geffen was the tallest of the tall—which news when relayed to Sonny only humiliated and angered him all the more. Besides his private asset, Geffen boasted a curly mop of hair, a sharp nose, and prominent teeth, and a certain aura of confidence about him that made women feel supersexy in his presence. Little David, it seemed, had never lacked an admiration society wherever he cared to find it.

With his potent business acumen, David Geffen was the best person to help Cher get out of all the financial and legal entanglements that being an employee of Cher Enterprises had left her in. He became her manager, and that wound up costing *him* a lot in legal fees. In a town where money talked big, David's was truly a labor of love—while it lasted. David had also come up with some sharp concepts for Cher's solo show, which she was now, thanks to his help, free to undertake. The take-over–dispositioned, well-endowed Mr. Geffen romanced her, whirlwind-style, in full view of the world.

With David, Cher could do all the things she could never do with Sonny. Now she had someone to go out with. They went to parties, shows, discos, the theater, then back to the sack, where untold delights were to unfold with delicious, spicy unpredictabilities thrown in if Cher's retrospective indications were to be given credence. And there were the new, fresh, interesting friendships that David generated for her. For the first time in her life Cher began to feel that she had a circle of friends.

But three things eventually served to end her romance with Geffen. Yes, in her own way she loved him, but she was like a kid in a candy store: She wanted to try new things, meet new people, and sample new men. Men who had always aroused her fierce curiosity were now to be frustrating mysteries no longer. David Geffen had recharged her batteries more than he initially bargained for.

Also, after eleven years of marriage to one guy, Cher felt it was much too soon to be tied to any one person again. It also threw her off stride to find that David was as preoccupied, nay, obsessed, with business as the unlamented Sonny had been—more so, in fact. Holidays and weekend trips were cut short when David had to leave Cher to go off and see—personally, attentively—to some client's trouble or demand or whatever. Cher had been that route; she would not be left in some hotel room as she had been in Las Vegas. The new Cher knew what she wanted and didn't want.

Another problem with the Geffen romance was that Cher had a residue of feelings for Sonny, with whom she had worked intimately for years and who, after all, was the father of her child. She would wind up working with Sonny again. That eleven-year bond had turned out to be too strong to be broken that easily. David, feeling matters were slipping, proposed marriage. Cher's answer was no. Sonny must have been delighted when he heard *that* news.

Sonny, his manhood and most private aspects affronted mightily, always held Geffen responsible not only for the initial breakup of the act but for the breakup of his marriage. "I had always thought in terms of us forever. It just never dawned on me that we would divorce. . . . But then along came David Geffen—that little antagonist. There were times I wanted to kill him. I think it was a very bad period for Cher. He was a bad guy to be with. I thought of punching Geffen out but restrained myself when everybody said no." But money being the sexiest commodity of all, Sonny couldn't restrain himself from laying a juicy twenty-four-million-dollar suit on Cher for breach of contract.

Many people actually thought that both men had been used and discarded by the heartless man-mad Cher. That view is simplistic, a trifle unfair perhaps, but not entirely inaccurate, as Cher would have been first to admit. When Cher first met Sonny, she had been one of the millions of people who have vague ideas of attaining stardom but lack the drive, persistence, hard ambition to bring them to the top. If it's true that there would have been no Sonny without Cher, it is also true that without Sonny there'd have been no Cher. It was Sonny who provided the impetus and know-how that took them to the top. Cher indeed had the superior talent, but without Sonny?

To give Geffen his due as well, he was there when Cher needed him. He pointed her in new career directions, assuaged her loneliness and confusion, satisfied her sexual appetite, *and* got her finances in order. He gave her back her life. But he didn't do it on his own; the decision, the strength to break free from Sonny had been Cher's and hers alone.

There are, of course, three sides to the story: Cher's side, Sonny's side, and the truth. Cher's side carried much weight. There was no point in her remaining miserable with Sonny when she had outgrown him. She had knocked herself out to make Sonny understand; she'd given him chances, opportunities, insights into how to renew their togetherness that he had not picked up on. It was time to move on.

She wobbled back and forth concerning her feelings for the sexy, take-charge Mr. David Geffen, telling people later that maybe she should have married him, that besides being a super-lover, he was a hell of a nice guy, etc., etc. But always she concluded that he wasn't what she really needed. Publicly David could hardly have suffered, squiring a major TV star around Hollywood to posh affairs and parties. Cher, in short, must have seemed like a trophy to David. And if she broke his heart, well, people can't control whom they fall—or don't fall—in love with. Geffen (who has gone on to become one of the richest men in Hollywood, thanks to shrewd business deals) and Cher have remained friends over the years.

During her protracted divorce proceedings and custody battle with Sonny, Cher picked up a lot of knowledge, hard learned, hard earned, that she was not averse to sharing. Neither was a woman named Esther Eller, who appeared on ABC-TV to give advice to women like herself who had lost custody of their children in divorce suits, settlements, and other forms of torture. Listening in was Cher, who empathized so strongly with Esther that she called the station to offer the lady "full and free legal aid." Cher went even further than that: She contacted her lawyers, Rudin & Pearlstein, and instructed their New York associates to take on Eller's case at her expense in the best we-gals-must-stick-together style.

After their big split Sonny and Cher were not through with television (although at the time it wanted no part of them). Sonny especially was not about to give up what he had worked so hard to attain: stardom. He moved to a different network, ABC, kept the same producers and basically the same repertory company, and debuted in September 1974 on Sunday evenings. It was pretty much the formula of the old show, with female guest stars filling in for the missing Cher. The result, *The Sonny Comedy Review*, was, to most critics, pitiful. Audiences reacted in the same way, so the show was canceled after only three months, accompanied by much unkind-to-Sonny humor. He later repetitively lamented to anyone who would listen that to his horror he had come to work one day and had found that he had lost his parking spot. Respect, he lamented, is the first thing you lose when Hollywood greases the skids.

There had been advance intimations aplenty on what was to come. Howard Cosell had guest-starred on one of the shows, prompting a critical observation that it was surely appropriate to have one no-talent try to prop up another. When Cosell stood in for Cher in an Indian number, whining that Sonny wouldn't let him reveal his belly button, the bit was considered tasteless. A skit in which Sonny was tapped by authorities to become a new James Bond was dismissed contemptuously as a lowest-of-the-low commercial plug for the telecasting of *Thunderball*, which was to follow (with a concomitant mammoth increase in the ratings). Sonny got depressingly gooey and fudgy when he expressed his ecstatic reaction to being back on TV and got demerits for hopeless "maudlinity" via a horribly sung paean to a "lost love." One of the relatively kinder critics wrote: "Obviously he's wearing his heart on his sleeve for Cher." One cynic commented: "Yeah, like an agent with one client that's blown."

The chorus of critical damnation of *The Sonny Comedy Revue* was led by the New York *Daily News*: "A segment of ABC's Sunday night (Bono Show) is called 'Sonny's Bloopers.' Not included, unfortunately, is the hour telecast itself . . . to call Sonny's appeal 'Chaplinesque' is blasphemy."

Yes, the regulars of Sonny and Cher's previous show had gotten themselves brief reprieves, but it was soon back to the unemployment lines. Kay Gardella, the TV columnist, asked Cher, in the New York *Sunday News*, what she thought of the Sonny TV debacle. "I didn't like it!" she snapped. "I didn't think the producers gave him a fair shake at all!" The part of Cher that still cared for Chastity's father, couldn't take heart in his failure; instead, as she told friends, Sonny's slump "made me want to throw up!"

Cher's solo show, produced by George Schlatter, of *Laugh-In* fame, seemed to appear with magical celerity as soon as Sonny's show was off. It came on early in 1975 as a mid-season replacement, then returned for a second season late that year. Schlatter had definite ideas on how this latest Cher venture should be handled. In his words, "This [is to be] a personality show, not a format show. We want to capture and spotlight Cher herself, as she really is. Cher has always been photographed by a third-person camera. We're going to turn her around and let her face the first-person camera, let people discover the nameless, vulnerable kind of quality beneath the somewhat brassy exterior."

Despite this flamboyant, hyperverbal effusion by Schlatter, Cher embarked upon the program, which was dubbed, simply, *Cher*, filled with apprehensions. "I really started getting scared when ABC canceled Sonny," she lamented. "Now the closer I get to going back to work, the more I miss him and the scareder

I get. Professionally, I mean." Already Cher was preparing herself in her inmost consciousness for an eventual professional reconciliation.

The pilot for *Cher*, shown in February 1975, got mostly positive notices. *Cher* became a regular series in April, with Wayne Rogers, Raquel Welch, and Tatum O'Neal as guests. *Variety* thought that "Tatum O'Neal stole the show" and that Welch's "I'm a Woman" duet with Cher "stretched 'family entertainment' under today's overly sensitive definitions—but okay by standards that Ed Sullivan set for years on same basic time period."

It was around this time that various, mostly fundamentalist, pressure groups began lobbying for less sex and violence (what little there was of it on 1975 TV) and applying pressure on the networks' broadcast standards departments. As Cher told Mark Bego in *Cue*, "The censors have always been on top of me to make sure that I don't show anything, but somehow when they're worrying about showing something, we stick something in with a line or whatever. There are so many options on television because, on one end, you have the faction that's trying to get sex off the air, and on the other end, you've got everybody in America who wants to see tits and ass, and violence."

The censors got Cher in trouble with Raquel Welch on the first regular episode. They wanted to cut the suggestive "I'm a Woman" duet, but the producer convinced them it was too important. However, there was no such luck with Welch's sexily performed solo number. Cher wasn't in *it*, so it got axed.

Welch worked up a head of temper steam when told that Cher had ordered her number cut. Even when Cher assured her that it was the decision of those prim-and-proper idiot censors, responding to the ludicrous demands of "mid-America"—the same middle America that supposedly was shocked by her bare navel and flesh-revealing costumes—Welch refused to believe her. Welch got so worked up that she hung up the phone on Cher, at which time Cher shrugged and gave up. Even a call from the head of the network didn't appease Raquel.

Cher played hostess, of course, to other, less sensitive guests. She did her bit to bring rock into the mainstream by having David Bowie on. She had on other rock stars, too, helping give the rock field a certain "respectability." Now parents could *see* the rock stars their children kept talking about and could judge for themselves. Certainly, meeting and performing with these people helped cement Cher's eventual desire to become a hard rocker herself. It also prepared and conditioned her for a marriage to her second husband, rock star Gregg Allman.

Then something amazing—or maybe not so amazing to the informed—happened. Cher gave Sonny a call and asked him if he would consider joining her on TV for a new version of *The Sonny and Cher Comedy Hour.* At the time Cher told *TV Guide*'s Rowland Barber: "It was *me! My* idea! I made the decision after I'd done four *Cher* shows, last fall. Nothing to do with the ratings. Doing a show alone was more than I could handle. I had to be into everything, from helping on scripts to picking the music. And they had me doing a monologue. That's not like me, to be out there alone making with the jokes." She told *The New York Times*: "It's not much fun working without Sonny. When I wanted to ad lib, there was no one there. I'd rather have more fun and half the glory."

Cher may have been saving face here. Her show was badly slipping in the ratings. The public was appalled at the continuing soap opera of her on-again, off-again marriage to rocker Gregg Allman, which she was carrying on at that time. The show was suffering; Cher had to leave the rehearsals to fly off and help Gregg recover from his latest drug binge. The *Cher* program was heading for the same dumps *The Sonny Comedy Revue* had landed in. It had survived a second season but probably wouldn't make it to a third. Producer George Schlatter likened working with Cher Bono Allman to working with Judy Garland, whose life was a mess of drugs (her own) and man trouble—and you can't get much more judgmental than that.

But there were other reasons to do a show with Sonny than

Cher's sagging ratings and diminished public image. The romance with Geffen hadn't worked out; her marriage with Allman was a mess. And she had a lingering need and affection for Sonny. Even when she first started her solo show, she was saying: "After the trauma of the separation I didn't come down for a while. Then I started finding out things. About myself, mostly. Then the trip to Europe. Everybody says I had fun, so I guess I did—dancing all night in Paris, all that. But I didn't feel like me. I was going around in a daze, sleepwalking." She claimed that she missed working *professionally* with Sonny, *only*, but a Trilby can't escape her Svengali—emotionally at least—all that easily.

When Sonny heard from Cher about the possibility of re-uniting, he was doing a predictably mediocre solo stage show in Lake Tahoe. He couldn't have been more surprised to hear Cher's proposition. "I thought—and I said, 'As long as I know you, Cher, I will never cease to be amazed by you.' Then I said, 'Well, why not?' Doing a show together made a lot of sense. I wasn't having any fun by myself, and I knew the terrible demands on Cher of doing a single. I saw her going down. They were trying to make a producer out of her. Cher is an intuitive performer and terribly insecure if she's made to do anything else."

Cher undoubtedly had mixed motives and feelings about reaching out for and to Sonny. Yes, the demands of a solo show were rigorous. Yes, it was more fun doing comedy routines with a partner. Yes, she was insecure, still somewhat shy in front of an audience. And there was the possibility that she saw reuniting with Sonny as the only way to save their television careers. *Cher* was heading for cancellation, she knew that. Without Sonny she'd just wind up a TV has-been. With him? Well, the network couldn't resist all the publicity value in a *divorced* couple reuniting for a second stab at a TV series, so she might save herself from disaster. It was also possible that in spite of her many negative feelings, the court battles, and hateful words, she was still grateful for what Sonny had done. Perhaps she couldn't bear to see him reduced to pathetic solo acts in Lake Tahoe and was throwing him a lifeline with her offer. But there must have been times when she herself would wonder if she had gone utterly crazy. Sonny! Back in her life again!

There were certain conditions to be met first. Sonny had to drop his lawsuit against Cher; Cher had to go on a publicity tour with Sonny. (This condition was jettisoned when Cher got pregnant by Gregg Allman.) The situation was extremely bizarre and seemed to illustrate, as Rowland Barber put it, "the sanctity of divorce." There were Sonny and Cher, a formerly married couple who'd had one child together, back on TV doing their usual—but, then, not so usual—stand-up shtick—and Cher was obviously pregnant by another man! Sonny even made jokes about it during the opening of the first show.

Sonny's life at that time was not without romance. He had had a number of women, using his "star" stature, or what was left of it, to bed one lovely lady after another. "Sonny, no matter what age he gets to be, will never get a prostate problem," one of his friends joked.

At this point Sonny was keeping company busily with Susie Coelho. He told Earl Wilson that his love for Cher was like "A brother and sister love now. But with Susie, I love her like a *lover*! But we're not getting married. She doesn't want to get married any more than I do. Ten years ago we would have. I believe in marriage. I'm probably in the minority. I believe, though, even with my own daughter, I'd prefer she live with somebody first, to be stable and sure."

At a party at the time Sonny, basking in a throng of admiring journalists, including me, proclaimed: "I'm a philosopher about women now. They come; they go. Something big will come along for me again in that department. I'll be ready for it, and I'll recognize it when it does." He said he was glad to be back working with Cher because "I'm sentimental. And we always made a good team together." A month later he was telling me, "I'm an eternal optimist. Work and love. What goes around comes around; often it comes up roses. I look for the positive every chance I get; when negatives pop up—and who can escape them?—I roll with them, then go on."

Liz Smith, who'd once seen Sonny and Cher as the "perfect couple," wasn't surprised when they got back together and hinted in her column that the relationship might be turning out to be beyond the professional when they took what started out as separate vacations in Palm Springs. As Liz would have it, "Once [Susie] split, the ex-husband and wife . . . were together constantly. Sonny and Cher dined and danced romantically at Zelda's, the hot disco, and held hands three nights in a row at Melvin's restaurant in the inn."

Liz pooh-poohed those who hadn't even seen the professional reconciliation coming, as she had. "What do Sonny and Cher have in common? Well, years of wedlock in which he Svengalied, bullied and pushed her to stardom (Cher is basically a relaxed, less frantic type than the energetic Bono). Likewise they have a mutual adoration society going for their daughter, Chastity, whom they call 'Chas.' And then there is the pull of all that big money to be made from appearing as a team rather than apart. These seem," Liz concluded, "like three mighty compelling reasons for possibly keeping 'that old feeling' still in your heart."

The new *Sonny and Cher Show* was another mid-season replacement in February 1976. "Sonny and Cher are back together, and the excitement is underwhelming," said *Variety*. "Not bad enough to be camp," wrote the New York *Daily News*, "and not good enough to be solid entertainment." Said *Cue*:

> There was a time, and not so long ago, when divorce was accompanied by good, healthy vituperation. No more. Couples now separate and remain good friends. Blame it on group therapy, transcendental meditation or joint tax returns—the fact exists. What is most startling is that such post-marital chumminess now may be seen on television, which many of us assumed to be the final bastion of middle-class morality on earth. In short, Sonny and Cher are back together, for the sake of business if not for love. . . . On the show, Sonny and Cher seem to like one another, so I presume they DO like one

another, since neither of them has shown any indication
of acting ability.

Many critics praised the pacing and production values, as well
as the rapport that the couple illustrated when they sang together.
As usual, opinions of the comedy sketches were highly subjective,
with *Cue* finding them "uniformly sophomoric and unfunny,"
and *The New York Times* finding the skits amusing and better
written than usual.

But it was no use. People tuned in to see the first couple of
shows out of curiosity: What would they do? How would they
handle it? Once the audience got the answers to these questions,
the ratings took a dive. The show got on the fall 1976–77 schedule
on CBS but didn't make it to a third season. Now there was
nothing keeping Sonny and Cher together.

Cher has no regrets. "Even though I haven't been too crazy
about some of the things I've done, I'm not ashamed of them
either. I am not ashamed of *The Sonny and Cher Show*. I don't
think it's *Gone with the Wind*. Actually I don't think *Gone with the
Wind* is *Gone with the Wind*, so let's just say it wasn't *Citizen Kane*.
It's just not what I wanted to do."

During the rest of the seventies Cher kept busy with a series
of solo television specials. She became friends with Kate Jackson
of *Charlie's Angels*, and the two made attempts to collaborate on
film scripts; but nothing ever resulted. As the specials got glitzier
and more and more overproduced, the reviews got worse. Kay
Gardella wrote of one 1978 special: "[Cher] bombs so badly that
one wonders who the guiding hand was behind this atrocious
hour. . . . Did the entertainer's childish fantasies take over and
dominate the direction of the hour? Her limited talents were always
skillfully camouflaged by Schlatter when he masterminded her
weekly variety series."

Cher shrouded herself behind powerhouse guests—Lucille
Ball, Elliott Gould, Dolly Parton, Shelley Winters—and in glamorous Bob Mackie costumes. The production numbers got wilder
and more imaginative: a montage of reproductions of magazine

covers she had modeled for; a battle between a rock group representing the forces of evil and Dolly Parton and a gospel choir representing the forces of good, with Cher's soul at stake. Cher brought in autobiographical statements, with her as a child lamenting to her "mother" that she's not blond and pretty enough to become a star. Her children, for good measure and (she hoped) heightened effect, appeared on her lap.

But Cher was unsatisfied. She did disco records and played Vegas, a city that she had always hated and that had bad memories for her but that paid her well. "I was thinking I should be fulfilled, but I wasn't. I wondered, 'What is the matter with me? Am I nuts? Why aren't I happy?' And trying to make a nice face for everybody—trying to do what everybody does in their normal life. Being so much more visible."

Cher continued to nurse her secret ambition, or maybe it wasn't so secret, for the clues were all around if people wanted to look for them.

Cher wanted to be a movie star.

But it would be quite a while before that would happen.

Whatever happened to Sonny Bono?

Sonny had also had his eye on motion-picture appearances. He was turned down for roles in *Earthquake* and *The Godfather, Part II*. He did win a role in the horror-fantasy film *Troll* in 1986. As one critic put it, "If your idea of entertainment is seeing Sonny Bono metamorphose into an *apartment* of foliage, this is the movie for you." He appeared in *Hairspray*, a John Waters film with Divine. In this he is the father of a blond bitch who's competing with Divine's daughter, Ricki Lake, for a coveted auto show title. Even after years of appearing onstage and on television and doing sketches with numerous professional actors, Sonny's performance is stilted and awful. He's even outacted by Deborah Harry, playing his wife. Harry gets into the outrageous caricature of the mother, but Bono is just stiff and unconvincing, putting too much effort (in the way of the essentially talentless) into too little. Divine (hardly a subtle performer) and Jerry Stiller, as Divine's husband, played their roles with just the right comic touch. The movie is charming (and has a more serious subtext) but didn't do anything for Bono's career, for which Bono has only himself to blame: It was Waters's first really mainstream feature and got a lot of attention and good reviews.

Sonny was married to three women after Cher and has two children with his latest wife, Mary, a sexy dark-haired woman with a Cher kind of sassiness about her. The fact that he was no longer married to Cher didn't keep him out of the scandal sheets. As recently as March 1990 one tabloid had him accusing his wife of having an affair with the manager of their restaurant in Palm Springs. Sonny Bono is now the mayor of that fair city and credits himself with taking a tired, apathetic town and giving it life— film festivals, the Virginia Springs competition, etc. Admittedly all was not beer and skittles even in this new career incarnation. He ran into some resistance with certain of his plans for civic betterment and complained that it was not so much that some worthy citizens of Palm Springs wanted things to stay the same as that change meant everyone had to give a little. "What's wonderful about [being mayor] is that forty thousand people put their whole lives and whole beingness [sic] in your hands," Sonny rhapsodized on one of his better days. "It sounds corny, but it's kind of spiritual—that people say, 'Okay, take care of us.' Something bigger than you takes over you, and there's a responsibility you have that's awesome and exciting." Svengali had turned messianic, it appeared.

In September 1990 Sonny came to New York to appear on *Regis and Kathie Lee* and to promote his new line of Sonny's chocolate chip cookies; this entailed a trip to Bloomingdale's. He plans to add more items if the cookies are successful. As for politics, he admits to onward and upward ambitions and has his eye on the Senate.

Sonny has aged well circa fifty-five, is still attractive (in his unique, inimitable way, Sonny *is* an original of a sort). He still has that boyish-sounding, nasal voice and is as vaguely awkward and disarmingly stumbling as ever. But Sonny adherents like to remind the public and those who "put him down" that it took balls to get where he did originally, that he did parlay his Cher into a great starring career, and that by the standards of the ordinary guy, he has been an energetic, an ambitious, a sexually and spiritually potent, never-say-die superachiever. Talent may have had nothing to do with it, but persistence, energy, determination, and an ego bigger than his stature all have put Sonny on the map and in the permanent records of show business and now in politics. "Sonny's always had a great self-awareness," a friend has said, "a strong narcissism; his attitude has been: *eat it!*" Those not interested in "eating it" may not get the real thing, but the cookies may take him farther than people think. Sonny never says die.

The last time Sonny performed with Cher was during a special reunion on *Late Night with David Letterman* in 1988. Letterman wondered to the world if Cher had any special tensions or feelings over the reunion. "I feel nothing," she said, but admitted that she and Sonny maintain to this day a strange relationship that no one—they included—can fully understand. Sonny concurred. According to all reports, Sonny is an attentive, concerned, and supportive (but not possessive or demanding) father to Chastity (now pushing twenty-two and, of course, a grown woman with her own agenda) and a substitute father, pal, and adviser to Elijah Blue, Cher's child by Gregg Allman, who is now weathering all the turbulences and torments of going-on-fifteen.

Sonny certainly seemed moved enough, on the 1988 Letterman show, singing "I Got You, Babe" with Cher. No matter what had transpired over the previous twenty-six years, they had been through a lot together. Cher was just a touch more distant. She could never go back to what she once was, and Sonny represented all that. Still, she seemed reasonably warm and friendly or, as one friend put it, "noblesse oblige, gracious. She could sure as hell *afford* to be!"

Sonny has said, "I can stand outside and say: I really loved the act. I love Sonny and Cher. I always did."

To many, Sonny Bono may have made his impression on Cher, but he does not play much more of a part, circa 1991, in this story of a tattooed lady. He is essentially a seventies artifact, a show biz casualty, a mild American curiosity.

Cher, on the other hand, is a *star* and very much on her own. From now on it's Cher's story alone.

FOUR
JUST SAY NO!

I'm alive! That's about it!
—CHER, commenting on the difference between her
  and Janis Joplin

*I just have the feeling that people can't cope with drugs. If they
could, it would be a different story. But I don't know anyone
who can handle them. Drugs handle people, not the other way
around.*
—CHER

The late sixties ushered in the beginnings of the drug culture—acid rock, head shops, grass, hash, and LSD. Psychedelic posters. Black lights in dormitories. Jimi Hendrix and Janis Joplin (two early casualties of the rock-drug life-style). It was "in" to be turned on. Ordinary alcohol would not do. Kids had to be different from their parents and get high or trip. Of course, it was just the same old thing—an escape from dull, everyday reality—but the youth of America didn't see it that way. Their idols—the Beatles, the Rolling Stones—used drugs, sang about drugs, glorified and glamorized drugs, and helped popularize their use. Drugs became commonplace. Even parents, cops, politicians lit up a joint now and then. Little did anyone dream of the nightmare he or she was starting.

Is it possible that Sonny and Cher could have predicted the

escalation of the drug problem? Could they have known where the romanticizing of the drug culture would lead? Did they know something nobody else did?

The explanation is simpler. Like most people over thirty at the time, Sonny couldn't see what people needed with drugs. They didn't interest him. He felt no peer pressure. Cher went along with Sonny. Neither of them was really a hippie. Both had no use for drugs. Undoubtedly they believed—as has been proved true in many cases—that the use of "soft" drugs, such as marijuana, led to the use of "harder" drugs, such as coke or heroin. Being in the music business, Sonny and Cher saw more than enough junkies and cokeheads. They didn't like what they saw and had no desire to wind up that way. "I went through the whole drug bit before I met Cher," Sonny said, and gave up drinking and smoking.

Sonny and Cher were phony about everything else, but not about their antidrug stance. About LSD they said, "It's a crutch that we don't need." Sonny went so far as to urge a youth commission on drugs at the 1968 Democratic Convention.

Cher has admitted to experimenting with drugs in the early days. She tried marijuana and Quaaludes, got sick on amphetamines when she was fourteen (seems that girl would try *any* thing at fourteen), and has gotten excessively polluted on alcohol on occasion. She was only human. "Drugs are not a very important part of my life," she has said, however. "I feel I have to be clear to handle things.

"I really don't know about drugs firsthand," she confesses. "I've gone through it. I think one of the saving graces is that drugs don't agree with me, they just don't. I'm already in a real strange place anyway. I like to be who I am."

Cher has never tried what is perhaps the most popular drug in Hollywood, cocaine. "I would never do it because I've never seen anybody I know who thought they could manage it that did. I love the idea that I've never done cocaine. There are other things I can't handle in my life. I don't want to add something else." Coke would hardly fit into her "health addict" life-style anyway.

Cher was "pissed off" over comedian John Belushi's drug-related death. "If he was here I'd slap his face for being so stupid. This is not Janis Joplin time—how could he do that? I had some really good times with him." Because of that tragedy and so many others, Cher is committed to doing something about drugs.

"I am going to do my best to see that my kids don't do drugs," she has said, telling daughter Chastity: "Chas, do me this favor. If you're going to do anything, please come home and we'll do it together, because if you have to do something, I don't want you to do it alone, and if I can talk you out of it, I will."

Cher acquired her antidrug convictions the hard way. The woman who had had hardly any use for cigarettes, alcohol, or even soft drugs like marijuana got married to a junkie! But even before that she had gotten a frightening firsthand look at the tragedy and waste of drug abuse in Hollywood.

In September 1974 Cher went to a club called the Troubadour to see a rhythm and blues group called the Average White Band. After the performance Cher was one of several people invited to a party in the Hollywood Hills along with members of the group. The host was to be one Ken Moss, a Gary Lewis look-alike who was known as the dropout stockbroker. Moss had dropped out of Syracuse University, claimed he'd made 1.5 million in the stock market as an options trader for Vogel-Larber, then become founder of Freelandia, Inc., a charter airline that featured water beds and organic food. The airline didn't make it in spite of much media hype. Moss was a Hollywood character of the type that Sonny Bono had always shielded Cher from before. And his party was the type of party that Sonny never wanted her to go to.

But Cher didn't think that at the time. She was out having fun, socializing, meeting new people, going to a real Hollywood party instead of sitting home alone with Sonny. She walked around the living room, talking and laughing with people she knew, as well as to strangers, and felt herself fitting into the groove, so to speak. Until . . .

Ken Moss came out with a bottle of white powder that he told everyone was cocaine. Many of the people at the party did not have to be encouraged to take a good sniff. When it was Cher's turn, she refused to have any. (The police confirmed this.) Within fifteen minutes what had been a lively but amiable party scene suddenly turned into a horror show. Moss had actually—and fatally—given his guests China White heroin!

The band's drummer, twenty-eight-year-old Robbie McIntosh, was taken to a Howard Johnson motel in North Hollywood by his wife after partially recovering but died nine hours later. Bruce McCaskill, the band's business manager, didn't call the authorities to the hotel until noontime. Bryan Russell, who had danced on *The Sonny and Cher Comedy Hour*, was said to have become so ill that he checked himself into the hospital. Cher was one of the few people who kept their cool during the ensuing panic when people who'd sniffed the heroin started keeling over. She couldn't help everyone, but she did take the band's lead singer, Alan Gorrie, home to her mansion in Holmby Hills, where she saved his life by applying ice packs to his body and walking him around so he wouldn't lose consciousness, as a doctor she called suggested. If not for her, Gorrie would certainly have died.

Cher must have thought at the time that all the evil things Sonny had told her about Hollywood and the people *out there* were absolutely true.

It wasn't until five months later that the tragedy fully hit home. An album the band had recorded before McIntosh's death hit the top of the charts; the Average White Band's single "Pick Up the Pieces" was number one in the nation. But McIntosh wasn't around to enjoy it.

Ken Moss allegedly fled to British Honduras, leaving the authorities—and Cher—with many unanswered questions. Had Moss known that the "cocaine" was actually China White? Had he deliberately served stronger stuff for kicks and thrills, to see what would happen? Did he anticipate such a horrible reaction? Or did he just think everyone would get superhigh and be happy?

Cher was left with other, lasting questions: Why did people do that to themselves, take that stuff into their systems? You didn't even know what you were getting; maybe your host didn't even know.

She vowed she'd never try cocaine—or whatever on earth it might be—and she never did.

After this frightening experience with heroin it was indeed to be something of an irony that Cher's second husband turned out to be a heroin addict. But he was. His name was Gregory Le Noire Allman, and he sang with the Allman Brothers Band. He had formed the group with his brother, Duane, in the sixties, and it became very successful. One of their most notable numbers was called "Midnight Rider," an irresistible soft-rock ballad that summoned up images of swift riders over moonlit plains, outlaws, beautiful senoritas, and the vast outdoors of the old Wild West, as well as a haunting subtext of a man forever on the run and doomed to loneliness because of it. In some ways it was the story of Gregg Allman's life.

There were tragedies in Gregg's past that would forever haunt him: the murder of his father years before and the death of his brother in a motorcycle accident in 1971. Another member of the band died the same way the following year. Gregg couldn't take this mixture of tragedy and performance pressure, and that was the beginning of a downward slide that even the love of TV goddess Cher couldn't halt for long. Her marriage with him may conceivably have caused her more anguish than her eleven years with Sonny.

It started when Allman asked if he could meet her when she came to see the band at the notorious Troubadour. He asked her for a date, and she said yes. Gregg was unpolished, awkward, folksy—not at all a seeming match for a TV glamour queen—but Cher found him appealing. For years people have wondered what she saw in Gregg, but the answer is really simple. She saw herself as she used to be: awkward, gangling, messy—a real slob. Her TV image, after all, was not the real Cher. She had been the girl who lay around in Sonny's apartment without lifting a finger to dust, throw away candy bar wrappers, or even change her clothing. She found Gregg's down-to-earth qualities appealing. Maybe, she felt, she wouldn't have to put on an act with him; she could be herself.

But there was a limit to what she'd put up with. When Gregg got a little too friendly in his car—his impression of Dr. Octopus no doubt—Cher made it clear that she expected *some* class. As the evening progressed, it just got worse. Sure, Gregg was a change of pace from Sonny and even David Geffen, but he was *too* much in the other direction. She wanted a nice country boy, maybe, but not a farm animal.

Anyway, before *that* particular session with Gregg was over, Gregg had passed out, his head falling forward into a plate of Chinese food. Cher fled.

Yet there was something appealing about the guy. And he was not without his share of rusticated sex appeal. Cher, confronted with a younger man with evident little-boy problems, wanted to play mother for a change. When he had the gall to call again and suggest another date, she, who had once been Sonny Bono's "little girl," said yes to this new "little boy" on her horizon. As long as they were on the dance floor, they were all right. Making conversation with Allman was, alas, a disaster. Cher was hardly an ultrasophisticate, even by that time in her life (1975), but at least she was a grown woman by then, twenty-nine years old, in fact. Gregg, only a year her junior, seemed in some ways a decade younger than that, hence qualified as the first of her older woman-young man relationships. There was also something charming, she had to concede, about a twenty-eight-year-old (at least physically) man coming on like an eighteen-year-old. And he *acted* like a little boy. He was so cute and cuddly, so charmingly awkward; yes, boyishness, she decided, had its own intrinsic appeal. Certainly he was not bad-looking, with blond hair down to his shoulders and a pink, smooth face.

His boyish surface hid some basic truths. Gregg Allman had already been married twice, and he was a bull in the bedroom, highly experienced in pleasuring women, especially the frustrated please-awaken-me variety, among which Cher, pushing thirty as she was, reluctantly numbered herself.

This young buck, when he finally got Cher into the sack, gave a masterly account of himself, making her erupt with a fully realized, exorcising passion she had never known before. When she and Gregg made love, it was a real workout, thorough and complete, absolutely nothing left to chance, a variety of calorie-burning exercise that Jack La Lanne had never conceived of. Gregg didn't make love like older-man Sonny, that was for sure, or even like a twenty-eight-year-old; he was more like that boy of eighteen she had seen in him. Experienced as he was, Gregg was not jaded; he drove into her like a passionate teenager. This was a new one for Cher: a guy who knew his way around a woman's body yet remained self-intoxicatedly conscious of his own, as self-enthralled as any kid who had found that first major thrill life had to offer. This kind of boyish sexual atavism got Cher thoroughly hooked. *Here* she was not learning the true essence of love that that older, protective, nurturing Sonny had tried to teach her. *Here* with Gregg, was the true essence of *passion*, and that beat everything! *This* was no slam-bam-thank-you-ma'am one-night-stand joke. *This* was no Warren Beatty trying to prove himself at her expense nor other varieties she had known that seemed almost perfunctory, mechanical, compared with *this*, with Gregg Allman. . . .

Many later thought that her total sexual and emotional enthrallment with Gregg Allman—the second man, and the last, to leave her a child to remember him by—was for a long time her undoing; only her strong character prevented it from becoming her unraveling.

Or as one of the more heated fan magazines put it, "It is far more likely that our heroine's head has been turned around (and around and around) by love—or sex (or both!). It is most always through sex that a man gains his initial power over a woman, and it is usually love (hers for him, that is) which enables him to hold on to that power." Gregg held the power for a long time. The overall result was that people thought that Cher was being too manlike aggressive with Gregg; she who had been led by other men was now herself doing the leading. Trouble was, many opined, Cher was thinking with a part of her anatomy other than her head. How else, in their eyes, could this overwhelming all-encompassing attraction be rationally explained?

Supposedly Cher was totally unaware of Gregg's drug problem when they first started to go out. When they were at a restaurant and Gregg would nod out at the table, Cher would explain to the other guests with a little smile, "Isn't that cute? Gregg had such a hard day at work, he can't stay awake." Finally one of her friends cued Cher in that Gregg's habitual drowsiness might be due to reasons other than hard work!

Even when Cher found out about his drug addition, she still didn't drop Gregg. She was unable to move out of his over-powering sexual aura and get a handle on herself and what she was doing. Yes, Sonny had held the power of the father surrogate, the parent figure; Gregg's power—well, far from *all*, but primarily—the power of youthful vigor and virility, was all between his legs. She had fun—of many kinds and, yes, outside the bed—with Gregg, fun of the kind she had rarely had with Sonny. Even David Geffen endowed with a fair share of sex appeal, paled by comparison. She wanted Gregg all to herself; she never wanted the fun to end.

So she married him—this man many believe wins hands down, in retrospect, as the great love of Cher's life, one of many loves, to be sure, over the years, but still the greatest, the champ of 'em all, the truest taste of genuine passion Cher was ever to know. . . .

On June 27, 1975, Cher was granted a divorce from Sonny Bono. On June 30, 1975, Cher—or Chooch, as Gregg called her—became Mrs. Gregg Allman. The fact that the wedding took place at Caesars Palace in Las Vegas perhaps indicates how impulsive and "serious" it was. Nevertheless, the twosome were able to rustle up a wedding party of several people, including managers and Cher's sister, who was maid of honor. Years later Gregg insisted that the marriage was all Cher's idea, that he just went along with it and made a foolish mistake. If anyone made the mistake (now that all the returns are in), it was Cher.

"I think I married Gregory," Cher said later, "because I was so tired of having someone tell me what to do that I chose someone who couldn't even tell himself what to do and couldn't try to be dominant over me."

And what did Sonny Bono think of this new young man in her life? Oddly, he liked him a lot better than he had David Geffen. "Gregg is not the bad guy" was Sonny's summation, recognizing as he did the man's serious problems. Sonny actually felt sorry for Gregg.

Cher's blithe assumption, as she got deeper into her marriage with Gregg, that she could get him off drugs turned out to be as naïve as Phyllis Gates's assumption that she could keep husband Rock Hudson away from men. Even many of her friends and associates believed that Cher would have her work cut out for her weaning Gregg off heroin, that it was as hopeless a task as if she'd married Liberace and expected him to give her children. Though the drugs seem to have made Gregg even more bullishly imaginative and insatiable in bed, the dark afterside of it—his mood swings, his manic frenzies—proved even too much for tough-gal, seen-it-all, man-wise Cher. Nine days after she had made Allman all hers, Cher Bono Allman filed for a dissolution of the union.

That wasn't the end of it. Barely a month had gone by after that when Cher decided to reverse herself, and Gregg was back in the sack with her, making love with the same physicalized eloquence that had hooked her in the first place. Gregg had also given in on the drug argument and agreed—sulking little-boy style—to do something about it.

Meanwhile, Cher was busy trying to salvage what remained of her solo TV show. Her producer, George Schlatter, was having conniption fits, what with Cher putting more in-and-out-of-sack energy into Gregg and her loser marriage than into her show. Moreover, the negative publicity (is Gregg in or out this sunny morning, dear listeners?) was playing havoc with the ratings.

Certainly the fan mags and the press were having a field day with the Allmans. Most people might have continued to accept Cher after her blockbuster split with Sonny and his ongoing charges of ingratitude, perfidy, or whatever else he came up with, but this thing with Gregg Allman was wreaking havoc with her credibility cross-country. It made her seem flighty, unstable. The less responsible columnists even suggested that it must be Cher who was on the drugs—a canard. That got her angry and retaliatory in print—that is, when she could find a journalist who thought truth was more exciting than lurid fiction, and these were in short supply, in 1975 or any year. One article suggested that Cher had surrendered to her more self-destructive impulses and was following in the footsteps of her mother, in fact, trying to outdo her image as "manizer supreme."

Then there was the speculation that Cher might remarry Sonny when she finally got Gregg out of her system and his masterly lovemaking out of her heart. After all, the fan mags speculated busily, hadn't the old lady married Cher's daddy three different times? Like mother, like daughter—those two dizzy broads were *man-mad*! And so it went. The general consensus certainly was that Cher wasn't thinking straight that summer of '75 and for some time after that. Years later she agreed.

The marriage reeled on for two more years (1975–77), oiled by Cher's generously self-indulgent obsession with Gregg. Gregg, with his finger in his mouth (temporarily) like a naughty small boy, let himself be persuaded to go to a drug addiction clinic in Buffalo; Cher left her show to be with him and help him through it. Her determination to stick with the marriage was reinforced by his suddenly expressed resolve to cooperate with the doctors and get his life "back under control" (had it ever been? some people wondered).

But Cher couldn't, after all, play nursemaid in Buffalo forever; she had professional commitments to meet. So did Allman. He wobbled off on a tour. Soon the word came that he was going hog-wild on smack.

In his own right a rock star for some years, Gregg was no stranger to press, fans, groupies, crazy people who practically tore his pants off after a performance (one wild girl had even unzipped his fly, reached in, and grabbed the precious family jewels before being pulled off his crotch by frantic cops; she left a scratch, mercifully light and surfacy, on his scrotum). But being the husband of Cher was another matter entirely. This was fame really blown up to epic proportions, and Gregg cringed from it, hated it. At her end Cher began getting minor nervous breakdowns from incessant returns to the mansion she had wrested away from Sonny only to find the joint full of cokeheads and junkies, Gregg's companions in nightmare. By this time not only was Cher's solo show dipping ominously in the ratings, but Gregg's band was falling apart. Personally and professionally the lives of the Gregg Allmans had become disaster areas.

Soon Gregg was heard from in the press. *She* had been quoted all over the fucking place; now was *his* turn, he indicated. He let it be known that being "Mr. Cher" had been "a big obstacle in the beginning" (as the whole country knew, anyway). He went on: "During that first year Cher and I were together, the Allman Brothers Band broke up. The organization of the thing got out of hand. On the last tour there were 28 roadies, each drawing like $500 a week. We went on a 52-city tour and came back to count it up and we had $100,000 between the six of us. We worked our asses off for nothing!"

Gregg Allman's body had always been on the sexily chunky side, with small pocket areas of baby fat, but his weight began to fluctuate severely as the marriage dragged on. After Gregg had kicked heroin, he promptly went alcoholic and ballooned up to two hundred pounds for a time. When he kicked the booze in turn, he lost some of the excess avoirdupois but was never at his "fighting weight."

Whatever their problems, the two did stick up for each other. Not only did Cher prove her loyalty and devotion time and time again by staying by him and desperately trying to get him off the drugs, but Gregg rushed vociferously to Cher's defense when people accused her of being responsible for the breakup of the Allman Brothers Band. He made a point publicly and often, of putting the blame right where it belonged: internal organizational problems. He may not, it is true, have been as open in assigning some of the blame to his ongoing drug problems.

Cher stuck up for Allman again during a controversial trial that pitted Allman against his former bodyguard John C. Herring, who was accused of trafficking in cocaine. Apparently Allman had switched from heroin to coke at one point, thinking it might be less addictive and more "respectable," and Herring had been his supplier. Under promise of immunity, Allman testified that Herring had sold him cocaine on several occasions.

Cher bristled when people suggested that Allman was the true guilty party, that it was he who had got Herring involved in the drug scene, not the other way around. Allman's turning "stool pigeon," as certain quarters saw his action, so angered various parties that his life was even threatened. Result: U.S. marshals searched everyone who came into the federal courtroom in Macon, Georgia. "This is an overabundance of precaution," argued the judge in the case, who had become mightily irritated by the excessive publicity and security measures. Herring was eventually convicted, but his sentence was overturned. He and Gregg later were reconciled.

When Sonny and Cher got back together for their second TV show, it put an additional strain on Cher's relationship with Gregg. Gregg could hardly help realizing that there was still a strong personal bond between the former husband and wife. Because of the new show, Cher was spending more time with Sonny than with Gregg; she knew that she had to devote her full attention to the show, or it would wind up in the ratings cellar, where *The Sonny Comedy Revue* and *Cher* had been. Special planning meetings had to take precedence over everything, even marriage. She had done her best for Gregg; now he would have to return the favor and understand her situation. Instead, he moaned about being left home alone all the time. At that point he didn't have the band or a tour to occupy his time, and Cher lived in constant dread that he would fill up that loose time with booze and/or drugs. But

Gregg Allman did something a little less predictable. He filed for divorce.

This time around might have spelled the finish for the Cher-Gregg marriage, except that Cher was pregnant with her second child and her first and only by Allman, Elijah Blue. As always the most romantic of sensualists and the most sensual of romantics, Cher worked up fond hopes that the pregnancy would save her marriage, because she was still deeply in love with Gregg. The usual pattern of her life reasserted itself, this time in heightened form; Cher needed to be in love. She needed to be needed. Her relationship with Gregg was diametrically opposed to the one with Sonny. *He* had been Superdaddy; now she wanted to go on being Supermommy. But she also realized that she was fighting a losing battle against Gregg's assorted addictions. She swore—yet again —that she wouldn't reconcile unless he made a sincere, total, and final effort to cure himself.

Her resolve was really put to the test—one she failed to pass—when she took Chastity on a "get-the-fuck-away-from-it-all" vacation to Hawaii. Premature labor pains put her in the Kapioloni Maternity Hospital in Honolulu for a week. She was extremely agitated, having already gone through the trauma of two earlier miscarriages, but the doctors assured her that she would be okay if she took it easy. She was, nevertheless, a badly fright-ened woman, so she called Gregg in Macon, Georgia, whence he had currently fled. Summoning his manly resolve, moved by and concerned about this woman who loved him deeply and obses-sively and was carrying his child, he flew to Hawaii to be at her side during what, for her, was one of the most difficult periods of her life. There, surprisingly, Cher and Gregg rediscovered the things they liked about each other. For a while it looked as if the marriage might be back on track.

July 1976 brought the birth of Elijah Blue. His birth seemed to cement the love that Cher and Gregg felt for each other, and when twenty-nine-year-old Gregg, confused, tormented, guilt-ridden over his out-of-control life, cuddled his baby son, he felt a wonderment, a reaffirmation of his manhood of a kind he had never known before. Like Cher, a sensitive artist with a creative capacity that was depthless (yet never was to be fully tapped), Gregg Allman tried to summon from within himself a determination to fulfill his manhood in ultimate, permanent terms. For several months proud, devoted parents, Cher and Gregg felt subconsciously that they were making yet another of their (ultimately doomed) last stands for happiness.

A year later Cher and Sonny's second stab at a TV series was put out of its misery by CBS. Secretly this was what Gregg had always wanted. Now Cher could stay home and fulfill the womanly, nurturing side of herself, taking care of him and their son, "my two boys, my two babies," as she called them.

But on his rocky road of the spirit, still filled with good intentions foredoomed, Gregg was still fighting not always successful pitched battles with Demon Coke. When he saw the fear and hurt in Cher's eyes one day, he knew that once again he must try to "make like a man" and in August 1977 entered a facility in New Canaan, Connecticut, the Silver Hills Foundation. This was the same place where such equally tormented luminaries as Joan Kennedy and Rita Hayworth were to be patients.

The treatment, which, to his credit, Gregg weathered heroically and purposefully at the time, seemed to work, and the Allman-Cher alliance seemed reinforced. With their boy a year old, they reexplored what she called "that sublime mutual passion," which had deepened after all they had been through together. Soon there was a rumor that another Allman tyke would be on the way—a rumor that proved false.

Gregg and Cher were deep in plans to do an album together. He was thirty now, he told himself, time to put away the boy for all time and become, again for all time, the husband and father, the *man* he was. The title they chose for their album was amusing, but poignant, too: *Two the Hard Way*. There was some controversy over the billing. "Gregg and Cher," they decided, didn't have quite the right ring to it. They decided it would be clever to bill themselves on the album as "Allman and Woman." Not everyone was amused. Said Cher: "My publicist said I couldn't possibly have a record without my name on it, so I fired the publicist." While plans for this project were underway, Cher hoped as she said later, that pairing with a man whose artistic talent equaled, indeed probably exceeded, her own, would reap even greater dividends than the efforts with willing, diligent, disciplined—but essentially untalented—Sonny Bono had. . . .

Love can make people guilty of crucial mistakes, can blind them to certain realities and imperfections, and this sadly became the case with Cher, Gregg, and *Two the Hard Way*. The public had never taken to the romance, the marriage, the off-again, on-again pairing of Cher and Gregg Allman. In their private world the love-pierced pair thought of themselves as rivaling Dante and Beatrice, Elizabeth Barrett and Robert Browning, Romeo and Juliet, Abelard and Héloïse. Delirious in their mutual ecstasy (when things were going well, that is), they wanted to draw the whole world, by osmosis into its mysteries. But the world did not want to be drawn in; it saw only the negative aspects: the drug addiction of Gregg; the "foolish obsession" of Cher; the frequent partings; the startings and stoppings. If the public didn't like these two making "beautiful music" in the figurative sense, they didn't like them doing it literally either.

Not that *Two the Hard Way* could be called beautiful music when it finally debuted before a hostile world. To put it simply, it bombed with the critics. Another problem: Hard rock didn't seem—at that time—to suit Cher. The public of 1977 knew her as a glamorous pop queen; they wanted its Cher to stay that way.

The cover for the album drew much comment, and it is as hilarious as it is sexy. Cher and Gregg are half naked, entangled, Cher looking like a sophisticated hooker and Gregg like the good ol' boy who never changes his underwear. Passionate, potent, fierce, and in his way handsome, certainly sensitive and charismatic, Gregg Allman this time out just didn't register—not at all. Critical consensus: He wasn't "glamorous-looking," a verdict with which both parties of the ecstatically intraobsessive pairing passionately disagreed.

But it was the tour for the album—a losing proposition from the first—that led to the final, abrupt breakup. Gregg, forced to come to terms with the realization that Allman and Woman was no substitute for the Allman Brothers Band, began drinking again—heavily. Cher, brokenhearted yet again, saw him sliding back into the same old self-destructive pattern. She also realized that she could not stand to see him go through it all over again. She knew her man well by now—only too well. And now there was their son, the symbol of their love, to add a painful complication to what was already a heartbreakingly poignant dilemma. And would Gregg soon be back on coke? Heroin? No, it was just too much. When they returned from the tour, Cher, death in her heart, illusions crumbled to ashes, told him they were through.

She later looked back on this, the saddest of her life disappointments to that date, more calmly and objectively and said, "I realized it was never going to be any different. . . . And I finally became bored. That sounds capricious of me or whatever, but I knew I was the one who was trying to put the strength into him. I would leave him and go back, leave him and go back. Finally I just said fuck it."

Cher was tired of being lied to all the time. Gregg would never stick to his promises. "If someone lies to you ten times, you start becoming numb to whatever they say, but it took me an awful long time." She stayed with Allman, to be sure, as long as she could—until she "just didn't have the juice anymore. I wouldn't have gone through it, except that nobody ever made me feel as happy as Gregory did. God, he's wonderful. I don't understand why he can't see it. He's the kindest, most gentle, most loving husband and father. But then he forgets and everything goes to shit."

Cher knew that *this* time around, when she broke it off, she could not go—could not *dare* go—only halfway. She didn't even want to know where he was. "It's better not to know what he's doing because it's just too hard for me. If I knew, I'd want to be with him and help him."

Cher, in the final analysis, broke it off with Gregg for the same reason that she had broken it off with Sonny: emotional survival. If Sonny had nearly driven her to fling herself off a balcony, what would living with a slowly disintegrating drug addict and alcoholic have eventually driven her to do? she wondered. Gregg refused to help himself and only plunged their existence back into misery just when things looked as if they might well start getting better. She felt she had no choice.

When Gregg Allman left what for him, as for her, was one of the "great loves," he also didn't look back. For a along time he cut off all communication with his ex-wife and son. Over the past fourteen years, Gregg has seen Elijah Blue, this child conceived of a once-ecstatic, all-enveloping love, only about half a dozen times, if that often. Cher and he are supposedly on good terms, though, probably because they see each other rarely. Cher, calmed after the great storm and after the passage of all those years, believes now that going through that brief simmering volcano of a marriage was worth it for no other reason than that she got her "beautiful baby boy," Elijah Blue, out of it. But when she looks into the child's face, she sees the memory of a promise sadly unfulfilled. What are her feelings at such a time? These she has not shared with anyone. . . .

Cher has also said that she still likes everyone whom she's ever loved. Indeed, she and Gregg spent one New Year's Eve together long after they were divorced. Whatever communion, spiritual or otherwise, the former lovers achieved on that sadly isolated occasion, they have kept to themselves.

Cut to 1990, thirteen years later, after their love had died. Gregg Allman and the Allman Brothers Band returned with a new album, *Seven Turns*. Part of their tour was a concert at New York City's Madison Square Garden in September. Gregg was now forty-three years old. The group previously tried a comeback in 1985, and while an appearance at a special jam show brought in offers, they all seemed too nostalgia-based to interest the band, the members of which wanted to move forward, not into the past. In 1987 the group got together again in New York for (ironically) an anticrack benefit but felt in retrospect that they were not at their best. The new band consists of Allman, Dickie Betts on guitar, Butch Trucks on drums, and newcomer Warren Haynes on slide guitar.

Butch Trucks told Jim Farber of the New York *Daily News*: "Gregg is no more difficult to work with than other people. In fact, Dickie was just telling someone the other day that even though he once said he'd never play with Gregg Allman again, he said the same thing about his brother after he broke his bicycle and he got over that, too."

Gregg Allman broke Cher's heart. But she recovered—partially. Since those unhappy two years Cher has had many relationships with men. But she has never remarried.

FIVE

YES, BUT CAN SHE SING?

When I sang, they said I couldn't act. Now that I act, they say I can't sing.
—CHER

"I'm not the best singer in the world," Cher has said, and she's absolutely right. But she's not the worst either. In over a quarter of a century she has recorded twenty to forty singles (ten with Sonny, ten solo), three-million-selling singles, one-million-selling album (with Sonny), and four-million-selling solo albums. Around twenty albums in all and about thirty single records. Not bad for someone who can't sing.

"I can't listen to my voice. I don't like it," Cher said. "You see all your mistakes when you hear your voice. You see all your imperfections."

Cher began her singing career as a backup singer for records produced by Phil Spector. These included "Da Doo Ron Ron" by the Crystals and "Be My Baby" by the Ronettes. Her last backup record was "You've Lost That Lovin' Feeling" by the Righteous Brothers.

Cher didn't use her own name for her first record, "Ringo, I Love You." She was billed as Bonnie Jo Mason because Sonny really thought the record was stupid. The song was supposed to be a confession of adoration from a starstruck fan to Ringo Starr of the Beatles. As Sonny had expected, it went nowhere. The whole thing was just a tax write-off for Phil Spector, who thought Cher singing "Ringo, I Love You" was a colossal joke. For one thing, Cher had yet to develop any firm control over her voice. The record did nothing for her career.

Neither did "The Letter," which was released in the spring of 1964. This was the first of two releases in which Sonny and Cher were billed as Caesar and Cleo. On their second record, "Love Is Strange," Cher showed some signs of improvement, but she still had a long way to go.

It was back to the chorus in late 1964, with Cher once more singing backups on the all-star recording of "Yes, Sir, That's My Baby." The act was billed as Hale and the Hushabyes but actually consisted of many major rock and roll and soul stars of the period. Like the earlier recordings, it has become a collector's item.

"Baby, Don't Go" was the first official Sonny and Cher record in 1964. Cher was supposed to record it alone, but she was so nervous that Sonny joined her in the sound booth and cut it with her. Cher's voice was beginning to exhibit some of the confidence it developed in later years.

Cher's first real solo (not counting "Ringo, I Love You") was "Dream Baby." Her voice was subjected to multiple tracking and all sorts of electronic tricks, resulting in a record that sounds as if it were recorded underwater. She was billed as Cherilyn because Sonny was afraid her contract with Imperial Records would restrict Sonny and Cher from recording on another label. Later records had the name Cher on them. Cher's deal with Imperial was her big break to that point.

Sonny and Cher's next record, for Atco, was "Just You," but the one that sent them hurtling into major success was the one after that, "I Got You, Babe." It became the biggest hit in the country in August 1965, and America's "hippie" couple was on its way. With this record Cher began adjusting her voice to match Sonny's. Since Sonny was practically tone-deaf, the results were less than felicitous. Sonny and Cher turned out several other records, but the two that did the best were "Bang, Bang" in 1966 and "The Beat Goes On" in 1967, both of which are fondly remembered by even casual fans today. Their other records have basically faded into obscurity. During this period, there were also a few albums: *Look at Us*, Sonny and Cher's first album; *All I Really Want to Do*, Cher's first solo album; and her second, *Sonny Side of Cher*.

Sonny and Cher made a few more records together in the seventies, none of them particularly memorable. "All I Ever Need Is You" was recorded in 1971 to cash in on their new TV show, as was "A Cowboy's Work Is Never Done" (1972), which was their last hit record as a team. They followed it up with "Mama Was a Rock and Roll Singer" (and an album of the same name), and it was a bomb. Sonny stayed out of the sound booth with Cher until 1977, when they recorded "You're Not Right for Me," another commercial failure and a disco record, to cash in on their second TV show together, *The Sonny and Cher Show*. As recording stars Sonny and Cher—as a combo—had a very limited run.

In his exhaustive survey of the career of Sonny and Cher, J. Randy Taraborrelli nailed it down: "With 'I Got You, Babe' and the hit records that followed it, Sonny and Cher, along with the Byrds and the Mamas and the Papas, became West Coast purveyors of the folk-rock sound Bob Dylan had defined and popularized on the East Coast. In terms of rock and roll, they were the bridge between the dying Phil Spector girl-group sound and the new American music as it recouped its losses after the British invasion. Historically, though, Sonny and Cher have never been recognized as part of the revitalization of American pop, or as being at all integral to contemporary Sixties music."

Massive volumes covering the pop and rock scene of the sixties mention Sonny and Cher only in passing; they are not considered terribly important or serious by rock authorities and chroniclers of that era. Many think Sonny had a greater impact on the rock music world than Cher did; in histories of rock music there are only the barest references to Cher Bono. Sonny's casual "plagiarisms" had ensured that whatever truly noteworthy records he wrote or produced would be overlooked.

"I personally was not very fond of Sonny-and-Cher music," Cher told the New York *Post* in 1977. "From that period of my life there were only two albums that I liked." Presumably they were the Cher solo albums.

Today Cher is a little more mellow in her opinion of the music she made with ex-mate Sonny, if just as realistic: "I always liked what Sonny was writing about. I thought it was kind of appropriate, and yet I'm not so much proud of the creative part, or my part of it, but we were a really interesting team. We were larger than the thing we were doing, because what we did wasn't that great. It's never going to go down as great music, but we made an impact on a generation, so we must have been doing something more than just singing."

Sonny and Cher had their share of imitators, such as Friend and Lover, a boy and girl duo that recorded "Reach Out of the Darkness," a painfully obvious hippie-we-all-gotta-love-each-other kind of song. Most of these imitators have long since faded into obscurity.

Cher had spent so much time singing backup for black soul groups that it was only a matter of time before she recorded an album devoted to that kind of music. *3614 Jackson Highway* came out in 1970 and is probably remembered, if at all, for Cher's Indian drag on the cover. The album was not successful. What did people need with Cher singing that kind of material when Aretha Franklin, Gladys Knight, and so many genuine black artists were doing it already—and doing it better?

But Cher really hit her niche with her next single, "Gypsies, Tramps and Thieves," written by Bob Stone, which came out in 1971 and was a smash hit. Although the sales certainly weren't hurt by the fact that Sonny and Cher's TV show, with all the resultant publicity, had just gone on the air, the song is so good that it probably would have hit number one in any case. A snazzily produced and beautifully arranged number, it's a lively and irresistible ditty about a Gypsy girl living in a caravan on the outskirts of town. The sanctimonious townspeople call her and her comrades insulting names during the day, but at night all the hypocritical husbands sneak back to the caravan to pay her for pleasure. She winds up with an illegitimate child who's doomed to the same squalid and hopeless existence.

It's debatable if the song has much to do with the actualities of Gypsy life—it seems about on the level of some movie with Jane Russell and Victor Mature—but its catchy melody, handsome orchestration, and attitude of repressed anger and unrestrained sensuality are memorable.

"Gypsies, Tramps and Thieves" capitalized on Cher's wild, Gypsy, do-anything-for-a-good-time image, and her voice on the record is strong and throaty and exhibits an insolent sexuality. "Gypsies, Tramps and Thieves" was the biggest-selling single in the history of MCA Records, according to *Record World*.

Two albums followed in quick succession. *Cher*, which featured the ambitious single "The Way of Love," said to be indicative of Cher's new growth as an artist, and *Foxy Lady*. Next was *Bittersweet White Light*, a disaster in which Cher recorded a number of old standards in what sounded like the old-time tone-deaf approach she employed while singing with Sonny. Behind the scenes Sonny put the package together and made the mistake of including "The Man That Got Away" in the list of numbers. Recently the much-maligned Pia Zadora gave a fairly good account of herself doing this classic number, but any woman who essays it is really taking on the ghost of Judy Garland. In spite of Garland's melodramatic excesses (in both her life and in her acting) and her over-gesticulating when she sang, the fact remains that Garland was a great singer and Cher was not then, nor ever will be, in her class. Had Cher not been in such thrall to Sonny at that time, she might have known better. Or would she? *Bittersweet White Light* could have been better described as "acrid black butchery." It's a miracle that it didn't end Cher's recording career right then and there, but not enough people bought it to realize how really awful it was.

"Half-Breed," a 1973 single that also became a big hit, was an attempt to re-create the excitement of "Gypsies, Tramps and

Thieves," with Cher as another angry outcast wailing about the iniquities of life. It wasn't as memorable as "Gypsies," but it certainly sold well.

Her next album, *Dark Lady* (1974), was nailed down by *Rolling Stone*: "Two catchy hit singles, *Dark Lady* and *Train of Thought*, highlight . . . the newest set by Las Vegas's leading contralto whose stylistic forte is the blasé whimsicality with which she approaches any and all material. . . . Cher seeks to entertain on the lightest of levels." But it added: "Cher's voice is so attractive that one senses possible future directions, e.g., a commitment to country soul, assuming a desire to shuck off her television persona."

By this time Cher had lost much of the stylistic patterns of Sonny Bono, but she had developed distinctly unappealing quirks of her own, such as singing out of the side of her mouth.

Wrote *Variety*: "Cher's vocalizing . . . accentuates vowel sounds in a manner reminiscent of [Keely] Smith." (And, to a certain extent, Lena Horne.)

Cher did not just accentuate her vowels; she folded, spindled, and mutilated them. She'd circle each note in a zigzaggy fashion, going from sharp to flat to sharp again, as if she were a weasel suffering torture. Part of this was from a desire to sound "jive"; years of singing backups with black singers had caused her to stretch out and play around with her vowels just as they did. Coming from a glamorized, glossy white woman, the effect was strange, to say the least. She approached every song as if it were a spiritual, but of course, she hadn't quite paid her dues.

What made it worse was what this vowel stretching did to her face. Her mouth made extremely unattractive contortions—lower lip to the left, for instance, as the upper lip stayed where it was; then the lower lip to the right while the upper lip went up —as she sang. It looked as if she were *chewing* on the notes, masticating the music until what came out was different not only from the songwriter's intentions but from what nature itself intended. If only she would just sing a song straight, she might sound natural and melodious.

Still, her voice had its good qualities. She had lung power, that was certain. In addition, her voice was sassy and sensual. Her vibrato has been criticized, but it gives her voice a certain punch and vibrancy. She can belt out a song if it comes to that. What was needed was a certain subtlety and grace. Subtlety has never been Cher's strong point.

Cher did two unusual records in the mid-seventies. The first was a new recording of the Ronettes' "Be My Baby"; only Cher did the lead instead of backup. Cher did a slow version of the song, which was a mistake. The melody of "Be My Baby" can't really stand up to close inspection and wasn't strong enough to handle the new arrangement. The song requires an upbeat, sexy tempo and fast pacing. The flip side, "A Woman's Story," was no more successful. Phil Spector was the producer, but the reunion produced nothing especially noteworthy.

Then Cher did yet another new version of an old song: "(A Love Like Yours) Don't Come Knocking Every Day." Despite the publicity value of having Cher team with then-popular Harry Nilsson on the song, the record was a failure.

Nobody could say that Cher didn't have nerve. All her life she had loved Sondheim and Bernstein's score for *West Side Story* and dreamed that one day she'd sing all the parts on television. She did just that on a special in 1978. The result was not good: "If we harbored any doubts about it *not* being her voice," wrote the New York *Daily News*, "we don't know now after listening to her struggle valiantly through *West Side Story*. What guts! She actually has the effrontery to sing all parts, including those of the Jets and Maria. To hear Cher's rasping, deep tones fight to reach those high notes, like a captain of a sinking ship shouting his last orders, is an experience not easily forgotten."

Though Cher had always been accused of having limited range, not everyone agreed. In *Life* magazine TV reviewer Cyclops rushed to her defense; he thought not only that Cher was "more beautiful and sings better than almost anyone else on television" but that she brought "a little Elizabethan bawdy into Plasticland, with a vocal range that ascends from the diesel truck to the clarinet, pit stops in every curve."

Cher's next album, *Stars*, was released to cash in on the publicity surrounding her new solo TV series, *Cher*. Her new boyfriend, David Geffen, had gotten her the deal, and Warner Brothers had high expectations for the record. The reviews were not good, and neither were sales. The critics seemed to see the album as a summing-up of all that was wrong with Cher's singing career.

"Cher is a stylist without a true style," wrote Janet Maslin in the *Village Voice*. "Her vocal tricks have always sounded profoundly unmotivated and arbitrary, devoid of emotional continuity. . . . Almost all the songs on *Stars* are too well-known in other versions for her to hide behind them without sounding second-hand. . . although selections seem jarringly disparate at first, most of them either accentuate or humanize her standard pose, [sharing] a sense of outrage with Cher's Indian outcast or gypsy dancer."

The *Christian Science Monitor* said: "No matter how hard she and producer Jimmy Webb try to prove otherwise on this record, Cher is just no rock and roller. . . . Image, not music, is Cher Bono's main ingredient for both records and TV." Trying to sing Eric Clapton and Neil Young, Cher was "out of her element and outclassed in both cases."

James Spina was merciless (and on target) in his review for *Women's Wear Daily*:

> Cher is solid (plastic) proof that 600 fingernails and 600,000 costume changes can do wonders for a flat singer. Now Bonoless, her musical guidance has totally vanished, resulting in her worst of many bad records. . . .
> On hearing her redo the Everly Brothers' *Love Hurts*, one gets the impression that Cher is reading the lyrics for the first time, backed by a limp orchestra that has been playing the songs for three years straight. Her mild pretense of some vague uphill battle in every piece is horrendously fake. . . . You can lead a hoarse voice to

a song but you can't make her sing it well. Maybe next time she'll at least give us a chuckle by redoing "Sonny" and changing the inappropriate words. . . . Didn't anyone realize that these songs have nothing to do with Cher's video-village style?

Cher seemed to be having one debacle after another. Her next album was *Two the Hard Way*, the ill-advised entry with husband Gregg Allman, the two billed as Allman and Woman.

Yet Cher has a different opinion about these last two albums. She felt she was at her professional peak, was recording music she loved and wanted to do. She told Andy Warhol: "I did a tape with Gregg Allman and I did another album called *Stars* that I love—but that's it."

She didn't care about what the critics thought—they had never liked her very much even back when she was with Sonny—but she couldn't help wishing the albums had sold better.

Her old producer, Snuff Garrett, replaced Jimmy Webb for her next Warner Brothers album, *Cherished*. Cher fought this album every step of the way. *Stars* had been the first step toward her dream of becoming a real hard rocker, and she didn't want to relinquish anything. Warner Brothers argued that had *Stars* been successful, it might be a different story, but the comparatively low sales indicated that her fans wanted more pop stuff like "Gypsies, Tramps and Thieves" and "Half-Breed." Cher came into the studio and dragged through a variety of numbers, such as "War Paint, Soft Feathers," meant to re-create the sound of her biggest early-seventies hits, but her heart wasn't in it.

One sound engineer recalled, "She was pleasant enough when she first came in, but by the end of the session she was snapping at everybody. I didn't want to go near her. You could tell she would really have rather been doing just about anything than recording those particular songs. A lot of us thought she was being self-destructive, but I could understand. When you feel you've moved on to another point, a new phase, creatively speaking, it's difficult to go back and do the same old stuff."

It was all wasted effort; *Cherished* was no world beater on the charts. Even the single releases from the album were unsuccessful. Warner Brothers threw up its hands; it had had enough of Cher.

Two years later Cher signed with Casablanca, primarily because her friend Gene Simmons of Kiss was with the label. Against all reason Cher was still determined to be a hard rocker, but Casablanca executives knew another album like *Stars* would be a disaster. The pop follow-up, *Cherished*, hadn't done too well either. Which direction to go?

The answer was provided by the president of Casablanca, Neil Bogart. Disco was the big thing in the late seventies. The voice, the singer, didn't matter; all that mattered was that the music had a strong, sexy beat and that you could dance to it. The disco market at that time was dominated by wailing, heavy-breathing black ladies like Donna Summer and countless clones, but why shouldn't a white woman, especially one with the exposure, reputation, and hollow glamorous aura of Cher, do just as well?

Cher hated the concept and hated disco music, even though it was gaining some mainstream respectability, just as rock had in the early seventies. Donna Summer's song, "Last Dance," which was heard in the movie *Thank God It's Friday*, actually won the Academy Award for Best Song. ("Last Dance" is utterly mediocre schlock, not even a particularly good disco hit; that it won an Oscar—the result of hype, a lack of taste among voting members, and the generally debased tastes of the seventies—was a scandal). The powers that be at Casablanca sat Cher down and said, "Look, your last two records were bombs. Do you want to sing? Do you want a hit record? Do you want a *career*?" Cher saw herself as having no choice.

Bogart brought in Bob Esty, the writer-producer who collaborated on "Last Dance," to work with Cher on the new album. He wrote a song called "Take Me Home" about those three words spoken by the most forward woman in the singles bar. The song helped cement Cher's image as a good-time girl and I'll-do-anything slut even though she was not in the habit of taking strange men home from bars, or vice versa. This was not a good period for Cher professionally. She could barely get through her sessions in the studio and was not enjoying herself the least bit. This was not the way it was supposed to be. She wanted to do rock music, but no one could take her seriously as a rock performer.

When *Take Me Home*—both album and single—became a hit, Cher, at least publicly, seemed to recant on disco. "I never thought I would want to do disco. People keep saying, 'There's no such thing as disco!' It's like saying the world is flat! It's here . . . people should know it. It's terrific! It's great music to dance to. I think that danceable music is what tells everybody what's *in*."

Nothing like a hit to change a person's attitude. In spite of the success, most people today remember the album mostly for its outrageous cover: Cher dressed as Brunhilde, the Valkyrie, complete with breastplate and horns.

Bob Esty tried to come up with a follow-up hit album for Cher, but his efforts were stymied by Cher's continuing private distaste for disco and her unabated desire to be a rocker. Now that she had had a hit record again—*Take Me Home* was a best seller for almost half of 1979—she felt she had a stronger platform. The fans might give her a chance to do what she really wanted to do.

No such luck. Esty wanted to do an album, *Mirror Image*, that would have fun with Cher's media image and her relationship with the press, the flood of publicity perpetually surrounding her. Bit by bit Cher kept putting in rock songs that had nothing to do with the basic concept. Esty found himself losing control of the project. If Cher had stuck with the original conception, she might have found herself with a second hit album. But what resulted, *Prisoner*, was too much of a discombobulated mess to achieve the same popularity. The cover showed Cher in chains, presumably a "prisoner" of her image in the media.

Cher's next venture was as ill advised as her project with Gregg Allman and also came about because of love: Cher's love for rock and roll, which no one would let her sing, and her love for a young man named Les Dudek. Dudek was in his late twenties when he met Cher, and like Gregg Allman, he was a rocker. Earlier in his career he had played guitar for the Allman Brothers Band, as well as Boz Scaggs and the Steve Miller Band. He had recorded five solo albums for CBS but so far was more a critical than a commercial success. Cher started going with Dudek while she was sharing an apartment with Gene Simmons in New York (her affair with Simmons had fizzled); and the arrangement seemed to be fine with all three.

To give Cher credit, she was more concerned with being true to her "art" as she saw it than with commercial success. (At this point she probably had enough money to take chances.) If doing an act called Allman and Woman with Gregg Allman could be considered an attempt to alter her image, the act she came up with for her and Les Dudek could be considered total obliteration. The two formed a group called Black Rose. Cher was lead singer, but she received no billing. However, when the group appeared on television, it was pretty obvious who that gal with the microphone standing in front of the boys in the band was, in spite of her somewhat altered appearance (her long black hair was exchanged for a short, ghastly "punk" look). Cher and Les weren't making any money, but Cher was having a great time. She was finally doing what she felt she had been born to do: *rock*.

But nobody else was having a good time. The record never even made it off home plate, let alone to first base. Getting concert dates was almost an impossibility. Cher knew that if she lent her name for promotional efforts, everyone would come expecting her usual glitzy pop and costume show. But without her name for publicity value, hardly a soul was interested in Black Rose. (What Cher may not have been willing to acknowledge was that at this point fans would have stayed away in droves even if they'd known Cher was connected to Black Rose.)

In the end the group could secure no concert dates except as an opening act, and even there it had difficulty. Hall and Oates finally took pity on it. Cher's Black Rose did not have much impact on the music scene. It is totally forgotten today and never did more than the one album.

Cher and Les remained together for several more months in

spite of the Black Rose debacle. After Black Rose split up, to the consternation of no one except maybe Cher, Dudek went to L.A. to make a new solo album. Since Cher was in New York rehearsing for a play, the two carried on a bicoastal love affair. "I don't think things are cooling," Cher said at the time. "It's just a matter of careers. If I didn't want to leave him, I would have had to give up the play, and I didn't want to do that."

Things eventually did cool, although the two remained cordial. Cher got Les a (very) small role in her film *Mask* in 1985, as Bone Tyson, one of the bikers. The screenplay of *Mask* inspired him to collaborate on a song about the picture called "Take Me Along." In the end, however, that's just what Cher *didn't* do. Les was discarded.

Cher's next album, *I Paralyze*, was one of her favorites. After *Stars* and *Two the Hard Way*, she told Andy Warhol, it was "the only thing I've ever done that I've really been proud of." She had just heard the final mix the day before and was extremely pleased with it. "I was astonished when I listened to it yesterday. I listened to it with John Loeffler (a current flame) and his music is so brilliant I thought, shit, I'm really embarrassed to listen to it with him, but I wanted to ask him some questions." She was thrilled when John told her he liked the record. That was just as well because no one else did. The title of the album was often misprinted as *I'm Paralyzed*, which may have been a more accurate monicker. Reviews were not good, and the record went nowhere.

That wasn't the end for Cher. In early 1987 she contacted Jon Bon Jovi (of the rock group Bon Jovi) to ask if she could record one of his songs for a new album. It was agreed that Jon would also produce the number (Richie Sambora and Desmond Child would be coproducers on the album), but there was trouble coordinating his schedule with Cher's. He was busy with a tour; she was off making a movie. Jon was nevertheless excited at the prospect of working with Cher. "I think it's cool," he said. "I think she's got a great voice."

The album was put together in pieces. While Cher was busy with her movie, Jon did music tracks in New York and guitar overdubs in Los Angeles. Cher would "slap some vocals down," as he put it, the following month. *Cher* (her second album to have that title) was a Geffen Records release. The song titles sounded like chapters of a mini-autobiography of Cher's life: "We All Sleep Alone," "I Found Someone," "Give Our Love a Fighting Chance," "Dangerous Times," and "Had Enough Getting Over You." (Cher also did yet another version of "Bang, Bang.")

Cher approached the new album with apprehension. "I was really nervous at first. I didn't sing for about five years, not even in the shower. I would rather think of singing as a hobby. Singing is much more organic a feeling than acting for me. Acting is more about being prepared. That's not saying it's unemotional, but it comes from a different place. Let me explain it this way: You can be happy and sing around the house, but you can never be happy and act around the house."

She added: "I liked the idea of being able to be around long enough to make a copy of my own record of "Bang, Bang" some twenty years earlier. I don't think anyone else has ever done that."

Finally Cher had another successful record, and *Cher* became her tenth gold album.

She followed up *Cher* with *Heart of Stone*. "I wanted to have songs that really suited my taste. When I sing a song, they're always about me. That's not narcissistic. It has to be personal. I have to hear how it relates to me." One of the songs, "After All," became her fourteenth gold single. Two other songs are especially memorable: the catchy lament for things gone by and opportunities missed, "If I Could Turn Back Time," and "Just Like Jesse James," another irresistible pop song that may be her best since "Gypsies, Tramps and Thieves."

There are some people who think that Cher has gotten a raw deal, that whatever the limitations of her voice, she has made a contribution to the music world just by virtue of her staying power, by her willingness to try new styles without regard to commercial considerations, and by her own hell-bent desire to do rock and roll (even when no one wanted her to). She's a woman who has been entertaining millions of people for more than twenty-five years. She must be doing something right.

Cher has lasted where other female vocalists have fallen by the wayside. Nancy Sinatra made vicious fun of Sonny and Cher at the beginning of their careers, but nowadays Sinatra gets publicity only when she writes a book about her father—not for any records. Ronnie Spector has only recently emerged from obscurity, and again, that's less for her music than for her tell-all autobiography about her life with Phil Spector and her bout with alcoholism. Some of the biggest records of the sixties were sung by Marianne Faithfull, Lulu, Bobbie Gentry, Dusty Springfield, none of whom is still active in the recording field. One of the strongest female vocalists of the sixties was Petula Clark, who had pipes, power, diction, and energy far in excess of Cher's, but even she has faded into obscurity.

One of the aforementioned women—who has asked not to be named—claims there's a reason why Cher has survived and the others have not. "Publicity," she says. "Cher always kept her name in front of the public. First there was the TV show, then her marriage to that druggie what's-his-name. . . . Cher has survived mostly on hype . . . and vulgarity. If I were running around getting tattoos, showing off my rear end, having affairs with young good-looking guys who probably just wanted to use me —and calling a press conference each and every time—I'd probably still be making records and appearing in movies today."

There is a great deal of bitterness in some quarters over Cher's survival, which is often seen as a result of her willingness to play clown for the press and her opportunistic nature. Yet her supporters insist that she survived because she kept struggling and knocking heads against the wall when most others would have just given up—and did. It has to be remembered that Cher did not always have an easy time of it. The TV shows made her a national joke, and far too many of her albums bombed. Others would have thrown in the towel after just one failure.

It also has to be remembered, however, that Cher was consistently bolstered by the money from her divorce settlement, Las Vegas stage shows, etc., and could afford to keep trying and taking chances, a luxury that most performers don't have. The true secret to her survival is luck, connections, a certain amount of talent and ambition, and an undeniable persistence and willingness to take risks and even fail. Anyone who got the reviews some of her records did and kept going has to be, grudgingly, admired.

There's no denying that Cher's voice has its limitations. Some of it is *self*-limiting; she refuses to accept that her obsession with hard rock fails to provide her voice with its proper showcase. At a recent benefit concert for environmental concerns, "Mothers and Others for a Livable Planet," taped at Los Angeles's Greek Theater on September 13, 1990, for later telecasting by ABC (as *An Evening with . . .*) Cher bounded out and strutted across the stage, wailing out two rock numbers she had previously recorded: "I'm No Angel" (originally a Gregg Allman song) and "Fire down Below" (both numbers are about hard-lovin' rebels). Neither number was particularly well sung, with Cher just shouting (barely) over the band and the backup singers. All her worst habits—vowel stretching, whining, straining—were in evidence to negative effect.

Virtually all the other guests also did at least one number. That Cher was outsung by a smiling, melodious Bette Midler ("Friends") wasn't surprising. Or even sunshiny Olivia Newton-John ("Magic"), the pop queen who took a page from Cher's book and found bigger success being "Physical" and sexy. But Goldie Hawn (who was excellent doing "It Isn't Easy Being Green")? Finally, when actress Meryl Streep came out with a chorus of "It's a Wonderful World" and also sounded much better than Cher, you would have thought our tattooed lady would have given up and gone home. The final number brought all the women together onstage, but Cher, uninterested, preferred to chat with Lily Tomlin while the others did their solos and opened her mouth only during the chorus. After Goldie did her solo, Cher nudged her as if to say, "Good show, kid," the professional patronizing the amateur when, to judge from each of their performances that evening, it could have been the other way around.

Cher is probably one of those singers, like Tina Turner and many others, whose recording career will rise and fall according to the material. No one buys a Cher album to listen to the pure, dulcet strains of her voice, as they might do with Barbra Streisand. As long as Cher keeps coming up with numbers like "If I Could Turn Back Time," the public will retain its interest in her.

If not, there's always the film career.

Cher has said that her ambition is to do torch songs at Carnegie Hall. (Perhaps it could be billed as "Lady Kills the Blues.") The realization of such an ambition isn't likely. Not in this life.

But who knows? The next "Gypsies, Tramps and Thieves" could be right around the corner.

Even though Cher and Hollywood mega–mogul David Geffen broke up long ago, they remain good friends.

One of Cher's post-Allman boyfriends, musician Les Dudek

Cher had a fling in the early eighties with then-unknown Val Kilmer, who went on to play Jim Morrison in Oliver Stone's *The Doors*.

Here Cher is seen with her co-star from the film *Mask*, Eric Stoltz. The two were rumored to have been a couple.

Before Cher's recognition as a serious actress, Cher stayed in the news by virtue of her relationships with a succession of young Hollywood studs.

Chastity, Elijah Blue, Cher, and Josh Donen, the man she almost married

Cher with Rob Camiletti (twenty-three at the time of this photo), attending the 1988 American Music Awards. Ironically, that night Cher presented an award to Bon Jovi, whose lead guitarist, Richie Sambora, would replace Camiletti as Cher's beau.

Cher in 1983, before surgery on her nose and teeth

Here she is seen leaving a screening for *Beverly Hills Cop* with then-boyfriend Josh Donen.

Two of Cher's "looks" in the eighties

Here she is seen leaving a New York City production of Shaw's *Arms and the Man*.

Chastity Bono stops to make sure the photographers get a good shot of herself and her unidentified male friend after the premiere of *Cinema Paradiso*.

Georgia Holt (Cher's mother), Cher, Chastity, and Sonny reunite in 1983 at Sonny's Los Angeles restaurant, Bono's.

Cher and her son, Elijah Blue, take in an Andrew Dice Clay
concert at the Universal Amphitheater in Los Angeles.

SIX

BROADWAY BABY

Cher on Broadway? What next? Gary Coleman as Othello?
—New York *Sunday News*

All along Cher's dream had been to be an actress (or at least a movie star). Before she teamed up with Sonny Bono, she was even studying acting. But according to Cher, her acting ambitions were quashed by Sonny Bono. "He asked me to give it up because he didn't like the idea. And when we became famous, he didn't want me to do anything but be Sonny and Cher with him."

The problem, as Cher saw it: "Afterward, when I was just Cher, people thought I might be talented, but they were afraid to take the chance. I had the *stigma* of being Cher."

It was a stigma she was determined to overcome. Many other people would have been satisfied with being a pop celebrity who made lots of money doing stage shows and now and then had a hit record. Even with its assorted problems, her life was hardly a pitiable one. Cher was after the same thing that had driven her ex-husband Sonny for so long: She wanted to be respected.

One would have thought that she would try for the movies, which seemed a logical next step after "conquering" television.

The fact is that Cher did try. But it didn't matter which picture she was interested in; she got turned down every time. And there were some pictures that even she wasn't desperate enough to want to appear in. Usually what she was offered were dopey sitcom-like movies or grotesque novelty items that would have costarred her with talking fish or giant gorillas and assured her of career suicide. She knew she had to be careful about what she appeared in. The wrong role would destroy whatever small amount of credibility she had left.

The two films she had already made were not the stuff to build a film career on. *Good Times* was little more than a glorified series of sketches of the type she later did on *The Sonny and Cher Comedy Hour.* *Chastity* had always embarrassed her. "I remember going to a preview and seeing everyone laugh at the serious parts. I left crying and said I'd never do another film."

Well, now that she had changed her mind, it was Hollywood that didn't want her to do another film, at least not a good one.

Cher wasn't the type to take no for an answer, but she knew the odds were stacked against her. Whereas most actresses in her situation would have settled for guest shots on *The Rockford Files* or maybe *Dallas* and considered themselves lucky, Cher came up with a daring scheme. Hollywood wouldn't give her a serious part until she was considered a serious actress. Did serious actresses do night-time soap operas, cop shows, or sitcoms? No, they tried the boards, appeared on Broadway, performed onstage every night without benefit of cinematographic tricks or editing. They *acted* for real. Cher was convinced—well, almost convinced—that she could do it. And if she couldn't, at least she had tried.

Cher had another reason for moving to New York: She hated L.A. "It's beautiful, but it's boring. No one there is really doing anything." She also felt that the people she knew in L.A. didn't want to see her—or anyone else—succeed; it was suffering from a citywide disease of self-centeredness and envy. New York to her seemed less cutthroat and more supportive.

It's no wonder that New York seemed comparatively benign to Cher. She certainly didn't have to pound a lot of pavements to find a stage vehicle. In countless interviews she has told the story of how she took classes at Lee Strasberg's Actors Studio, did a scene from *I'm Getting My Act Together and Taking It Out on the Road* for Joseph Papp, worked hard to sharpen her technique and study her craft, but the fact remains that she got the part in *Come Back to the Five and Dime, Jimmy Dean, Jimmy Dean* because her mother was friends with Robert Altman's wife. Producer Joseph Clapsaddle admitted that they were hoping to expand attendance by using Cher's name as a draw. So much for getting ahead the hard way.

It also must be said that the vehicle Cher chose—or that was chosen for her—to begin her brief stage career, was hardly what one might call serious. *Jimmy Dean* was not Eugene O'Neill or Tennessee Williams, but a campy, largely humorous (intentionally and otherwise) play about a reunion of a Jimmy Dean fan club. In true sitcom fashion, laughs and tears were intermingled to create a crowd, if not a critic, pleaser.

Of course, Cher was in love with New York; she thought she was on her way to gaining the respectability she craved. Her career was back on track. She was aching to show everybody who had laughed at her that she was not a joke.

She moved into Gene Simmons's apartment while she searched for one of her own. She discovered that next to finding an apartment, being taken seriously was a breeze. Adding to the turmoil of finding a new place to live was the difficulty of finding a buyer for her West Coast mansion, which she was determined to sell. While this went on, Chastity, who was studying at the High School of Performing Arts at the time, moved in with Lee Strasberg's widow, Anna. Cher told columnist Cindy Adams, who noted that in the harsh dressing-room light Cher hadn't "one blemish, line or enlarged pore," that East Coast audiences in general were sharper than those on the West Coast. "New York's the hippest of all," she added. "Here everything's different. I walked out in a beaded wig, a blanket around me, no make-up, and construction workers hollered, 'Heeeeyyy Cherrr!' They ran up for autographs. L.A. doesn't do that."

For Cher, New York was a great ego assuager. But that was no help in securing a new apartment. Driving through Central Park in a cab one afternoon after an unsuccessful search on the East Side, Cher thought (as she later told reporters), "I'm so special. Why doesn't someone just give me an apartment?" (Cher may have been special, but no one in New York gives anybody an apartment.)

When Cher finally found a place, she hung on to it tenaciously. She didn't even care if *Jimmy Dean* closed on opening night. "I'm staying in New York for a year, regardless of what happens. I've spent months looking for an apartment, and I'm not giving it up now that I've found one." Her move to New York almost became permanent. At the time (1982) she never wanted to go back to Hollywood and its unpleasant memories and associations.

"L.A. is kind of like heroin," she said, "a beautiful, quite peaceful feeling, and then it kills you. Nobody wants to say anything good about you." As for New York, "I've met the best people since I've been here. This is the first time in my life that I ever had a friend." Cher found that in Manhattan people were more willing to take her at face value; she wasn't Cher the glitzy pop star who'd fallen (her last album in 1982 had been a bomb, and her TV show had long since been history) but a woman and an actress attempting a new life and fresh start. Of course, even if she was a little bit tarnished, many people were secretly delighted to have a real Hollywood-type star in their midst. Cher went to parties, met a lot of new people, and made friends fairly easily. She felt she was *really* on her own at last. The friends she had weren't Sonny's, or David Geffen's, or Gregg's; they were her own.

No wonder she spent eighty-five thousand dollars to move to New York, which included rent, plane fares to and from California, schools for Chastity and Elijah Blue, payments for the movers, and a substantial amount for the upkeep of her mansion, which she still hoped to sell. She explained: "It was a part of my life I don't particularly want anymore. I don't need to be quite so grand. That [house] was a substitute to help me live with the fact that I wasn't doing what I wanted to do in my work."

That was no longer the case now that *Jimmy Dean* had come along. The Broadway production was not the first time the play had been performed. There had been several successful regional productions, including one in Columbus, Ohio, that starred Barbara Loden and *Candid Camera*'s Fannie Flagg.

Producer Clapsaddle didn't have an easy time raising the money to open on Broadway. The director, Robert Altman, contributed $204,000 of his own money during play rehearsals, all of which he lost when the play was closed. Clapsaddle said that he and Joel Brykman, the play's general partners, put in a little over $50,000, but "the rest of the checks bounced because my investors changed their minds." Other major backers of *Jimmy Dean* were Don Fisher and Jack Lawrence, who provided the balance of the $850,000 needed to open the play. Other "angels," including Rip Taylor, contributed $10,000 or more.

Robert Altman was an odd choice to direct *Jimmy Dean*. Although he had directed several motion pictures, including the highly popular *M*A*S*H*, he was a neophyte on Broadway. Altman, too, seemed to be trying to prove himself or to be fleeing from something. Perhaps it was from the way he perceived Hollywood as having turned on him. For a while Altman had done no wrong. Pictures such as the 1971 *McCabe and Mrs. Miller*, though they confounded audiences, were praised to the skies by film circle sycophants. Although Altman did make a couple of interesting and worthwhile movies—*That Cold Day in the Park* (1969) and *Images* (1972) are two intriguing oddities, and *Popeye* (1980) is a charming film—too many of his movies were clumsy, slow, and undramatic. By the time he was making such episodic bombs as *A Wedding* (1978) and *H.E.A.L.T.H.* (1979)—(a barely releasable item)—he had fallen out of favor with critics as well as with the audience. Circa 1982 Altman as a filmmaker had virtually no public or critical boosters.

So Altman and Cher both were refugees from what they perceived as a Hollywood that had rejected them. It wasn't strange that they had this odd unspoken alliance, for the whole production was built around the two of them. Without their participation *Jimmy Dean* would probably have been mounted at an Off-Off Broadway theater, if at all. They got the major share of the publicity. Altman had basically put together the whole show: He chose the play and the cast and even came up with the concept for the set. Cher was his insurance that people would want to come see the play. He knew his name as director would have curiosity value, some publicity worth, but not much more than that. He needed a *star*. Cher was his star.

None of the other cast members was too thrilled with this. They had worked hard to get to where they were, and they resented the fact that they were in a sense playing second fiddle to Cher, who hadn't paid her dues. When a cover story about the production came out in *New York* magazine, it was titled "Cher and Altman on Broadway," as if the others involved didn't exist. Still, nobody wanted a flop, and if Cher's public relations machine could prevent that, so much the better.

Come Back to the Five and Dime, Jimmy Dean, Jimmy Dean takes place inside a Woolworth's in a small Texas town, McCarthy, in 1975. Twenty years before, several women were members of the Disciples, a James Dean fan club that formed in 1955, when the star and sex symbol came to a nearby hamlet to film scenes in George Stevens's *Giant*. Mona (Sandy Dennis) stayed in town to work as a clerk in Woolworth's. Sissy (Cher) works as the counter waitress and is proud of her Dolly Partonesque boobs. Edna Louise (Kathy Bates) went off to get married and have (many) children, but she has driven in for a reunion with the others, accompanied by a friend, Stella Mae (Marta Heflin). Juanita (Sudie Bond) is the owner of the store. The last arrival, Joanne (Karen Black), is an old acquaintance in a startling new guise.

As the play—and the reunion—progress, the women tell each other lies and are finally forced to confront them and admit the painful truth. Bosomy Sissy has had a mastectomy, and her most prized possessions are falsies. Mona's "retarded" child was not fathered by James Dean when she worked on the *Giant* set as an extra but by Joe, a homosexual who was run out of town by Juanita's husband and others. Then Joanne reveals that *she* is Joe, who has had a sex change operation. From homosexual to bisexual to transsexual in a hop, skip, and a jump; Graczyk was covering all the bases. Before the night is over, just about everyone in the play is emotionally shattered.

Jimmy Dean was just the kind of campy, anything-goes exercise with larger-than-life characters that would appeal to a certain kind of audience. Many people loved the play without taking it very seriously. Indeed, it seemed that Cher had not come that far from *The Sonny and Cher Comedy Hour*, for in many ways *Jimmy Dean*, basically a freak show and burlesque of true drama, was little more than an overgrown television sketch.

Still, it was the right part for Cher to test the waters with. Even she was smart enough to know that she wasn't ready for Blanche Dubois or Maggie the Cat in such fine, well-written, and incisive dramas as *A Streetcar Named Desire* or *Cat on a Hot Tin Roof*. The role of Sissy was something she could have fun with; it was all wisecracks and sharp retorts. The heavy drama she could build up to and handle if she had to.

Rehearsals for the play didn't get off to an auspicious start. Cher nearly died, for one thing. It provided a bit of melodrama that was as scary-funny as anything in the play. She was taking her daily dose of rather large vitamin pills when she got careless. Wanting to avoid the unpleasant taste of the pill (after she'd already chewed two others), she swallowed it whole, only to have it lodge in her windpipe. The other actresses had already accused Cher of being overly flamboyant and mannered in her performance and didn't at first know what to make of her doing what appeared to be a Carol Burnett impression of somebody drowning. She had already tried to move the pill down her throat with a piece of bread and some water, but nothing worked. She stumbled toward Altman, her hands flapping, body faltering. "Help me," she rasped.

Once he figured out that Cher wasn't doing some impression or being cute, Altman sized up the problem and wrapped his hands around her chest from the back to perform the Heimlich maneuver. This succeeded only in making Cher spit up the piece of bread she'd eaten. Luckily the pill shifted position and allowed the entry of air into her lungs. She could breathe, but she certainly couldn't go on with rehearsal with something still stuck in her throat. (One of the backstage crew suggested that it might have improved her performance.)

The rest was like something out of one of Altman's seriocomic movies. He rushed outside with Cher, hailed a cab, threw her in the backseat, and told the driver, "St. Clare's Hospital!" The cabdriver was well on his way when for some reason Altman decided it would be better or faster to go to Manhattan Eye and Ear. The driver swerved around and switched directions. Meanwhile, Cher was gasping and sweating and wondering why Altman couldn't make up his mind.

Finally they arrived at the hospital, and Altman got ready to rush Cher from the cab into the emergency room. "Don't bother," she said. "I coughed it up." After this incident, which Cher called "terrifying," she switched to liquid vitamins. Altman became her "hero."

There are indications that if Cher had choked to death, not all her costars would have cried about it. Cher just didn't act like a trained stage actress; she didn't seem to know how to do anything. Early on Altman didn't have much confidence in the production or in Cher. He arrived at rehearsals and told his players not to expect much feedback from him; either he was losing faith or he was just too busy with the blocking to tell them how to act. Cher asked him for feedback all the time. "Should I do this? Should I do that?" More experienced performers like Black and Dennis, both of whom had worked with Altman before (Black in *Nashville* and Dennis in *That Cold Day in the Park*) knew that whether he was directing a movie or a play, Altman was more concerned with how things looked, with the actor's (or camera's) movements, than with the "motivation" of the characters. That was the actor's job; he didn't want to hear it. Cher didn't understand that she was expected to come to grips with her characterization, to understand the waitress Sissy, on her own time. Altman was too busy with other things. Privately Cher was frustrated; publicly she said, "It's fantastic to work with him. He's so supportive and gives you the chance to work things out."

But one observer, watching Cher rehearse, had a highly positive opinion of her. This was the producer-director-playwright Robert Dahdah, who happened to drop in one afternoon. Watching from an aisle seat, Dahdah was impressed. He told me, "I was very surprised to find that Cher was a natural actress and a real pro. Her talent came naturally to her, and she *projected* wonderfully. I had never really thought much of her as a performer up to that time, but when I saw her rehearsing in *Jimmy Dean*, my estimation, of, and respect for, her went up one hundred percent."

Altman continued to encourage Cher's inventiveness; whatever she wanted to try was all right with him. If it didn't work, he would have it drummed out of her somehow by opening night. Meanwhile, he continued to concern himself primarily with other aspects of the production. He was making a few changes from previous stagings of the show and wasn't sure that they would work. Originally it had been planned that younger actresses would play the characters in 1955, but Altman decided this was unnecessary. Undoubtedly, considering that he had put up so much of his own money, financial considerations entered into it. A second slew of actresses would have really overtaxed the budget. Instead, he used one or two doubles (who appeared infrequently for scenes when certain characters had to be present but didn't have any lines). These stand-ins wouldn't have to be paid as much as actors with speaking parts.

Another major change he made was in the lighting and the set. Instead of using one kind of light for the "past" scenes and a different kind of light for the "present" ones, Altman designed a set (with considerable help from David Gropman) that was half 1955 and half 1975. Each half consisted of the same section of the interior of the Woolworth's store; the actors would go upstage for the present scenes and move downstage for those set in the past. This wound up being just as confusing for audiences as

Altman had been afraid it would be. For one thing, there could not be any time for makeup or costume changes for the actors as they crossed from one set to its mirror image and traversed twenty years in five seconds.

Altman upset the playwright, Ed Graczyk, when he stopped fooling with the structure of the set and started tinkering with the structure of the play. He moved several 1955 sequences into the first act, then made a shift of time right in the middle of an important speech. Graczyk was walking out of rehearsals in fury until he finally realized that Altman wasn't really indulging in major rewrites; the play remained essentially the same. He could only hope the changes wouldn't alienate the audience.

The early rehearsals, as Dahdah remembered, took place at St. Clement's Episcopal Church on West Forty-sixth Street; later they were moved to the Martin Beck Theater. There was no heat, and the actresses had to remain dressed in their hats, overcoats, and mufflers so that Altman had trouble telling them apart. Cher fell off a ladder at one point (before the incident with the pill)— she had stretched too far putting up Sissy's decorations—and tumbled into a big cardboard box. The set went silent. Would Cher have to be rushed to the hospital? Luckily, she got up hurt but smiling.

After a while things warmed up. The actors had taken stock of one another. Still, Cher became friends with only one of them. Marta Heflin assured a reporter that there was no rivalry among the three main stars, Cher, Black, and Dennis: "I was prepared for that, but it never happened. It's been lovely." But Heflin could judge only behavior, not inner feelings.

Cher became friends with Sandy Dennis, and the two of them chatted constantly on the set, often to Altman's annoyance. Dennis, of course, had risen to prominence (and won a supporting Oscar) as the eternally upchucking Honey in the 1966 film version of Edward Albee's play *Who's Afraid of Virginia Woolf?* Another bright spot in her career had been the lead role in *Up the Down Staircase* (1967). Dennis saw Cher loosen up and learn to trust and share with others as the rehearsal progressed. "She has learned

156

that you have to sacrifice your own moment on stage sometimes for the sake of the play. She's learned, too, not to sacrifice too much," Sandy told Arthur Bell, of the *Village Voice*, adding, "She's darling. She has this great voice. She just knocks me out. It's like working in the Girl Scouts again."

Cher's relationship with Karen Black was another story. Karen was a veteran film actress by the time of *Jimmy Dean*, and though she had never achieved major stardom, she had given some highly creditable performances in films from *Easy Rider* to *Airport 1975*. Black is one of those actors who can always be counted on to give their best in a film or play. Chances are she was not crazy about playing second fiddle to someone like Cher, who at the time was better known for her clothes, pop songs, and comedy show than for her film roles. Although there were no major public quarrels and the two seemed to get along for most of the time, even enjoy each other's jokes and company, there was no real warmth between them. Cher admired Black's performance, but she admitted that it was *all* she admired. As she told *The New York Times*, "Everybody was great, even Karen, whom I didn't like at all."

There was trouble right from the first, when Cher refused the role Altman offered her and it was given to Karen. "What's interesting," Karen said, "is that originally Bob wanted Cher to play my role. With her low voice and looks he thought she'd be just right to play the transsexual. But she wanted one of the other roles."

It has been said that it usually took time for Karen Black to warm up to people, but Karen's standoffishness was a nuisance to Cher. She was nervous enough as it was, and she wanted everyone's support; Karen, whatever her reasons, seemed reluctant to offer hers. Karen, for her part, found the first few weeks of rehearsal irritating. "It seems that no one ever did the same line in the same way twice. That took some adjustment. Eventually we all worked it out and learned that each actress uses just so much space and time."

But it was no secret that her costars were annoyed at the way

Cher seemed to hog the whole show as if she were back in production on *Cher*, her TV show of the seventies. They found her
too expressive on occasion, too loud, too boisterous—too *much*,
in short. Why couldn't she tone it down just a little? Nevertheless,
Black told one reporter that Cher was working out okay, that she
was "very natural." Black also found amusement in the way Cher
said whatever came into her head: "She just tells you stuff. She
doesn't hide at all. She says, 'Bob, don't you think . . . Bob, can
I ask you a question? . . .'"

Altman didn't want the fact that Black played a transsexual
to leak out. Bell, the often acidic gay columnist for the *Village
Voice*, interviewed Black and Dennis and point-blank asked Black
if Cher was playing a sex changer. When she refused to confirm
or deny, Bell said, "I bet Burt Reynolds is playing Cher in the
first act!"

Sandy Dennis chortled in response: "Wouldn't that be fun?"

Sudie Bond took note of how Cher made good use of what
she was observing during rehearsals. "She's bright. She watched
us all like a hawk and absorbed everything like a sponge."

Kathy Bates, probably the least-known member of the cast
at the time, has more recently received publicity as the Oscar-
winning star of the film adaptation of Stephen King's best seller
Misery. Although she said she liked working with Cher, she discovered that performing with a pop star could have its drawbacks
once the show opened. "It's her fans," she said. "They bring
flashbulb cameras to the show—every night. That just isn't done
in Broadway houses." The constant dazzle of flashbulbs while the
women were trying to perform was a perpetual irritation. It was
more like being onstage at a concert than in a drama.

Cher admitted that she studied her fellow actresses carefully.
"I watch all the other girls. Working with Sandy Dennis is the
thrill of my life. I've never worked with anyone in my life I've
liked as much. I learn something from her every single night. I
suck up all the little things I see, and I watch everything."

Although privately Cher was apprehensive, she put up a good
public front. "I'm not threatened by Broadway," she told re-

porters. "An artist isn't intimidated." One thing on her side was that she felt totally at home on a stage. She figured if she could have stood on a stage for so many years—decades, really—as just plain Cher, she wouldn't have much trouble getting out there and being someone else.

"Being in a play is so different from anything that's ever happened to me before," she said. "There's an audience out there, and yet you don't have to pay any attention to them, and it's wonderful. I much prefer it to nightclub work, where you have to play to the audience *all* the time." She added, "I don't really know what I'm doing most of the time onstage, and if I stop to think about it, I won't know what I'm doing at all. When we started, everyone was talking about preparation, and I didn't know what that was. What I do is sort of turn my mind to pretend. I thought I'd hate having to be the same character every night, but then I found it was natural. There was a lot of freedom in it." She actually enjoyed not having to sing. "Having to sing for money takes the fun out of it."

No, Cher didn't have her voice, herself, or her natural Cher persona to hide behind. She had to *become* Sissy, the waitress. No matter how confident she may have acted with the press, privately she just felt like throwing up. If there was anything she could hide behind, it was her boobs—the enormous falsies she wore as Sissy. She used to keep them on when she went out on interviews, inviting people sitting with her to reach out and give them a squeeze. She got a big kick out of it.

On one occasion she told writer Mal Vincent, "Did you notice I left my boobs in the dressing room? They may win a Tony as the biggest stage props of the year. I don't know how Dolly Parton walks. I've never had the problem myself. That's *real* acting."

Later some would snip that her boobs *did* do most of the acting.

As opening night loomed closer, various publicity ploys were created in order to keep public attention as high as possible. Jack Lawrence, the sixty-two-year-old composer of "Tenderly" and "Linda," was coaxed out of retirement to write a new jingle for the play. Then producer Clapsaddle made an appeal to the papers to find anyone who had a good usable copy of the sound track record for *Giant*, so it could be used as background music.

On opening night the glitterati of New York, its trendsetters and celebrities, were not in evidence. Instead, there was a younger crowd consisting mostly of people who'd grown up on Sonny and Cher records and *The Sonny and Cher Comedy Hour*, people who bought Cher records and went to her concerts. It wasn't the play that interested them. This was *Cher on Broadway*, man! To them it was just another one of her stage shows.

Although this proved not to be the case, the audience seemed to love it nevertheless. It was like an *event*, a camp extravaganza. The three lead actresses were already considered to be walking parodies: Cher with her hair and crazy outfits; Karen Black of the uncertain stare; chipmunky Sandy Dennis, perhaps the weirdest of the lot, with her brave, homely face and distinctive twitches. This was something the most outré vulgarian wouldn't have dreamed up in his wildest nightmares. The opening-night audience lapped it up, annoying flashbulbs and all.

Not so the critics. *Come Back to the Five and Dime, Jimmy Dean, Jimmy Dean* opened on February 28, 1982, but it might have been better if they'd waited until the twenty-ninth (it wasn't leap year). The critics were universally savage.

Douglas Watt in the *Daily News* thought the play was "utterly preposterous and strangely unpleasant." He dubbed Altman's direction clumsy and the acting "mostly atrocious."

Frank Rich in *The New York Times*: "A dreary amateur night [that would] benefit from a new script, a total restaging and a revamped set. . . . Neither the gimmicky plot nor its clichéd characters are credible." Clive Barnes in the *Post* thought the set was "the ugliest and most confusingly cluttered on Broadway," with the play "full of pretentiousness . . . pompous simplicity and garbage-like symbolism."

Rex Reed damned the play as a "confusing, trivial and completely contrived piece of chicken fried silliness—just another

Texas tumbleweed destined to blow down Broadway and out of
memory faster than you can yell, 'Hook 'em, horns!' " Joe Shabutt
of the Associated Press put it simply: "A thin, labored collection
of unsurprising revelations. . . . *Jimmy Dean, Jimmy Dean* is no
good, no good."

While all the lead actresses came under attack, Sandy Dennis
was particularly vilified: "Mona is played by Sandy Dennis the
way Sandy Dennis has played all her roles recently: thinking hard,
saying her lines in a stop-go style and flashing her teeth in a grimace
for whatever emotion is called for." Some critics couldn't even
figure out what she was doing. A large part of the problem was
that the audience was halfway into the first act before they realized
that some sequences were taking place in 1975 and others twenty
years earlier.

Against this onslaught Cher and Karen Black came off relatively unscathed. "Cher handles her undemanding role compe-
tently," wrote *Theater World*. Another critic was less reserved, if
still cautious: "Cher's Sissy is, maybe, only a variation on her old
Sonny and Cher Show work as Laverne, but it is assured and vig-
orous. She also does quite well in her character's demanding sec-
ond-act soliloquy that takes her from anger to tears to raucous
laughter."

The only person whose career didn't suffer from appearing
in or being associated with Jimmy Dean was, ironically, Cher,
the least "professional" (in theater terms) of the lot. Black and
Dennis found that *Jimmy Dean* would not look very good on their
résumés, Altman became as much an outcast on Broadway as he
was in Hollywood, and Ed Graczyk presumably flew back to
Columbus, never to be heard from again.

Nonetheless, all hands on the show were nonplussed by the
negative notices. When they read over the reviews in Sardi's, some
of them passed up the opening-night party that had been set up
at real Woolworth's for later that same evening—or morning,
rather. Said Altman: "They didn't see the same play I saw. Somebody has got to be way off. It's me or them. . . . To say Cher is

not a commanding presence on the stage is ludicrous. . . . But I have to take the brunt of the criticism. I'm the one who put it together."

All week long a crew from TV's news show *20/20* had been following Altman and the others around to do a special segment on the show. A live remote was planned from the Woolworth's on Thirty-fourth Street where the opening-night party was to take place. Everything was proceeding well until someone started reading lines from an advance copy of the negative Frank Rich review over the air. Altman was furious. He claimed that *20/20* producer Martin Carr had promised him that reviews of the play would not be read on the program. While the crew tried to finish the broadcast, Altman was screaming obscenities in the background, "You bastards! You assholes!" being mild examples. Carr denied having made any such promise. The *20/20*-ers packed up and left in a hurry. It wasn't until they had gone that Altman let his three leading ladies into the Woolworth's. Their days of cooperation with the media were over.

Altman found himself in a media war over his participation in *Jimmy Dean*. Besides the fight with *20/20*, he screeched at the producer of another program who dared to reveal the play's character revelations on the air. Next, he clashed with *New York* magazine because he had wanted it to run a picture of him and all the actresses on the cover, and instead, it ran a photo of just him with Cher.

There are two truths about the critical reaction to *Jimmy Dean*. On the one hand, the critics probably were annoyed at the media circus that Altman had surrounded his show with: major articles; segments on *20/20*; a big glitzy party, and in Woolworth's of all places. It smacked not of serious legitimate theater but of one big whopping publicity stunt. Altman's vulgar attempts at promotion would have been more appropriate for one of his movies. Although *Jimmy Dean* was hardly the first Broadway show to be heavily hyped in various media, it was perceived as the product of "unworthy" film and TV personalities trying to "step up in class."

On the other hand, *Jimmy Dean* was no Pulitzer Prize winner either. Entertaining it may have been in a trashy way, but the critics couldn't just write their reviews on the basis of audience laughter. They had to examine the true worthiness and value of the piece, and on most counts *Jimmy Dean* came up short. Also, if the audiences were getting such a kick out of what they witnessed, there was also the matter of just who these audiences were comprised of. Certainly they were not, by and large, serious theater goers but people who came to see the camp cuttings-up of big-bazoomed "Sissy" and neurotically-twitching "Mona." Fans devoid of incisive critical skills can hardly be the final arbiters of a play's enduring qualities or lack of same.

Jack Lawrence, one of the four producers, put a practical face on the matter. He thought that if the show could be kept running for three weeks, no one would even remember the pans. The show's budget was $850,000; the producers had spent only $675,000. So, he said, that gave them that much left over to keep running. They had to take in $160,000 per week, though, to make it.

Continuing in his high-profile movieland approach to the Broadway theater, Altman called a press conference at the Backstage restaurant so that he and the cast could publicly rebut the reviewers. It was considered by many a tacky gesture. But Altman was thinking of all the money he personally would lose, given his large investment, if the show folded prematurely. Ticket sales were relatively brisk—the bad reviews only piqued some people's curiosity—but not brisk enough.

Cher missed five performances in one week because of an unspecified illness and three more in the show's final week in April. Since she was receiving such relatively low pay for her work in *Jimmy Dean*, she could not have afforded to stay in the production for very long even if it were a hit. At Caesars Palace she was paid thirty thousand dollars a night, compared with the four thousand dollars she got for each week of *Jimmy Dean*. The expenses incurred in moving to New York (she had still not sold the mansion) were just too high. Not that this made her one of the ten neediest cases.

It turned out to be a relatively short time and distance from the opening-night party at Woolworth's to the champagne fete on closing night, which Cher did not attend. She found the whole thing much too emotional and told Chastity to go without her. Later she said, "I was holding myself so much in check all day because I felt I had to give those people out there the best I had to offer. This was our last performance. I'd been so hysterical most of the day. I cried more that day than any other day in my life."

She had managed to get through the performance, but when it came time to leave for the party, she just froze. "I just couldn't do it. People kept telling me how sorry they were and that we'd all get another show and to keep a stiff upper lip. All the time I was trying to remain calm."

Cher had found a sort of surrogate family on Broadway. In addition, she felt that people were coming to see her not as a pop entertainer but as a serious actress who had managed to garner some reasonably respectful reviews out of the general carnage. She was working again, entertaining people, and both her professional and personal lives, for once, were going great. The closing of the show must have seemed like not only a defeat—couldn't her name draw enough people to the theater?—but a possible sign that her days of happiness were at an end.

She could not possibly celebrate this defeat. She told Sandy Dennis, who went to the party, not to "say shit about anything." Chastity, carrying a cinnamon walnut cake that she had made for the occasion, went in her place. "She's a lot more mature than her mother," Cher told Phil Roura and Tom Poster of the New York *Daily News*.

What was next? Andy Warhol wondered if she might like to do a musical. "I don't know," she told him. "I guess I would, but I don't know if I could really handle it. This sounds awful, but it's so little money and such small exposure and such hard work and it's so repetitive that I don't know if I am actually trained to handle it. Or dedicated enough."

In other words, Cher had had her fling with Broadway. Time to move on.

But as it turned out, her next major project was to be Robert Altman's film version of the play he had just directed. Cher was not crazy about making a film of a certified Broadway flop, but she felt an obligation to Altman. After all, she reasoned, hadn't he given her a chance to do legitimate theater (of a kind)? And she felt she would give a good performance on film. If she could do it onstage without any cuts or retakes, doing it on a camera, she reasoned, would be a piece of cake.

The movie version of *Jimmy Dean* cost $800,000 (half of which was recouped by a presale to the *Showtime* pay cable network) and was shot on a soundstage in seventeen days. At first the plan had been simply to videotape the play itself (as if it were something intended for PBS's *Great Performances*), but Altman decided to shoot it in Super 16 millimeter so that it could either be blown up to 35 mm for a theatrical release or be shown immediately on television. New technology had made Super 16 less difficult to work with, and Altman knew it would be much less expensive.

From the first, Altman intended that this would not be just a photographed stage play, although he transferred some of his ideas from the Broadway production. He explained to *American Cinematographer* that on Broadway he had to stage the play so that it would satisfy all 1,322 sight lines (one for each seat) in the Martin Beck theater, but in the film version he need only concern himself with one. "We still use the theatrics of the play, but I am not forced to make compromises because of all those sight lines."

A carryover from the Broadway production was the double set of the store where the action takes place. A two-way mirror was placed between the "past" and "present" sections and the audience would be taken back and forth from one time period to another as needed by the camera. The "past" side had somewhat brighter lighting and a slightly bluer cast. The two-way mirror also acted as a kind of airbrush or filter so that when the actresses were shot through it in their "before" scenes they looked much younger. With the exception of a few close-ups, the camera stayed exclusively on the "1975" side of the set and shot "1955" scenes through the mirror.

Cher had previously done only two pictures, the last one thirteen years before, and she found herself not too much at home in front of a movie camera. Acting onstage and performing on TV or in concerts, she was again reminded, were entirely different disciplines from moviemaking, and she felt uncomfortable with the slow pace, the way everything was shot in bits and pieces. It had also been a fact that her last film director had not been a Hollywood veteran of dozens of pictures like Bob Altman; indeed, he had been as inexperienced as she was. Altman had no time to coach, guide, or direct her; she was on her own. He was even more preoccupied than he had been with the play. So left to her own devices, Cher simply re-created her Broadway characterization and was effective enough in the part. But she never felt comfortable; nor did she have the control over her performance that she thought desirable. Everything depended on the camera, what it did, what it saw, and on what Altman wanted his audience to see. So she went out and did her bit while cameras rolled— everything seemed complicated and confusing to her—crossed her fingers, and hoped for the best.

The reviews for the film were less generally excoriating than those for the play, but they were still mixed. Said Vincent Canby in *The New York Times*: "There are some interesting things [about the film] but they have less to do with anything in the screenplay than with the manner in which [it] was produced and with Mr. Altman's unflagging if misguided faith in the project." Canby continued: "Ed Graczyk's screenplay is small but less likely to be salvaged than the Titanic—the actresses are not treated kindly, either by the material or the camera. . . . Closeups emphasize an already distraught performance [by Sandy Dennis]. Miss Black and Cher are no more convincing."

The *Aquarian Arts Weekly*, on the other hand, thought that the film was "so well directed, so well performed and so technically astute that it ends up having quite a kick. . . . The chances for juicy acting are immense, and gleefully lapped up by the best ensemble cast since *Diner*."

Again, Cher received some fine notices for her work. "Cher

reveals once more, at least to me," wrote Andrew Sarris of the *Village Voice* with some prescience, "that she could have been a major movie talent with a little bit of luck," although he also thought that all the actresses were "merely star presences struggling with impossible parts."

Pauline Kael of the *New Yorker* found Cher as Sissy "direct and simple in her effects; she's stunningly unself-conscious." Wrote David Denby in *New York*: "With her smoky voice and cartoon smoldering eyes, Cher is the flagrant soul of cheap-waitress commonness; vulnerable, self-mocking, intensely likable, she's perfect for the role."

But none of this praise did Cher that much good, as she discovered. *Jimmy Dean* was not widely distributed and was far from a box-office sensation. Cher had survived her brush with Broadway, but she was still a long way from major movie stardom.

SEVEN

SHE'S A REBEL

I used to daydream a lot as a kid. I still do. I'm always the heroine of whatever I think about—and everything always turns out really good.
—CHER

The fates had always conspired to cast Cher as a rebel. The demands of her mother's career and her turbulent marriages not only drove her out of the house but forced her to fend for herself at an early age. Cher was on her own at sixteen, earlier than most kids. She was living with a man at sixteen, too, even if it was chaste. Cher grew up fast.

Later she was again seen as rebel when she walked away from her marriage and a hit TV show in the seventies. People thought it took guts and a really independent attitude to risk endangering the Sonny and Cher empire because she could no longer stand her husband's smothering control. Until women's liberation made an impact on the nation, most women seemed only too happy to let their husbands handle the finances and take care of those dull business affairs. In some ways Cher was perceived as a pioneer.

Her frequent liaisons with younger men, her outrageous wardrobe—all were indications of a rebellious nature. Still, Cher dressed and behaved one way in public but a different way in private. She felt no need to live up to her glamorous image twenty-four hours a day. She was happy to drive around town in a Jeep, but even there she had to be different: It was a black, custom-made number, which made her feel real "butch," as she put it, when she drove it.

Cher is a very feminine woman, very attracted to men, and she so admires masculinity that she herself projects a certain masculine aura. Like men, she dates and dumps a variety of partners. Like men, she refuses to be fussed over or "taken care of." Like men, she likes to call the shots and have control. Like men, she enjoys relaxing in work shirts and torn jeans. She even likes to wear tattoos. She is not interested in being a "lady" if that means taking a backseat or leading a dull life.

Cher combines the best qualities of both sexes. She can be a tough broad when required, then the next moment become the dolled-up glamour puss absolutely reveling in her ultrafemininity and the effect it has on the opposite sex. For these and many other reasons, Cher is seen as a rebel, and for once it is not just a pose or an image.

Her masculine qualities may have led to her casting in her next two pictures after *Jimmy Dean*. Although Dolly Pelliker in *Silkwood* was diametrically opposed to Cher's public image, she was not so alien from Cher's private one. Both women could be seen as down-to-earth. This was certainly also true of Rusty Dennis, the role Cher plays in *Mask*—a biker gal with a dubious lifestyle of men and drugs.

Although Dolly Pelliker was a made-up name, Dolly and Rusty Dennis were real people (Pelliker was based on Sheri Ellis), women who had been through suffering and loss far worse than anything Cher had experienced. In certain scenes in both pictures Cher was suddenly struck by the fact that a real person had gone through the ordeal, whether it was Dolly/Sheri being tested for radiation in a hospital or Rusty picking up her hideously disfigured son at camp. As Cher put it, "It makes you feel like you have to be true to these people because they really existed."

She got the part of Dolly Pelliker in *Silkwood* almost as easily as she had been cast in *Come Back to the Five and Dime, Jimmy*

Dean, Jimmy Dean. Director Mike Nichols was in a matinee audience of *Jimmy Dean* and was highly impressed with what he saw; he realized that night that Cher had what it took to handle a serious role in a serious picture. If she had any rough edges, Nichols could smooth them over; he'd handled an awkward and unpolished Dustin Hoffman fifteen years earlier and gotten him to deliver a fine performance in *The Graduate* that had led him directly into a starring career. Mike Nichols recognized Cher's basic ability, and while she might not have been in Hoffman's league for basic acting talent, he felt sure he could get her to do what was required.

Chances are that Nichols had commercial considerations in mind, just as Altman had with the play. Powerful as the true story of Karen Silkwood was, the film would still be a hard sell in an era of teen and action movies. *Silkwood* was *people*-oriented; it wasn't full of spaceships, flying supermen, or special effects. Kurt Russell and Meryl Streep, the other stars, were well-known but not major box-office attractions. Neither was Cher, but everything Cher did generated publicity. Ironically, Nichols hired Cher for her glitz, then proceeded to strip the woman of glamour.

Karen Silkwood was a pretty young woman who worked at the Cimarron plutonium fuel plant, run by the Kerr-McGee Corporation, in Crescent, Oklahoma. Her efforts to expose hazardous working conditions—Karen and others were exposed to cancer-causing radiation daily—led to run-ins with superiors and even other workers. One day in 1974 Karen had an appointment with a *New York Times* reporter to whom she planned to turn over some crucial evidence that would prove the plant was falsifying quality-control checks. On the way to meet the reporter, Karen was killed in a car crash, the cause of which was never satisfactorily explained. (For one thing, the documents were missing from the car.)

Steve Wodka, who worked for the Oil, Chemical, and Atomic Workers Union in Washington, D.C., characterized Karen Silkwood as a thorough, credible, and caring person, and he greatly admired her willingness to take risks. Silkwood today is seen as a heroine who sacrificed her life for the good of others.

She could have just quit her job and walked away from it all. Instead, she tried to make the plant a safer place for everyone.

Mike Nichols had already won his fair share of film-directing acclaim at the time of *Silkwood*. He had directed Cher's buddy Sandy Dennis, along with Elizabeth Taylor and Richard Burton, in an excellent 1966 film adaptation of Edward Albee's 1962 stage hit *Who's Afraid of Virginia Woolf?* He had won an academy award for the 1967 *The Graduate* and had guided Ann-Margret, another show bizzy singer with acting aspirations, though *Carnal Knowledge*, for which she had received much acclaim in 1971. He did do an occasional stinker—the 1973 *The Day of the Dolphin*, for instance—but his overall film track record was a lot healthier than Robert Altman's. Some time before, admittedly, he had turned down Cher for a film role, but at this time he was firmly convinced that he could do for Cher what he had done for Ann-Margret.

Still, Cher couldn't help being intimidated by her costars— one of them in particular. Meryl Streep by 1983 was considered one of the country's finest actresses, excelling in everything from dramas like *Kramer vs. Kramer* to mediocre thrillers like *Still of the Night*. Cher knew that she just wasn't in Streep's league (although later, more self-confident and cocky, she did say that she could have handled *Kramer vs. Kramer* and a lot of other "dramatic" roles).

Much of her initial apprehension about working with the woman evaporated, however, when Streep accorded her a very warm welcome on the first day of shooting. Cher for her part might have been surprised at the time to know that Streep was apprehensive about meeting *her*, for she thought of Cher as very glamorous, très chic, and so much the embodiment of Hollywood style that Meryl felt like a drab wren beside her, or so she indicated. How much of this was tact and a desire to put Cher at ease and how much genuine remains moot, as Streep was never without her own brand of self-possession and self-appreciation, in her case most justified. Streep later expressed her gratitude that Cher seemed down-to-earth, accessible, and unaffected.

Kurt Russell, the male lead, had started out as a child actor for Disney. His teenage years were a twilight period for him professionally and personally. He had found that he was out of step with the youth of America during the peacenik and rebellion period. He was regarded as reactionary and mocked because of it. When he reemerged as a successful leading man in the seventies and eighties, he was happy that *he* was "somebody" and the hippies who'd laughed at his "square" politics were "nowhere."

Cher's character, Dolly Pelliker, is based on Karen Silkwood's friend Sheri Ellis. In the film Dolly is a poignant figure in many ways; she is a lesbian in love with Karen but must remain at arm's length, the unrequited lover cast in the role of best friend. She wants to be part of the special feelings that Karen shares with her boyfriend, Drew (Russell) but knows she never can be. During the course of the film she does have a relationship with another woman, but it doesn't work out.

Whatever flaws she may have are not blamed on her being a lesbian; she's simply a sometimes troubled human being who happens to be gay and is thus one of the more positively portrayed homosexual characters in Hollywood films. Her sexual orientation is handled matter-of-factly.

The real Dolly Pelliker—ex-rodeo queen Sheri Ellis—didn't object to being portrayed as a lesbian but, when asked if she was gay in real life, replied, "I'm a virgin, and so is everybody else in Oklahoma." What bothered her were certain fictionalizations of her life, such as the affair with a hairdresser depicted in the picture. Even more upsetting was the implication that Sheri/Dolly betrayed Karen by telling the powers that be at the plant what Karen was up to. After Silkwood was killed, Sheri burst into the offices of Kerr-McGee with an unloaded .22 rifle. At the time of the film's release (1983) she was writing a book about Karen and had bought a house with some of the money she was paid by the producers for character portrayal rights. She and Cher had never met.

Cher didn't like the idea that she was to be so completely deglamorized for what she felt would be her first major film. Nichols made it clear that if she tried to get by with wearing makeup or fussing with her appearance, she wouldn't be true to

173

the character and her performance would suffer. At first Cher wouldn't listen. She behaved like Jane Wyman filming *Stage Fright* back in 1949; Jane had dolled herself up to compete with costar Marlene Dietrich and damaged her credibility in the process.

But there was no Marlene Dietrich in *Silkwood*. Karen herself was not a glamour puss, and neither was Streep. Dolly didn't wear makeup or dress in sharp outfits not because she was a lesbian but because she, like Karen, didn't particularly care about that stuff. Nichols had to convince Cher that not every woman was a slave to her vanity. These women worked in a plutonium plant, for pete's sake; they were not Manhattan career girls or ladies who lunched in wigs and lipsticks. Eventually Cher got the message.

But it wasn't easy for her. Cher had been a pimple-plagued teenager and still occasionally had bouts with bad skin flare-ups. She was used to being seen, by the public at least, at her best. The makeup artists had worked on her before she stepped in front of the cameras for her assorted TV shows and specials; she always looked great when she did her concerts (and her fans were not in a position to see her up close under those circumstances anyway). When she appeared in *Jimmy Dean*, she played a character for whom making up and looking sexy were second nature.

But playing Dolly Pelliker would expose her a little more than was comfortable. There would be no lying to the camera. No makeup, no glamour. It was an extremely difficult moment for her when she faced the fact that she had to go out there and eventually be seen larger than life exactly how she was—or rather, worse than she actually was because she wouldn't dream of actually letting anyone see her in real life looking as she did as Dolly. Was she just a gloss and glamour queen or did she have the right stuff? That was the issue here. Eventually she mustered all her Bette Davis courage and went out there to give a *performance*, and the hell with what she looked like.

With uncombed hair, a sullen (and scared) expression, baggy pants, a shapeless shirt, and a bulky workout jacket that she wouldn't have been caught dead in at Jack La Lanne's, Cher looked strange to the assembled cast and crew. Kurt Russell, trying to be friendly, poked fun at her (she really did look like something the cat had dragged in), and Cher hastily retreated to her dressing room until Nichols came to coax her out.

It was an undeniably amusing irony. Cher had spent her childhood absorbed in movie mags and Hollywood glamour, dreaming of the day it would be her turn in front of the cameras, like Lana, Marilyn, maybe Hedy Lamarr. Now, in her first big picture, she looked about as glamorous as an overaged tomboy. Heck, she wanted to look like *Joan* Crawford, not *Broderick* Crawford!

Nichols found that it was easier to get Cher to do what he wanted than he had anticipated. He decided, for instance, to add a scene in which Dolly begins to sob as she sees Karen's smashed automobile being towed past the restaurant where she's sitting. Cher immediately went into a panic. Nichols wanted to do it the same day he told her about it, and she was convinced that she'd never be able to manage it. By the time they were ready to shoot the scene, Cher was crying hysterically. "Let's just do the scene," Nichols said. "Don't worry about it." What Cher didn't realize was that she was in just the frame of mind to be convincing as the grief-stricken Dolly in the sequence, hence had no trouble doing exactly what Nichols wanted in front of the camera.

Cher liked working with Nichols. "Mike gives you the kind of space in which you can feel totally safe, even to make mistakes. So you really try to do anything he asks." Nichols would practically cry along with her if it would get her to give him what he wanted.

But Cher sensed her role in the film had little to do with crying. "I was the child. I was the darling girl. If any parts of it were funny or could relieve tension, they were my parts, and so everyone was happy when I was around."

This especially applied to Kurt Russell, who delighted in playing practical jokes on Cher, as if he were her older brother. He'd grab food out of her hand and take a big bite out of it, bang on her dressing-room door and then run and hide, playfully punch her in the shoulder. Their roughhouse relationship was similar to Dolly's and Drew's in the film. Cher and Meryl also became close, like their film counterparts.

Cher has recalled that there was a scene, near the end of the film, where she had to get up and leave because she was almost hysterical. "It was the scene when the doctors are telling Karen that she's not badly contaminated. I know the doctors are lying, and Meryl was made up to look like she was going to die. Suddenly I looked at her and thought: 'This happened to a real person. And if Meryl were dying, I don't think I could stand it!' "

Meryl Streep was very helpful to Cher, teaching her things about the craft of acting that Cher had never even considered before. She later recalled Meryl as "very generous when she's acting with you. There's never the feeling that one of you is going to be victorious. I always felt that she was hoping I was going to be as good in a scene as she was." When Cher asked Streep what was the most important thing about film acting she could pass on to her, Streep told her, "You should work harder in my close-up than you do in your own," and vice versa. "What Meryl was suggesting was the essence of real collaboration," Cher admitted with exaggerated humility, adding, "I didn't even know what a close-up was!"

Cher and Meryl were as close as sisters during the filming of *Silkwood*. There was not much to do in the small town where they were shooting, not far from Dallas (they could not stray too far from the set). Cher missed her children terribly and was often depressed. Meryl provided companionship and a shoulder to cry on. Cher was never to forget her kindness.

Although Karen Silkwood had been dead for nearly ten years when the picture came out, it generated a great deal of controversy from all quarters: the press; the critics; the real-life people whose namesakes appeared in the film. Steve Wodka, the union official, thought that Karen was a lot more "politically aware" than she was portrayed in the movie. Her father, Bill Silkwood, thought that the film made his daughter seem a lot less intelligent than she actually was and that it followed the lead of the Kerr-McGee lawyers by making Karen seem distracted and immoral.

The picture was also accused of taking certain liberties with the actual facts. One of the best, most chilling sequences shows the decontamination of Karen's house by men in protective white uniforms. They carry out all furniture and personal effects and strip the walls bare, registering everything with their instruments. While it was more dramatic to have this all take place in a day, the actual decontamination took three months! Also criticized was Nichols's ending, which shows a sinister pair of headlights bearing down on Karen's car, indicating a "foul play" that was never proved. (However, the suggestion that Silkwood fell asleep at the wheel was also never proved. The truth may never be known.)

There was less squabbling among the critics than there was among the journalists; *Silkwood* received almost unanimous praise, which it deserved. The film is one of Nichols's finest and is absorbing for its entire 128-minute running time. Understated for the most part in its approach, *Silkwood* is undeniably effective and features excellent performances from the leads and a large supporting cast. Although Cher's role is relatively small, her participation in this film is a plus for her.

Her notices for her performance were for the most part excellent. Rex Reed wrote, "It's fun to see Cher stripped of her forty-pound eyelashes and Cher drag as the caring home town lesbian who fills Streep's icebox with leftovers so mangy they've grown penicillin." The *Village Voice* termed her "first rate . . . in a surprisingly small role after all the hoopla." *Women's Wear Daily* thought she was "marvelous." *Newsweek* congratulated her for "her best work yet as a dramatic actress," and Kathleen Carroll in the New York *Daily News* suggested that Cher was "going to surprise people with her touching performance as the self-deprecating Dolly." To *Variety*, her intense argument and lovely reconciliation with Streep were one of her particularly wonderful moments.

Other reviewers were more reserved but still fairly positive.

"I'm not sure about her acting (I saw her under the blight of Robert Altman's direction in a Broadway play) but here . . . she is at least kept from false moves by Nichols," said the *New Republic*. *The New York Times* had a similar, but more admiring, reaction; "Whether or not Cher is a great actress I'm still not sure, but when you take away those wild wigs she wore on television . . . there's an honest, complex screen presence underneath." Wrote Pauline Kael in the *New Yorker*: "[Cher] has a lovely dark-lady presence, but Dolly is a wan, weak role."

Occasionally Cher found herself with a better write-up than Meryl Streep. *Time* magazine noted that Cher and Russell were "easier and more naturalistic performers" while Streep was "an actor of calculated effects, which work when she is playing self-consciously intelligent women, but interpreting a character who abandons three children, shares a house with a rather shiftless boyfriend and a lesbian, and shows her contempt for authority by flashing a bare breast at its representative, she seems at once forced and pulled back."

Cher received an Academy Award nomination as Best Supporting Actress for her work. The night of the Oscar telecast Cher was so nervous "it felt like being in an airplane when the pilot's dead." She had the misfortune of finding herself up against the troll-like Linda Hunt, who played a diminutive man in *The Year of Living Dangerously* and went home with the coveted statue. "The only time in the history of the movies that a woman plays a man, and I get put up against her!" Cher lamented. In this case she was no film historian, for women had at least posed as men in earlier films—to wit: Katharine Hepburn in *Sylvia Scarlett* (1936) and, in several sequences, Garbo in *Queen Christina* (1933.) And that same year, 1983, Barbra Streisand would be fetching indeed playing a man in *Yentl*. Cher hadn't a chance against the dwarfish Hunt doing her highly publicized gender-bender.

The other nominated actresses for that year were Glenn Close in *The Big Chill*, Amy Irving in *Yentl*, and Alfred Woodard in *Cross Creek*: None of these performances was necessarily better than Cher's. Cher did win a consolation prize, the Golden Globe Award, but against the Oscar it was small consolation.

Even Pia Zadora had won that one.

Anna Hamilton Phelan was at UCLA's Center for Genetic Research when she met a young man who touched her heart and imagination. His name was Rocky Dennis, and he suffered from craniodiaphysial dysplasia, a congenital condition that increased calcium deposits in the skull and proved so disfiguring that Rocky resembled a modern-day equivalent of the Elephant Man. His head was about twice as large as normal; his face lacked a bridge to the nose and had eyes set much too far apart; the condition was both grotesque and incredibly painful.

Yet Rocky was still a lovable youngster, in many ways a typical boy, with a sweetness and courage that Phelan found irresistible. Although she had come to the center to do research for another story, Phelan decided that the tale of Rocky Dennis and his devoted, if unusual, mother, Rusty, would make a powerful and inspiring motion picture. This, then, was the origin of the film *Mask*.

Cher had no difficulty in winning the role of the disfigured boy's mother. By being hired for *Silkwood* by the prestigious director Mike Nichols, she had won new respect in many circles. She was now taken seriously as a film actress. When she received the script from producer Martin Starger, she immediately fell in love with it. Here was a lead role she could really sink her teeth into. She later said of *Mask*: "Originally, I didn't want to do something with this much responsibility so soon. I wanted to wait before I did a starring part, to bridge it with something. But when this came along, I didn't have a choice."

Although Cher was to say that she didn't really identify with Rusty Dennis, the mother, there were certain similarities between the two women, such as their "gruffness and independence." According to Cher later, "It didn't seem like a major stretch. I knew the look, and I've known women in my line of work who were just as tough as Rusty; they just dress nicer. I have the capability of being tough. I don't have the necessity most of the time." Cher also felt that Rusty's relationship with her son was very similar to Cher's relationship with her own two kids—to wit, "Very unconventional, very loving, but not the typical parent and child."

There was one aspect of Rusty's character with which Cher parted company. Rusty was a drug abuser, and the character in some ways reminded Cher of her second husband, Gregg Allman, whom she had always perceived as being essentially self-destructive. But Cher was to rely a great deal on the original of Rusty in creating a true and believable portrait; Rusty became her "unseen director." Rusty also gave Cher a true sense of what lay beneath the words when Rusty and Rocky argued, a real handle on their special relationship. Rusty, who was on hand, did not hesitate to tell Cher, for instance, when the dialogue didn't ring true.

Rusty Dennis was a decidedly unconventional woman, who must have appealed to Cher, but in many respects she differed from the woman playing her. Rusty, of course, didn't earn millions playing Caesars Palace; she lived in a disordered trailer. She found her outlet not on the stage or TV but with biker gangs and drugs, the latter being a constant bone of contention between her and Rocky. But Rusty had always tried to do her best for her boy and was his biggest supporter. She was determined that Rocky should live as normal a life as possible. He would not go to special schools and be hidden away from society; he would go to a regular high school like everyone else. There was nothing wrong with his mind or with his personality, so why, Rusty thought, should her boy be shut away?

There are indications that Rusty had become so used to Rocky's appearance and loved him so much that she may have blinded herself to certain realities. One day she showed Cher a (group) picture of Rock when he was younger but obviously deformed and therefore immediately recognizable. Nevertheless, Rusty felt it necessary to tell Cher, "He's the tall one." Rusty also informed Cher that in her view it was better, on balance, for Rocky to have his brains and personality intact and look the way he did than to be a handsome, arrogant moron. Her faith in Rocky enabled him to make it through his relatively short life, with friends, some semblance of normality, and a certain degree of happiness instead of being shunted aside and treated strictly as a freak. Cher admitted that before she did *Mask*, her probable reaction to seeing someone like Rocky would have been to gasp and look the other way.

Something else that Cher found endearing and enthralling about *Mask* was the way the picture was all about *images*. The way people are perceived (Rocky as monster, the bikers as bums) was not necessarily how they *were*. This, too, she could identify with.

The director of *Mask*, Peter Bogdanovich, had made his film mark years before with a superb adaptation of Larry McMurtry's fine novel *The Last Picture Show*, about the inhabitants of a small Texas town (Bogdanovich did a sequel, *Texasville*, in 1990). He had had some experience working with singing prima donnas, having directed Barbra Streisand in *What's Up, Doc?* in 1972—the year after *Picture Show*—and felt sure that if he could keep a handle on Barbra, he could do equally well with the more down-to-earth and laid-back Cher. Instead, he found himself engaged in one of the biggest battles of his career.

Cher has said that Robert Altman was the kind of director who let you do whatever *you* wanted to and that Mike Nichols let you do only exactly what *he* wanted. Bogdanovich was something else again. He wanted Cher to do what *he* wanted, but he didn't have the patience to talk or fake her into it, the way Nichols did. It was inevitable the two would clash.

Cher was convinced that she understood the character of Rusty a lot better than Bogdanovich did, and she simply did not trust the director's judgment. This, in retrospect, is ironic because Bogdanovich had felt that Cher's persona—anyway, the public's perception of it—was a match for Rusty's: "free, outspoken, tough . . . but also a lot more vulnerable than she lets on." Cher thought that "Peter wanted to be doing my job but had to hire me."

Actress and director argued almost constantly for weeks. Cher was to say: "Peter reminds me very much of Sonny. You never know why they're being nice or mean, and you have to go along." Although she had respected Bogdanovich's work in the past, she decided that she didn't like or respect him during *Mask*. Every choice he made or insisted upon seemed to her the wrong one, and she refused to go along. Bogdanovich went so far as to tell her exactly how to read a line, and she found this intolerable. Finally she yelled at him, "Fire me or get off my back!"

Bogdanovich, for his part, opined that he felt Cher had problems with men, particularly men cast as authority figures, because of her bad relationship with her father; she didn't trust, maybe even hated, men because of her early experiences. The relationship with Sonny hadn't helped either. Possibly because of Bogdanovich's notorious and tragic relationship with the late *Playboy* model Dorothy Stratton, who had wound up luridly murdered, Cher felt that he essentially disliked women unless they were easily pliable and virtually subservient.

Certainly Cher was in no mood to worship at the shrine of Peter Bogdanovich—she was not one of his puppet women—and she continued to buck his demands. Although there were times when she found Peter more tolerable than usual—he did have his good points—she basically thought he was a pig.

It wasn't until halfway through the shooting of *Mask* that Peter Bogdanovich at last accepted that maybe Cher knew what she was doing after all; as soon as he realized he could trust her instincts, he began to relax and back off. Relieved, Cher found him easy enough to work with after that.

Cher later claimed that her assorted problems with Peter stemmed from other things besides the working relationship (problematic though that was). She felt that he was unsympathetic toward the characters in *Mask*, and this had led to a clash in their respective perceptions of the leading parts. Nor had Cher forgotten that years before Bogdanovich had done a not entirely favorable 1966 piece, a major one, on her and Sonny when he was in his magazine-writing phase. She felt that he had not understood her then and that he didn't understand her now. This outweighed any considerations of gratitude for her being cast in the film.

She had a much better relationship with costar Eric Stoltz, who played Rocky under a ton of hideous makeup and who proved to be extremely touching and effective in the part. The two became close during filming, and their constant hugging and kissing led many to believe that they were having an affair. Stoltz denies this, but what he doesn't deny is his admiration for the woman. "The way that Cher functions is quite extraordinary," he says. "There is absolutely no bullshit about her. She is incapable of self-censorship."

Cher has maintained that she and Eric developed a relationship similar to Rusty's and Rocky's, although Eric, half in jest, accused her of preferring him as Rocky to him as Eric, but it would appear that her feelings for the young man were far more than motherly. Cher was one of the only people on the set ever to see Eric out of his makeup. Richard Dysart, who played Rusty's father, told *Quirk's Reviews* writer William Schoell that he hasn't met the "real" Eric to this day but has seen him on-screen. Many have noted that the actor is in reality a lithe, handsome redhead who could never have known the kind of pain that comes from ugliness and that constituted Rocky's entire life. Certainly Eric and Cher dated; on the dance floor she wrapped herself around him and hugged him closely and fervently "like a lover," as one onlooker put it. Also, during the filming Eric moved into Cher's house, and the two became good friends and constant companions. *If* nothing physical ever happened between the two, it was probably because Eric didn't want it to.

Another similarity between Cher and Rusty Dennis was that both had had bad relationships with their fathers. Bogdanovich chose Dysart, who plays the head of the firm on TV's *L.A. Law* and is one of the finest character actors working today, to play this small but important role. "The character was far from what I am and what I usually do," says Dysart, adding, "That's why I wanted to play him." Dysart did a reading, along with Estelle Getty, who plays the mother, for Bogdanovich and got the part. He greatly admired Eric Stoltz and the way he endured those three-hour-long makeup sessions, saying of him, "He was a trouper, to say the least. He took direction well, made creative and intelligent suggestions, and kept in good humor throughout the ordeal." A scene where the two spend the day at Dodger Stadium was cut out of the film, but Dysart still found it "a great experience."

Dysart also liked working with Cher: "She was working strongly and clearly and well and *honestly*, and that is the key to her acting approach and ability—the honesty. I felt then, and have continued to realize, that with Cher 'what you see is what you get.' Superior talent."

Cher recalled that she and everyone on the set—including Rusty Dennis—had the feeling that Rocky, who had died sometime before, was on location with them in a spiritual sense, moving them to do their best and truest work, embodying the film with something extra and very special.

By the time the movie premiered at the Cannes Film Festival, Cher and Bogdanovich were at each other's throats again. The trouble this time was that Universal wanted to remove the Bruce Springsteen songs from the sound track (terms could not be agreed upon) and replace them with tunes by Bob Seger. They also wanted to cut a couple of scenes that Bogdanovich thought were essential. In Peter's view, it was important to use the Springsteen songs because "The Boss" was Rocky's favorite and it was important to the integrity of the film. Peter placed ads in the trades attacking the studio and demanded that Cher refuse to help publicize the picture.

In Cher's stated view, Peter Bogdanovich was badly overreacting. She accused him of being even more destructive toward the picture (and her performance) in the beginning than the studio was being now. Sure, it would have been nice to have Springsteen on the sound track, but the use of the Seger songs would, she opined, hardly destroy the picture. And if she could live with those scenes being cut, she averred, so could Peter. After all, she was *in* those scenes. Cher, in short, was getting even with Peter for his treatment of her on the set early in the shooting and for certain public statements he had made about her that she found offensive.

Bogdanovich had the real Rusty Dennis on his side, if not the fake one. Rusty, for her part, claimed that far from welcoming her help with her performance, Cher didn't even want her on the set, claiming she made her "nervous." Rusty had convinced herself that Cher was responsible for the cuts made by Universal, that Cher wanted to remove or downplay anything that might make Rocky the center of attention rather than herself. "It was supposed to have been ninety percent my son's story, not hers," Rusty complained. She also charged that Cher wanted one scene cut because she sang in it and was afraid it would remind people of her old image.

Indeed, Rusty made it sound as if Cher had, with cold calculation, conspired to steal the movie away from Bogdanovich and Stoltz's Rocky and transform it into a solid star vehicle for herself. (Rusty, some people think, may not have been far off the mark.)

Yet it was also true that Rusty herself had an ax to grind. Screenwriter Anna Hamilton Phelan and Bogdanovich both had turned over one of their profit-sharing portions to Rusty; but Cher did not, and Rusty was pissed off because of it, especially since Cher earned three quarters of a million dollars for acting out her story and she got only a measly fifteen thousand dollars for living it. Rusty, of course, was not privy (not that it might have mattered) to Cher's eternal fear of being poor and her tendency to overcompensate wildly by either hoarding whatever she made or spending it on herself, her children, or frivolous, unnecessary items.

Despite all this, Rusty Dennis did express herself as pleased with Cher's portrayal of her, even if Cher wouldn't return her calls when she phoned to tell her how great she was.

At Cannes the two camps each held press conferences: Cher and producer Martin Starger on one side; Bogdanovich and Rusty Dennis on the other. The result was that Bogdanovich dropped his lawsuit against Universal and Starger. When even his leading lady was against him, what good was it?

Cher proceeded to win the Best Actress Award at Cannes's thirty-eighth Annual Film Festival, but even then she was embroiled in controversy, causing a minor scandal with her blatantly showy outfit and the lack of graciousness she showed toward Norma Aleandro, the Argentine actress who was named co-winner of the Best Actress Award. The fur nearly flew out of hand when Cher realized that there was only one trophy between them and they would have to share it. "Sorry you have to share, Cher, *mon chère*," quipped the master of ceremonies. Cher was a Hollywood *star*; why should *she* have to share an award and a trophy with some Argentinian she had never heard of and who had starred in a silly foreign picture probably nobody would ever get to see? Aleandro was, of course, thrilled to win the award but was not so thrilled with her co-winner's behavior.

One writer described the general reaction to Cher's outfit: " 'She looks ridiculous,' was the consensus, as the onlookers gasped incredulously at Cher's short black skirt slit to her hip, knees generously termed 'knobby,' and a barely-laced bodice that looked like one of Miss Kitty's rejects on *Gunsmoke* and a crucifix dangling from her ear."

While the picture received mixed reviews from the critics when it opened in the States in 1985, Cher's write-ups were almost exclusively positive. "Cher is tremendous as Rusty," wrote Ed Sikov in the *Native*. "It is a performance that makes her highly touted work in *Jimmy Dean* and *Silkwood* seem like trial runs." Rex Reed found that Cher played Rusty with "ferocious trashiness. [She] doesn't call attention to her virtuosity: her no-fuss acting style matches Rusty's passionate lifestyle."

Kathleen Carroll in the New York *Daily News* wrote that "Cher has found a part that fits her like a black mini-skirt. . . . She has definitely put her heart into this performance, and the emotion shows through." And from *Variety*: "Cher's [fine] performance suggests a hard exterior covering a wealth of conflicting and confused feelings." *The New York Times* averred: "Rusty is played by Cher with a good deal of skill," with the *Christian Science Monitor* chiming in with "Cher gives another of her nuanced portrayals."

The reviews for the picture itself were generally less predictable, with the exception of Rex Reed's write-up. *Mask*, he wrote, is "a sad, wrenching story of human dignity and courage in the face of adversity. *Mask* is a film that instructs and uplifts the spirit." Other, more discerning reviewers were less impressed. "*Mask* milks the emotions as shamelessly—and as clumsily—as Pollyanna," wrote Vincent Canby. "Bogdanovich has the tendency to resort to the obvious when playing with the audience's sympathy," Kathleen Carroll noted. And David Sterritt found that "the film has little insight to offer beyond its upbeat outlook, and even this is achieved partly by glossing-over or prettifying grim details."

Everyone expected Cher to get nominated for a Best Actress Oscar, but it never happened. "I was really upset," she said later. "I wanted to throw up and die." (The term "throw up" appears often in Cher's quotes.) However, not everyone thought her performance was worthy of the 1985 Oscar—or even particularly good.

Doug McClelland, a major film historian and the author of such books as the current *Hollywood Talks Turkey*, had this to say:

> Cher did considerable bad-mouthing of director Peter Bogdanovich after *Mask*. However, although she was widely praised for her performance in it, I couldn't help thinking that she owed her stardom in this new medium to Bogdanovich and his editor. Her performance literally seemed to have been pieced together in the cutting room. Her big moments appeared to be comprised of bits of film on her all strung together; she didn't seem able to sustain a scene by herself. Sometimes there would be so many different shots of her getting through a single scene that the episode began to look like a montage! Bogda-

novich and Company obviously worked hard to make her look good, and they succeeded, though the recipient of their TLC would be the last to admit it.

Some feel it would have been ironically amusing if Cher in the end had wound up giving exactly the performance Bogdanovich wanted and didn't even know it.

At the Oscars, which had snubbed her, Cher showed up in, as writer Edward Guthmann put it, "a skin-baring, black-leather-and-feathers concoction that made her look like an S & M float at Mardi Gras." This was her way of thumbing her nose at the Academy that Oscar spring of 1986, although she enjoyed herself more that night, on balance (the result of the lack of competitive pressure), than when she had been nominated for *Silkwood* the year before.

Since her appearance in *Mask* Cher has been involved with the National Craniofacial Foundation, a charitable organization for children afflicted the way the late Rocky Dennis was. She puts pictures of some of the children next to the mirrors of her dressing rooms while on tour, beside photographs of her family. She has served as honorary chairwoman and spokesperson of the organization and attends its fund-raising functions.

Cher was never one to do the predictable. She had just made two major pictures, received a great deal of attention and acclaim for them, and been nominated for one Oscar. Most actresses would have thrown themselves right back into their work, but Cher wanted to relax for a while. Relax and have fun.

And for Cher, fun meant *men*.

EIGHT
MEN ON HER MIND

Men are luxuries, not necessities.
—CHER

"If I wasn't with a man before, I was looking for one," Cher has said. "Now we [Cher and her female friends] can go out, have a good night, and not have to be looking for men or going home to them. I'm starting to feel more respectful of women. I've always liked them, but I didn't respect them."

This may be a clue to why Cher seems to hang out almost exclusively with much younger men and for shorter and shorter periods. She has learned that she can have fun and find warmth, friendliness, and companionship with other women. Men can be reserved for a little sex and romance when it's called for. In this way, she is like a "typical" male who beds different women, has short-term affairs, loves 'em and leaves 'em, and basically prefers to spend time with the boys.

In Cher's case the "boys" she loves to hang out with have included Diana Ross, Kate Jackson, her sister, Georgeanne, her best friend, Paulette Betts (who was also married to a member of the Allman Brothers Band), her exercise partner, Angela Best, and

139

her personal assistant, Debbie Paull. Although some of these women have been accused of "fussing over Cher like a bunch of lesbians," their chief topic of conversation, in fact, is men.

Because of what are considered certain manly attributes—her tattoos, for instance—Cher is occasionally plagued by rumors of lesbian behavior. (Years ago a tabloid even accused her of having an affair with her own half sister.) Those who spread the rumors are seemingly unaware that nowadays (or even in the past) a woman's being independent, fighting for her rights, or living by a masculine code of behavior does not necessarily add up to lesbianism. Besides, some lesbians could be just as frilly and feminine as, if not more so than, their heterosexual counterparts.

Still, the rumors persisted. Cher learned not to talk too much about her women friends; the press made insinuations and blew things out of proportion. Conversely, she decided it would be best to be more open about the men she dated. She has, in fact, never kept a low profile when it comes to members of the opposite sex.

There is no doubt that Cher loves the company of men. She is no "slut," however. She has never been one for casual pickups (except in her much younger days, and even then she was comparatively prudent) and prefers short-term affairs to one-night stands with strangers. She likes to get to know a man first.

She has, however, gotten to know *many* men.

Cher has explained why she isn't too crazy about being with guys who are older than she. For one thing, they seem to ask her out only if they are married, and they have, unlike Sonny Bono, never seemed particularly nurturing. "I don't," she sums up, "particularly care for older men as a group."

Older men also remind her of her father and all the men she saw around her house as a child. "Men were something that you knew were around, but you couldn't quite figure out what their function was. And you could do without them easily—and most of the women [she knew as a child] did. All of the women who were my mother's friends were working women; they all supported their children alone." That is basically the situation Cher finds herself in today, especially in the case of Elijah Blue, Gregg Allman's son.

Cher isn't interested in marriage or being protected, but she does like romantic gestures and sweetness and concern, and she believes that younger men are more likely to have these attributes than older ones. Men of the younger generation were likely to have been raised by women who share Cher's outlook on life and male-female relationships; they can understand women "and power, women doing their own job, women who don't need men to take care of them."

She adds, "Younger men are more supportive and a lot less demanding, and they also have more time for their relationships. I want somebody who still wants to go dancing or spend the day at Disneyland, somebody who'll give me more than the little time he has left over after his day at the office. Younger men are more fun to be with, and they have a kind of softness I like."

The romantic aspect of her various amours fade away after about two years tops. "I guess I just can't make that heavy commitment," she says. She does manage to remain friends—usually—with most of her "exes."

Sonny Bono, David Geffen, Gregg Allman, Les Dudek . . .

And, of course, Gene Simmons.

Simmons, with whom Cher got involved after her affair with David Geffen petered out, wore more makeup than she did.

Of course, his was stage makeup, which he wore in his guise as bassist for the rock group Kiss. Simmons and three associates had been floundering around, playing sleazy nightclubs in Manhattan to less than packed houses, when they came up with a gimmick. They all would sport outlandish painted faces, and clothing to match, with each becoming a different kind of "creature." Simmons's makeup was of a demonic cast, a vampire in greasepaint. A rather ordinary-looking man was transformed into a striking, sensual ghoul with sneering lips and multicolored features.

Kiss was never famous for its music, but for its efforts at self-promotion and merchandising. Occasionally a halfway memorable song would come out of the stew of music they created, such as "Beth," but their "sound" was never taken very seriously by either critics or fans of serious rock. Nevertheless, Kiss had its devotees, mostly teenyboppers, who would also buy its comic books and make up their faces to resemble their favorite band member. The members of the band were careful not to be seen out in public or photographed without their trademark makeups.

Eventually the makeup gimmick was dropped, and Simmons became an actor in such films as *Runaway*, where he played villain to Tom Selleck's hero. Out of makeup, Simmons was not very striking, but the sneer and "attitude" were the same. Though by no means handsome, Simmons was tall and projected a kind of sexy and manly insolence found attractive by many women, including Cher, who was four years older than he was.

Cher met Simmons at a fund raiser for Jerry Brown. She didn't really know who he was and thought she was about to be introduced to the actress Jean Simmons. By that time the group had become extremely successful, with many hit records, and Simmons wasted no time cluing Cher in to it. Of course, Cher had heard of Kiss, but only because her daughter, Chastity, was a fan. She herself never listened to its music and knew very little about the group.

Cher, on first viewing, found Simmons affected; trying to impress her, he adopted a peculiar voice that was probably meant to be deep and sensual, but it sounded only as if he had a cold. Simmons wilted somewhat when Cher passed one of her famous blunt remarks about how "funny" he was talking. Still, his voice didn't stop her from letting him drive her home from the fund raiser. Along the way he stopped at his hotel to pick up material and paraphernalia that would prove to Cher what a sensation his group, Kiss, was. Cher wasn't terribly impressed with Simmons, but she liked him well enough to stay up late talking with him that night at her house, though his ego was affronted when she didn't ask him to share her bed.

Not much later Simmons took Cher and her actress friend Kate Jackson to a rock concert. Kate and Cher compared notes in the ladies' room and agreed that Simmons was trying to live up to his image as a superstud and was hitting on both of them at once. They also agreed that he was an asshole. Cher figured that would be the last she would see of Mr. Simmons, but a week later he was on the phone because he was afraid she possibly thought he'd been hitting on both her *and* her friend. *She* was the only one he was after, he assured her; he really liked *her*; he couldn't stop thinking about her. They had an all-night phone marathon, and Simmons phoned her every night for the next few days from wherever he was on tour. Finally he informed her that he thought he was falling in love and was taking time off from the tour to see her.

Cher had no idea that much of Gene's image was the truth; he had cut a swath through a sea of groupies since the band first formed. "He was the worst," Cher said, referring to his experiences with women. Gregg and Sonny couldn't hold a candle to Simmons, and they were no slouches when it came to womanizing. Being with women made Gene feel powerful and handsome, a stallion, but being with Cher did something extra for him: It did something to his heart. He had, it seemed, never really had a *relationship* with a woman before.

Simmons and Cher continued to date, and before long they were involved in an affair, a full-fledged one. Cher found that when he was with her, Gene behaved very differently from how certain members of the public saw him. He didn't drink or do drugs like so many rock stars; he was a gentleman instead of the standard chauvinistic "make-out" artist. He was, in short, what Cher needed at that point.

Cher was accused by the columnists of carrying on with Simmons strictly for career reasons. Joey Sasso claimed the affair was nothing more than an attempt by her to recapture the youth market (which Kiss had practically sewn up) and save herself from becoming a has-been.

In truth, Cher did have her uses for Simmons, and she probably never seriously considered him a candidate for a long-term romance. First of all, she wanted a male presence in her life, not someone domineering like Sonny or pathetically dependent like Gregg Allman or a nice-but-a-little-dull number like David Geffen; Gene Simmons, with his scintillating, pseudoscary image yet pliable personality fitted the bill. Cher did use Gene to get a recording contract with his label, Casablanca, after her last couple of records had been bombs and Warner Records had had its fill of her. Even after the affair was over, she stayed in Simmons's apartment while she was hunting for her own during her 1982 run in *Jimmy Dean* on Broadway. Simmons, still in love with her, did not object; the two had become friends, to be sure, but some who knew them wondered if the friendship was ever a two-way street.

Cher felt very secure with Simmons; he loved her, but he didn't make demands. Simmons continued seeing other women while they were going together—with Cher's blessing. Cher said publicly that Simmons's extracurricular involvements were no threat because Simmons always wanted the woman to "leave in the morning so he could get on with his day." Cher herself saw other men but limited these forays to companionship. Privately, it appears, Cher was hoping that Simmons would really fall for one of the other women—when she was through with him, of course—or at least stop being too much of a drag by focusing all his romantic attention on her.

Fundamentally Cher liked Gene but did not want to have an ongoing romance with him. Years later she dismissed Simmons with: "He was kind of too soft for me. Just very easygoing." Cher here proved the adage that "Women don't like tame men." Underneath his makeup, the macho stances, the vocal flourishes, Simmons was very tame, at least for her speed.

A pattern began to assert itself: If Cher could have a man too easily, she soon got bored with him. That's basically what happened with Gene. He would have to put his makeup on before he became exciting. He had often told Cher that when he was in Kiss-drag, his whole personality changed and she had better watch out; he had a tendency to be mean as sin to whoever happened by. The first time Cher saw Gene in his makeup he ran true to form and made a rude, nasty remark. Cher hauled off and slapped him. If that sort of thing had happened a little more often, she might never have let him go. Cher found him warm and lovable and very amusing but not the kind of man who had real staying power in romantic terms. "We didn't get married," she said, "because it wasn't true love."

Cher was almost relieved when Diana Ross showed up to take Simmons off her hands. She introduced the two superstars to each other at a birthday party she threw for Gene. Diana Ross has always had a thing for white men, especially for men who seem to embody a kind of incipient danger and authority; she bought into Gene's whole "act" without even thinking. For his part, Gene saw another chance for heavy "star-fucking." Soon the two were dating up a storm. Although Ross has been accused of stealing Simmons away from Cher, Cher couldn't have cared less. Eventually Diana also got bored with Simmons and, needing an excuse to break it off, accused him of renewing his relationship with Cher when the two roomed together (chastely) in New York a couple of years later. But there was nothing going on, according to Cher, who told friends, "We have a wonderful relationship. The only thing we don't do is fuck."

First Sonny. Then Gene. From 1980 to 1982 Cher had, it seemed, spent an inordinate amount of time living with men with whom she shared board but not bed.

When Cher came to New York in the early eighties, she found herself with more men than she could handle.

Not that it started off that way exactly. She found herself for a time a victim of the "oh, she must already have a date" syndrome—the belief among many men that there's no point in asking certain women out because they'll always be busy. Cher wasn't busy. This attractive, wealthy, glamorous woman spent a lot of nights just sitting home alone like some shopgirl. She probably could have told you what was happening on all the popular nighttime soaps.

The men she did meet told her she was "fascinating" but shied off from a date request. After all, she was *Cher*; she was too *famous* to need a date. Little did they know. . . . Finally she made up her mind just to go out and meet somebody. One of the first to cross paths with her was Ron Duguay.

Duguay was a shy but handsome hockey star of the New York Rangers, whose good looks galvanized both women and advertising people who wanted him to hawk their products on television. Commercials featured him surrounded by bimbos going "Look, it's *Ron Duguay!*" No actor was he, but his easy affability and sweetness, coupled with sexy looks, got him by and drew Cher to him. In some way she identified with Duguay; he, too, seemed overwhelmed, as she had been, by the bright, if hollow, lights of celebrity. But whereas Cher had learned to deal with it and had eventually risen above it, she worried that the same might not be true for Duguay. She even told Andy Warhol, "I don't know if [Ron's] ever going to be strong enough to outlive the whole thing that is going on around him."

Ron found it difficult, as she had, to put up with "superficial people who think you're beautiful, and [people] who want to fuck you so that they can say, 'I fucked Ron Duguay,' " as if that fact of having gotten into Ron's jockstrap made *them* better or more legitimate.

Broadway actress Patti LuPone (of *Evita* fame) had a hot and heavy thing for Ron and was not thrilled when Cher made a play for him. Stories circulated that Patti had thrown a fit—and anything she could get her hands on—at anyone who would dare mention her love rival's name in her dressing room. Patti knew that she was outclassed by Cher's Hollywood glitter but wasn't about to give up the "Battle of Duguay" without a fight.

There was no need for a hands-on cat fight, it turned out; Cher never really made first base. Although she felt Ron was as beautiful on the inside as he was on the outside, he never really responded the way she wanted him to. "I really liked him right away, and then nothing happened. And it was just like me, standing there waiting for something to happen that just never did."

Cher has lamented that this incomplete forward pass fiasco with "Duguay" left her "a little bit wary" of men in New York.

Still, Cher got Ron to come with her to the opening-night party of *Jimmy Dean* in 1982. Cher walked Duguay around like a prized possession. A joke (*not* told to Cher) made the rounds that guards were looking out for Patti LuPone in case she tried to crash the party.

A few months later, at the time of the play's early closing, Cher's "thing" for Ron had obviously run its course. She told one reporter that she was going to the Garden to "see the Flyers kick the shit out of the Rangers."

On Valentine's Day in 1983 Cher was invited to appear at "The Night of 100 Stars" at Radio City Music Hall. The show itself was no big deal, but Cher received two big thrills. The first was meeting dapper Jimmy Stewart, who told her how much he enjoyed her work. Cher, who shares a May 20 birthday with Stewart (some thirty-eight years apart) was so touched and excited by the then-seventy-four-year-old Stewart's gracious remark that she started to cry.

Thrill two of the evening was her meeting with John Loeffler, a twenty-nine-year-old composer and singer who did numerous jingles for such clients as Grey Advertising, Revlon, Canada Dry, and NBC. That summer he had recorded an album with twenty original compositions. He had also appeared on a CBS television special hosted by Linda Gray called *The Body Human*, where he was interviewed on what it was like to be single in Manhattan.

What first attracted Cher to Loeffler was no secret: He was a handsome blond with an aquiline nose, sexy lips, and a strong resemblance to actor Perry King. The fact that he was into music—a serious musician, in Cher's professional parlance—only made him more irresistible. Cher tried to remember to be "wary" of this latest New York man, but it wasn't easy. She said at the time that John "had the promise to be everything that anyone could ever ask for or want"—a statement that was superfervent for Cher.

John also had the shrewd grace to let Cher know he considered her a serious musician; he listened to her (universally panned) album *I Paralyze* and told her how much he liked it, even if he also admitted that he was surprised that he did. Loeffler, however, was not cut out for toady duty; he could be blunt with Cher. For one thing, he told her point-blank that he preferred her without her makeup (that left Cher, who thought it bizarre that he should say so, more than a little astonished). Then he informed her that he wished to take her away from the glamour, the glitter, and the effusions of her adoring coterie in Manhattan and treat her to a motorcycle trip to New Hampshire or Vermont. Cher almost did chuck it all and run off with him (if only for a weekend).

But there were complications from the muses. First she fell for a musician; now she was falling for an actor. And she couldn't make up her mind between them.

John Heard was a handsome blond actor of much promise who had already been married once, in 1979, to actress Margot Kidder (Lois Lane in the *Superman* movies). The marriage did not last long. According to columnist Suzy, Kidder dumped Heard after "five or six weeks of what must have been wedded unbliss." Heard was on the rebound and hadn't quite "made it" when he ran into Cher. Still, he had amassed some impressive credentials: costar with Jeff Bridges in *Cutter's Way*, a romantic lead in *Head over Heels*, and the role of Cassio in the production of *Othello* in Central Park in 1979. Heard was to hit a high note dramatically in a TV movie as the sexiest Reverend Dimmesdale ever to come down the pike in a version of Nathaniel Hawthorne's *The Scarlet Letter*.

Before long Cher was telling the world that she was in love with two men at the same time, both of whom just happened to be young, handsome, blond, and talented. What was a poor girl to do? Not only was Loeffler the ultimate, she rhapsodized, but Heard had "the most amazing mind and gentle quality about him that makes me feel totally safe."

At age thirty-six, Cher was coming on as strictly high school hot pants sixteen, promptly falling in love with virtually any good-looking man who was halfway nice to her—anyone, in short, who didn't remind her even faintly of paternally domineering Sonny and fucked-up adolescent Gregg. On the contrary, the Messrs. Loeffler and Heard seemed like two very "together" fellows.

Anyway, Cher couldn't make up her mind about the two blond apparitions. Andy Warhol, who had as good an eye for male appeal as Cher, shrugged and told her he just hoped that they had money.

Heard then (half-seriously, one assumes) told Cher that he thought it would be great if she, Loeffler, and he just lived together "like Kerouac." This gave Cher some pause.

Eventually Mr. Loeffler and Mr. Heard went the way of the other male phantoms in thirty-six-going-on-seventeen (at least romantically) Cher's scheme of things. Nothing had turned serious; they would have to be categorized with the former "wonderful, handsome, talented, amazing" Ron Duguay of the hot hockey stick.

Certainly Cher was a woman who would have no trouble attracting a man with her own considerably flashy attributes. But she was also a major star in both records and, now, with *Jimmy Dean*, on the stage. The lady had "connections," as everyone around her could not have overlooked. Heard and Loeffler wouldn't have been human—or particularly good careerists—if they hadn't considered those connections while maintaining their triangular relationship with Cher. She admitted later that both the Heard and Loeffler "things" had fizzled for lack of "substance" (obviously she meant emotionally, not physically).

It was while Cher was dating the three aforementioned men—Duguay, Loeffler, and Heard—that she met Val Kilmer, and that one stuck for a while.

The year was 1983. Cher was thirty-seven. Kilmer was twenty-four.

She was ripe for Kilmer by that time, and he for her. Her pattern, just prior to their meeting, was somewhat confused and uncertain, romantically, even for her. She claimed that she had not had sex with any of the threesome—Duguay, Loeffler, and Heard (not until she made up her mind about them, as she never really did)—but that she would sometimes sleep over, cuddling chastely in bed with one of them until morning. One day, after one of her sexless sleepovers, she decided that enough was enough. She didn't understand men any better than she ever had. She was going nowhere in this department. She toyed with giving up men for a while.

Then she met Val Kilmer at a friend's house. She didn't make her move or show any interest for quite some time. But she realized she was not giving up men after all.

Kilmer was a sexy-looking blond with regulation handsome features, full lips, a thick, rumpled mop of hair, and a basket that was a conversation piece in certain circles all over town. Although in some pictures he looks about as appealing as Jimmy McNichol (cute but not "hunky"), he was actually one of the best lookers Cher had ever taken up with.

Kilmer, who had writing aspirations, had cowritten a play, *How It All Began*, which was seen by Joe Papp and eventually presented at the Public Theater with Kilmer in the lead. He appeared in Papp's *Henry IV, Part I* and made his Broadway debut in *Slab Boys* with Sean Penn and Kevin Bacon. At that time (1983) he had not yet appeared in such major films as *Real Genius*, *Top Gun*, and *Willow*.

Young Mr. Kilmer was a man of many talents (he published a book of poetry) and had a strong interest in social causes and international concerns. Part Cherokee, he wrote a screenplay about Native Americans. Then he turned down film roles and used three hundred thousand dollars of his own money to make a documentary that asked, "How do we prevent nuclear war while maintaining national security?," exploring this controversial dichotomy with panache. Here, obviously, was a young man whose brain was not in his crotch.

This time Cher felt she had finally found her prince of the dream. Kilmer's combination of talent, ambition, and social concern tipped the balance for her. He wasn't just a pretty face; he wasn't just interested in the necessarily self-involved world of acting. He wanted to help people and do things. "My hero . . ." Cher muttered to herself meekly. He made her feel so—well, humble. She was in love with his intrepid idealism and doubtless what she conceived to be his boyish naïveté, considering the realities of the world and the human condition. People whose main goal in life is to make enough money so that they can shop galore and stick their tongues out at detractors (such as Cher) always stand in awe of people who know what they don't like about the world and set out to change it, whether the "cause" is won or lost. Cher has admitted that she thought Kilmer, though thirteen years her junior, was a lot more together and mature than she was.

But the age difference didn't really help. And there were other problems. No mincing courtier or effusive attendant was Val Kilmer. He liked his privacy—and his space. Cher blamed herself for the problems between them: "I came with a lot of baggage; I've been famous the major portion of [Val's] life." Cher also had two children, and should things get serious and permanent, they would represent a major responsibility for a twenty-four-year-old who wanted not only to make it big in pictures but to leave his mark on the great wide world. In the end he proved to be too dedicated to his main interests. Hero he might be and remain for her, but husband material he was not.

In 1984 Kilmer got his first big part in the zany spoof *Top Secret*, but Liz Smith reported that he and Cher were going to "separate screenings." Kilmer went on to play Jim Morrison in Oliver Stone's film about the Doors; in 1988 he married *Willow* costar Joanne Whalley.

Having breathed the rarefied air of heroes, Cher was ready for more temperate climes once the Kilmer thing had ended, and she didn't have to go far to find consolation.

Only as far as Kilmer's agent.

Joshua Donen had worked for the prestigious William Morris Agency since 1981 and when he met Cher already had clients who included David Bowie, Tim Curry, Billy Dee Williams, and director Matthew Chapman. Donen was the son of director Stanley Donen and a graduate of the USC film school. He had a pleasant face—nice looks, glasses, certainly a more low-key attractiveness than that sported by such male voluptuaries as Kilmer and Heard—but he was warm, friendly, appealing, and, for Cher, soothing. When Cher and Donen first met, it was not love at first sight, however.

At one point Cher had wanted to retool an old film to suit her talents. She had decided the way to go was along the lines of the Streisand remake of *A Star Is Born* in 1976 (though that had not been well received). Donen arranged the screening of a picture for her and a studio head. When the final credits were over and the lights came up, Donen and the studio boss discussed the possibilities while Cher yawned and opened a magazine. She gave the studio head a mere grunt as he left the screening room. Donen couldn't understand her behavior. Why was she being so antisocial? Why was she acting so uninterested? He was so angry he could have killed her.

Cher up to that point had not liked Donen particularly. Whenever she saw him, she found him rude and unfunny. Yet people seemed to like Donen, and she couldn't understand why. Did they perceive him as powerful? What was his secret, if any?

After the screening Donen and Cher had dinner to discuss the project, but the two just nibbled at their food and didn't speak. Finally Cher decided to confront the matter. "I'm sorry you think I'm just a bitch," she blurted out. Donen realized that she was trying to say that she couldn't help the way she was or the manner in which people perceived her; he concluded that she was shy and even "afraid of people."

In reality Cher was never all *that* shy. Her rudeness in the screening room was more likely due to the fact that she didn't cotton to Donen at the time, coupled with a feeling of being shunted aside, cut off from the decision-making process, the business end of things, with the two men going on about *her* project as if she weren't even there.

Indeed, even if they had included her in the discussion, she would have put up a wall, maintained her distance. Men discussing business, making decisions about her career, smacked too much of Sonny Bono and *those* days.

At dinner she realized that she was being self-destructive not to meet Donen halfway; she reversed gears and opened up to him. He remembered being enthralled by her frankness and honesty and by the inner nature she revealed that night. Cher, however, saw Donen as another David Geffen. Cher seemed to divide her time between men she wanted to use for sex and those she wanted to use for career reasons. Her days of being used *by* men were over, or so she believed.

The Cher-Donen relationship continued for a couple of years. They gave out gushy public statements about their love for each other, how they couldn't bear to be separated, and so on. Josh Donen became the Coast production vice-president of ABC Motion Pictures and read many scripts, hoping to find one right for Cher. Although she was wont to complain that the constant script analyses infringed on the time they could have been having fun together—movies, nights out with friends—she probably would have panicked if he had stopped reading them altogether. Somewhere in that pile was there a follow-up to *Mask*? After all, there was still an Oscar to be won! Meanwhile, Josh was telling all comers that his relationship with Cher had "filled all the holes in my life."

The same, alas, did not hold true for Cher. Although she had said that Josh was the personification of all the best qualities of her previous lovers, that he seemed so much older, so much more mature and wise for his years, etc., in the end that wasn't enough to hold her. His admirable qualities were great as far as they went; trouble was, they didn't go far enough—not for her.

Not that she didn't have fun while it lasted. The two sunned on the Riviera in August 1985 (to demonstrate his love for Cher, Donen had even gotten tattoos to show off on the beach). They went speedboat riding, partying, zooming along with the jet set.

The real trouble started when Josh told Cher he wanted to get married.

According to rumor, the two even got engaged—for proof, the press highlighted a huge diamond and platinum ring that Cher had started wearing—but it seems unlikely that Cher would have seriously considered such an offer. She simply had no interest in getting married yet a third time. Then Cher told the press she didn't want to marry Josh but wouldn't mind having his baby; this was promptly blown out of proportion into a major story about Cher wanting a "love child."

Cher was adamant about not making it legal. Her reasoning at the time: "People get married because the stigma is too much and they don't want their children to be bastards. Joshua wants to get married, and I feel it's an awful lot of pressure." At thirty-nine Cher may also have felt that the biological clock was ticking away against her.

Josh could not have been pleased that Cher wanted his baby—but not him. It wasn't long after this that the relationship fizzled.

Once Josh and Cher had been involved in a four-car crack-up in Massachusetts, occasioned by a drunken driver. It was a violent and frightening accident, with their car spinning dangerously out of control. Both escaped without serious injury. This was not to prove true, emotionally speaking, for Donen when the relationship with Cher—another spinning, out-of-control "accident"—ended. He nursed the hurt of his "rejection" for some time.

Donen is now executive vice-president of production at Universal Pictures. He positively refuses to talk to anyone about Cher; it is said that he is (perhaps understandably) "bitter."

Cher got together with her next man because of an illness.

She was basically a highly intelligent woman, and no one could quite understand why her early school records had been so poor. Had Cherilyn just been playing the rebel, refusing to stand still and learn anything, refusing to cooperate with her teachers?

Or had there, always, been a deeper problem? After all, she had barely learned to read by age eighteen.

When daughter Chastity exhibited signs of the classic poor student, Cher took her for testing. Perhaps some sort of learning disability was the explanation. It couldn't be that she was stupid; Cher knew that wasn't true. Also, Chastity's personality was entirely different from her mother's. She wasn't the roughhewn, feisty, don't-tell-me-anything rebel that Cher had been.

Cher got a surprise from the doctor. Not only was Chastity dyslexic, but so was Cher. So it had been an inherited genetic defect all along, something entirely divorced from "character" and "motivation." Now Cher knew why she had had such trouble in school, why she had even had difficulty making change or putting through long-distance calls, why she had been forced to compensate via her sharp memory. From that day forward dyslexia became one of Cher's "causes."

Another movie star suffered from the same problem: Tom Cruise. Cher had pretty much decided to write finis to the Donen affair when she met Cruise at a fund raiser for dyslexia in New York in 1985.

Cher was thirty-nine. Tom Cruise was twenty-three.

The Tom she met that night had already graduated from the boyishness of *Risky Business*; he was about to make *Top Gun* and become a major movie star. In *Risky Business*, made when he was twenty-one, and in other early films Cruise's looks had not yet "settled," his face seemed full of baby fat, and his whole aura and stance smacked more of boy than man. But by 1985 a butterfly had emerged from the gawky, unformed cocoon, and *this* Tom Cruise was strikingly handsome and full of confidence and inner assurance where before he had been, at best, smug. Cher was riveted when she saw him: handsome in a manly way, yet with oddly boyish expressions and mannerisms. Like Cher, Tom Cruise had known a chaotic early life, his father having deserted the family when he was quite young. His dyslexic condition had subtly complicated his young life, and he had had to survive expediently, as best he could. All this Cher could identify with. At the fund raiser they found themselves comparing notes on their dyslexia-ridden early years. Later their conversations were to have little to do with learning disabilities.

The two dated, off and on, for several months. During this period Tom was "two-timing" Cher by also dating another older woman, Mimi Rogers, a decade his senior. Stories began to circulate about Tom and Cher's getting into juicy—and vulgar—kissing scenes at Hollywood parties while the "old guard" of movieland looked on in disapproval (though Tom had some excuse, considering his relatively "tender" years). Cher thought Tom adorable and irresistible, but it is debatable whether she ever took him all that seriously as a lover.

Some months later Tom married Mimi Rogers (they are now divorced), and his thing with Cher—whatever it was—ended. Tabloids have continued to suggest that Cher was so crushed by his rejection of her that she has never gotten over it and compares every man she dates with her "lost, beloved Tom." According to these fictions, no subsequent relationship can ever last for her because no man can compare with Cruise.

The reality is that Tom was only one of a series of younger men whom Cher has played around with, and while she liked him a lot, she, unlike the more vulnerable and romantic Mimi Rogers, would never have considered him husband material. Her ego, true, may have been slightly damaged when Tom chose Rogers over her (but then Rogers had *wanted* him more), but her heart remained intact. In retrospect, what really drew Tom and Cher together initially was their shared dyslexic incapacity and their respective memories of all the horrors of insecurity and unconventionality the affliction had pushed them toward, though, being survivors, they had, in time, transcended them all.

Cher clearly bears no bitter feelings toward Tom as of 1991. She told columnist Jeannie Williams that she felt genuinely sorry that Tom hadn't won the Oscar for *Born on the Fourth of July*, adding, "He deserved it so much!" She might also have been thinking of how a "stunt" performance—Linda Hunt playing a man; Daniel Day Lewis as a man even more handicapped than

Cruise had been in *July* (in My Left Foot)—had cheated them both of awards. "But I got one [an Oscar] eventually," she told another writer, "and so, I'm *positive*, will Tom!"

"Have him washed and brought to my tent!"

This is supposedly what Cher said when she first caught sight of her next lover, Rob Camilletti. Cher claims that if she did make that remark—and she has to admit it was funny—it would have been strictly tongue-in-cheek. She didn't date young Rob until three months after she had first laid eyes on him.

It was her fortieth birthday, May 20, 1986. The big four-o. Cher was celebrating (if that is the word for it) at a Manhattan nightclub. And then she saw this—this *vision*.

"He just kind of rocked my socks, you know? I've never felt a physical impact like that," she added, oddly following up with "except maybe when my children were born."

Rob got her juices flowing and body humming, that was sure, but she found herself hesitant about getting involved with him. She knew people were already calling her a cradle robber, and now that she had turned forty, the rumors would get *more* vicious. If Cher had merely been into casual sex, it all would have been simplicity itself; she could have gotten him into bed and been done with it, but as always, she preferred to know the guy first. Was he *worth* knowing, though? She remembers one of her first impressions being "I thought he was probably *not* a good thing to waste my time on."

Of all Cher's many boyfriends, Rob Camilletti is probably the one who has most excited public interest and curiosity. He was lean and "so handsome it was not only illegal but a major felony," as one Cher entourage member put it, and he sported dark hair, strong masculine features, and that certain air of confidence that Cher has always found intriguing. He was twenty-two when he first met Cher; he had been bartending—and collecting his share of propositions from all comers—when a brief earlier brush with a rock career had failed to work out. At the time of their encounter he was studying acting with Stella Adler and supporting himself with odd jobs, working in a bagel store, waiting on tables, "picking up the coin wherever it fell, and it fell in some strange places," as one cynical onlooker put it. He had come from a nondescript lower-middle-class Italian family in Queens, his father being a construction supervisor for Con Edison.

Rob was to express surprise at Cher's initial interest. "What the hell could she find interesting in a guy like me?" he said. "I'm just a mook from Queens." He *was* wise enough, instinctual enough, to question how much they might have in common once Cher got past the physical attraction to him or "out of the pants and into the brain," as one friend put it. She, after all, lived in an entirely different universe from his—a universe he defined as "working class, struggling-actor, part-time waiter, 'nobody.' " Camilletti had extreme reservations initially about getting involved with Cher (despite what she might be able to do for his career), and he later said that he wouldn't admit to himself that he found her attractive. He probably saw her at the time as a ditzy, glitzy shallow superstar.

And then the *ages: she* forty, *he* twenty-two.

Rob couldn't know that Cher had strong reasons for wanting to get to know him better. Not since Sonny had a man produced such an effect in her. Of Sonny she had said: "He was like an apparition because everyone who was standing around him just faded." If *Sonny*, homely, paternal, nurturing but *older Sonny*, had made such an impression on her long before, it is easy to see how, in a far more physicalized way, she turned on to hunk Camilletti. They started dating, and before long were carrying on such a red-hot affair that the tabloids, "legit" press, and gossip columns were hard put to keep up with them. This time Cher came up with a pet name for her boy toy: Mookie. She called it an affectionate nickname spoofing his Queens background and self-image; the papers were less cute—and kind. To them he was known as the bagel maker. Soon Mr. Twenty-two and Ms. Forty were dividing their time between her Beverly Hills mansion and her New York apartment.

And how did Rob feel about Cher? Well, Cher may have

been moving on into her early forties and he into his early twenties as the affair progressed, but she was hardly what anyone would call an ugly old pig. He was undoubtedly flattered by her attentions and appreciative of her kindnesses, and of course, she showed herself the sexiest of lovers. Cher even told friends that he excited her far more than any man since the long-departed Gregg Allman.

Later Rob wasn't precisely sure of what had motivated him to turn his whole life over to Cher. Yes, she could help his career—that is, if show business success was his aim. Certainly living high with Cher in L.A. and New York beat living in a dump or with his folks. He could not be blamed for trading in his risky, uncertain former life for one of glamour and opportunity. Cher, in short, was manna from heaven for Rob Camilletti of Queens.

But every silver lining is cursed with its proverbial cloud. With Cher and Rob it was the unrelenting publicity. Rob found himself getting more and more attention (always, alas, as the "former Queens bagel maker"), but the acting roles he yearned for were not materializing. Being Cher's boyfriend had its drawbacks; no one would take him seriously. Rob grew more and more upset as the press made merciless fun of Cher's boy toy, portraying him as a seedy hustler and a cheap opportunist.

Finally Rob managed to get a role in a picture, appropriately entitled *Loverboy*, but he wasn't the star; the appealing but nerdy Patrick Dempsey hogged the action in this 1989 release as a pizza delivery boy who, as one critic put it, "turns on a bevy of frustrated older women." ("And a role poor Rob was *born* to play, too!" clucked one observer.) Rob, however, almost didn't get to play in the picture, for he wound up, briefly, in jail.

It all had started when some nutcase using the name Peter Nelson began making phone calls to TV stations and newspapers to alert them to Rob and Cher's alleged "upcoming nuptials." (Rob at the time was twenty-five, Cher forty-three.) This was news to the couple, who had no intention of getting married. No matter how much Cher's publicist, Lois Smith, denied the phony story, no one would believe her. Finally all the stations, papers, and tabloids rushed reporters and photographers out to Cher's house to spy on "Mr. and Mrs. Cher III," as they were unkindly dubbed. The mission: to find out at all costs when the "marriage" would take place.

With reporters busily going through her garbage, Cher had to resort to subterfuge just to keep a doctor's appointment. While she hid in the backseat of a friend's car, Rob took her Ferrari out and drove it around as a decoy action. A photographer under assignment from the *Star*, Peter Brandt, followed the Ferrari but eventually gave up and turned around.

When Camilletti returned later that afternoon, he saw a mess of newsmen and photographers lying in wait on the road just in front of the entranceway to Cher's estate. Rob's story is that he thought at first just to drive past them but then decided to "drive up fast, make a wide turn, and cut it quickly up the driveway" so no one could get a picture of him. What happened was that when he hit the brakes so that he could make the turn into the driveway, the brakes locked, and the Ferrari wound up skidding off the road and right into Peter Brandt's Honda.

The police reaction to Camilletti's story was dubious, to say the least. Rob had already smashed Brandt's camera in a prior incident. Brandt, who was not in the Honda at the time but outside standing by the car, claimed that Rob not only deliberately smashed his car but even tried to run him over in the process and that after the accident Rob ran after him, shouting that he was going to kill him. According to one witness, Camilletti had rammed the other car on purpose.

Camilletti was arrested and booked for investigation on the charge of assault with a deadly weapon. The following day Cher called a press conference. "I *know* Robert," she informed one and all. "He is *not* a violent man!" She resented, she said, comparisons between Rob and Sean Penn (then the husband of Madonna and ready at all times with his fists and feet). Then, probably wondering about Penn's low boiling point, she hastily added that he, too, had been a media victim and had struck out accordingly.

This was, obviously, the case with Rob Camilletti, the bagel boy, boy toy, Mr. Cher III candidate, all of which terms had been applied to him in cold, black print.

Cher didn't stop there. She took to screaming at Brandt, calling him "you scum" and adding, "You people would do anything for money!" Brandt, quick on the comeback, shot back that between her perfume (Uninhibited), Rob, and her scanty dress, he believed Cher herself had already done everything for money. Net result: Rob wound up paying a fifteen-thousand-dollar fine and doing community service.

Then it was on to the aforementioned *Loverboy*, with Rob playing an exchange student from Genoa with a thick Italian accent, who makes pizza in the shop from which Patrick Dempsey operates as the delivery boy/stud. He had to be taught how to throw the dough just so, in order to look authentic when they filmed his brief scenes in an honest-to-goodness pizza parlor near the beach at Venice, near Los Angeles. Although Rob comes off as rather attractive, sweet, and perfectly competent in the role, the picture did nothing for his career—or Patrick Dempsey's, for that matter. *Loverboy* was, unfortunately, the kind of comedy in which the biggest laugh comes when somebody's hairpiece catches fire. Cher's friend Kate Jackson, Kirstie Alley, and Carrie Fisher were also in the cast, but Rob didn't have scenes with any of them.

Rob let it be known that Cher coached him for the picture, that he went home to her every night and talked over the day's work with her. The part being so tiny, Cher mustn't have had to give it that much time. Cher's reported advice to him was succinct and possibly ill advised: "Take direction and take it well. Understand exactly what the director is telling you, but also rely on your own instincts. If something isn't comfortable, natural, or right in a scene, speak up. It's important!" True, it may have been all right for a star or lead to "speak up," but someone who had little more than a bit? This may account, among other reasons, for Rob's failure to get a decent role to date.

Because of all the false hell-raising tabloid stories about their "marriage" and Cher's alleged "pregnancy" by Rob, he and Cher did discuss the possibility of wedlock and children. (At forty-three

Cher's baby-making time clock was running out, another factor in their thinking.) Coming as he did from a conventional Queens Italian background, Rob informed her that when he got married, it would be "forever." Cher, more realistic and worldly-wise, countered that she could guarantee only a few years' commitment. This put the chill on Rob's marriage intentions, which suited her just fine. She was soon telling the press that her two marriages had been so stinking lousy that she'd rather jump off the Empire State Building than ever tie the knot again.

The Rob-Cher relationship may have had utilizing aspects on both sides—she wanted his youth and sexual potency; he, her contacts and the life-style she made possible—but friends who knew both at the time felt there was real warmth and affection involved. Cher said she thought Rob "the most well-adjusted man I've ever been with" and seemed happy with him for quite a while. The age difference didn't seem to matter; Rob assured her often that it didn't. He probably meant it, too.

In the end Rob came to feel that Cher's attitude toward marriage being what it was, theirs was not a relationship with any solid or lasting grounding. Possibly he thought that now that he had appeared in a Hollywood film, he was "on his way" and soon would not need her so much. Possibly Cher feared doing too much for him because career considerations would take him away from her, give him too many options, expose him to too many beautiful women. Rob took to showing up with the proverbial lipstick—all shades—on his face and collar. Cher later insisted that the final decision had been his, that *he* had left *her*. But considering Cher's nature, as one friend has said, he would inevitably had been handed his walking papers even had he confined himself to behaving like a choirboy.

Liz Smith later reported that friends of Rob's in New York had it that he was deeply upset, while denying there had been a breakup at all. Cher's mother liked Rob a lot; but she had never had much influence over Cher's private life before, and that was not to change at that point.

Although nothing much has happened to Rob's career since

the split with Cher (he still does occasional bartending, at age twenty-six), he still serves as occasional fodder for the press. He got a mention in May 1990, when he served as a guest DJ at a New York club and went on Howard Stern's radio show to promote it in spite of the way Stern had made merciless fun of him and Cher when their romance was at its steamiest. He later showed up at a Hollywood premiere with a date who was said to bear a striking resemblance to Cher. And every time Cher had a fight with the man who came after Rob, the tabloids had him and her renewing their relationship and more passionate than ever. In truth, as of 1991, Cher and Rob see each other from time to time, are still friendly, and can't help feeling a certain residual affection for each other.

Not too much time was to pass before Cher found herself another man. This time a rocker.

Actors and rockers—they were her only weakness.

Cher met Richie Sambora—who is thirteen years her junior —when he coproduced her album *Cher* in 1987. Richie was a guitarist with the popular group Bon Jovi, which is headed by Jon Bon Jovi, a "pretty" longhair who has appeared on many of the "sexiest men" lists (which have not, however, included Richie). Cher had contacted Jon when she wanted to record one of the group's songs, and he and Sambora wound up coproducing the whole album. Many had wondered if sparks would strike between Cher and Jon, but it was Sambora who eventually caught her eye.

Before you could say, "Here we go again," the usual stories were in circulation: They were breaking up, they were back together; they were getting married, they weren't getting married; Cher was pregnant, Cher wasn't pregnant. Every time the two had even a minor argument, the tabloids had them rushing back to their "exes"—Camilletti and, in Richie's case, a sexy woman named Lehua Reid. Supposedly the two would see their exes just to make each other jealous. Meanwhile, the press, including the more "legitimate" daily newspapers (whose staff people were probably reading the tabloids themselves), reported the Cher-

Richie "thing" was "in splitsville" more times than Zsa Zsa Gabor got married.

Just as Cher had once been accused of breaking up her ex-husband's Allman Brothers Band, she was now charged with breaking up Bon Jovi. Certainly the other members of the group—especially the high-profile Jon Bon Jovi himself—were envious of all the attention their Richie was getting out of his Cher involvement, but it was unreasonable to expect the boys to break up a highly profitable act because of *that*; it was believed that it would have to be something a lot more serious to get them to break apart.

Early in 1990 the popular stories had Cher "pregnant, secretly engaged" to Sambora and sporting an enormous diamond engagement ring. Six months later Cher was reportedly "depressed" over his "dumping" her. Neither tale was true. Cher had long since made clear her attitude about remarrying ("Never!") and the alleged "supersplit" with Sambora proved premature. Late in 1990 he was her date at her sister's wedding, and during her concert tour in the eastern states she put up at his New Jersey estate. Cher was particularly livid over one tabloid story that had her on the verge of a nervous breakdown because Sambora had allegedly decided she was "too old" for him and split.

As of this moment, Cher and Sambora are not together, but that might not last, considering Cher's history. Sambora may not be slick, glamorous, or particularly gorgeous but reportedly he has a a splendid manly endowment and his own very special brand of sex appeal. Plus in a personality-interplay sense Cher reportedly finds him "as comfortable as an old shoe."

Considerations like that undoubtedly are important to her as she grows older (forty-five on May 20, 1991). Meanwhile, fans are still holding their breaths—half in anticipation, half in dread, of the inevitable time (if the past is any reliable criterion) when Cher and Sambora actually make beautiful music together. After all, she did it with Allman. She did it with Les Dudek. If Bon Jovi does break up permanently, Sambora will need a new outlet for creative expression. His voice certainly can't be any worse than Sonny Bono's.

Sambora has one advantage over Rob Camilletti. At thirty-one he's older, a little wiser, and farther along in his profession. He's made a lot of money playing guitar for his pal Jon's band. No one can fairly accuse him of hustling or gold digging. If he does have ulterior motives (and who can say he does?), he's keeping them to himself.

"I fall in love for about fourteen months, and then afterward I love the person; but I just don't want to be with them anymore. I move on. . . . When it starts to get too intense, I have to go . . . when it gets to be where you have to really make a commitment, then I have to go."

With these words Cher explained how she felt about her relationships with men several years ago. She's extended the time period for over two years per man, it would seem, but it remains to be seen if she will really sustain her feelings for, or make a commitment to, Richie Sambora or anyone who comes after him.

Cher, in fact, seems as confused about her love life as everyone else is. She used to say she had a father complex, but she has obviously gotten over that long since. She says that each time she meets a new man she wants to live forever and ever with him but then admits that in reality she feels just the opposite.

Cher gets angry when people or the press question her taste in men. She says she doesn't care about a man's looks but admits it's more fun to fall in love with someone who's beautiful. Although she told writer Carol Wallace that she had been "in love" with lots of men who had had people shaking their heads and wondering what she saw in them, almost all of her boyfriends have been lookers. Maybe when Cher takes up with Telly Savalas, we'll believe that she is primarily mesmerized by "inner beauty." But Cher is right when she suggests that her diehard fans would hold it against her if she ever did so. They *want* her to have a handsome boyfriend.

"I don't need a man," she says. "But I'm happier with one. I like to have someone I can touch and squeeze and kiss. But I don't fold up and die if I don't have a man around."

Cher's dream man? She claims her big crush is Sylvester Stallone, whom she considers "a wonderful actor." But the trouble is that the Sly she used to know is not the Sly who's around today. She spent some time with Sly once and thought he was amusing and adorable (of course, those are her words for practically every guy she's ever dated), but now she feels he's become too trapped inside his own image—that ultimately hollow physical perfection and the "attitude" of success.

Bruce Willis used to come to those big barbecues she threw at her house. He was the only one who helped her clean up later. Cher and Bruce Willis? Apparently nothing happened between them, but maybe it should have. They could handle each other. But Bruce is otherwise engaged at the moment, and Cher doesn't have a poacher's temperament.

Cher feels that you have to take each man on his own terms. It's not possible, she thinks, to "understand" men as a group, but only as individuals. She subscribes to the philosophy that if men and women only adopted that sane approach to each other, instead of trying to pigeonhole every member of the opposite sex they meet, the war of the sexes might have been over a long time ago.

Already Cher has doubts about her life-style. *Is* there something lacking in her character that has her living with one young man after another? Does she care? Has she ever worried about what people think? Should she? Was she turning into the female equivalent of the kind of man she had always hated, the man who traded in one woman for another as if they were nothing more than a different flavor ice cream?

Cher does not look forward to the future, to growing old.

She fears she may just grow old *alone*.

A stellar foursome in *The Witches of Eastwick*

Cher did not disappoint fans of her outrageous costumes at the
1986 Academy Awards. She was escorted by former boyfriend
Josh Donen, whose father, Stanley Donen, produced the 1986
ceremony.

OPPOSITE: For the unveiling of her perfume, Uninhibited, Cher
threw on this Nefertiti outfit to the delight of photographers.

Cher with *Moonstruck* co-star Nicholas Cage at a screening of the film in New York

OPPOSITE: Cher and Rob Camiletti seen at the Los Angeles premiere of the movie that would win Cher the Best Actress Award, *Moonstruck*

Cher with *Moonstruck* co-star Olympia Dukakis backstage at the
People's Choice Awards

OPPOSITE: Cher poses with Oscar after winning the Best
Actress Award at the 60th Annual Academy Awards show.

Cher and former boyfriend
Richie Sambora returning to Los
Angeles from Atlantic City after
her engagement at the Sands
Hotel.

Reports have surfaced that Cher
has gotten back together with
her ex-boyfriend Rob Camiletti
in the wake of her break-up
with Bon Jovi guitarist Richie
Sambora. Here they are seen
attending a performance of
Brooklyn Laundry, a play starring
Glenn Close.

NINE

FILM STAR

*Thank God I wasn't in the Olivia De Havilland days. I would
always have been on suspension.*
—CHER

Frrom a minor part in a beach party
movie with Sonny (or so the story goes) Cher had come a long
way. She had five pictures behind her by 1986. The two with
Sonny, *Good Times* and *Chastity*, could be dismissed, but she was
pleased with her work in *Jimmy Dean*, almost won an Oscar for
Silkwood, and got more than her share of praise for *Mask*.

What next?

Certainly at that point she was doing better than other female
vocalists who'd taken up acting. Bette Midler had gotten great
notices for the 1979 *The Rose* but had lost the Oscar, and although
she came out with a picture on a fairly regular basis, she was
criticized for making poor choices. Linda Ronstadt's performance
in the Broadway revival of Gilbert and Sullivan's brilliant operetta
The Pirates of Penzance (and the subsequent film adaptation) had
inspired Cher to try for her own Broadway show, but although
she could never compete with Linda's splendid, near-operatic warbling, she had made more pictures than Linda, who never seemed
to pursue the acting side of her career with any vigor.

Diana Ross had made a big splash, and was excellent, in the 1972 *Lady Sings the Blues*, but the soul superstar hadn't stuck with films. Dionne Warwick had appeared in one picture years before but drew more comment with her breast exposure than with her acting. Two other contemporaries of Cher's, sixties survivors, had limited success with their acting careers: Tina Turner had certainly engineered a fabulous recording comeback, but her roles in such films as *Tommy* and *Mad Max Beyond Thunderdome* didn't seem to lead to better film vehicles. Michelle Phillips, ex-girl singer of the Mamas and the Papas, seemed to appear only on nighttime soaps like *Knots Landing*.

The younger singers were faring no better. Deborah Harry had one lead role (*Union City*) before doing supporting parts in John Waters's films (with Sonny, of all people), winding up in a listless turn on the *Wiseguy* TV program as a washed-up rock singer. Olivia Newton-John had a brief run as a movie star with *Grease* and a couple of others but was also concentrating on the singing. And Madonna, although she'd appeared in *Desperately Seeking Susan* (and was to show up in 1990 in *Dick Tracy*), got a lot of attention but only lukewarm reviews; certainly she had shown herself no candidate for an Oscar nomination.

The field was wide open for Cher. There was virtually no competition from the ladies turned actresses of the recording field. She might be the first to break out and become a motion-picture superstar (Streisand was thought of as an actress first, singer later).

That is basically what happened.

Cher has let it be known that her favorite movies are *The Godfather* saga, *The Enchanted Cottage, On Borrowed Time, The Good Earth*, and *The Great Santini*. When asked what roles she wished she could have played, she answers: Patton, Rocky, and Scarlett O'Hara (she certainly would have been "interesting" in all three, one being female and two male).

There were a lot of roles Cher would have liked to play that she wasn't allowed to essay. She badly wanted to star in the remake of *A Star Is Born* in 1976. She felt she would have been perfect in the part, but Barbra Streisand had preempted that, being at the time more "box office." In the remake the lead character was changed from an actress to a rock singer, and Cher said the same thing about Barbra that was often said about herself: She's no rocker. Cher was also miffed because she thought the script closely paralleled her life, but the producers had dumped her when Streisand let them know that she wanted to do it. Most critics and audiences later gave Cher the satisfaction of agreeing that the net result was terrible and Barbra proved to be not very convincing as a rock star.

Streisand and Cher both had been considered for the lead in the remake of *King Kong* that same year (1976)—at that point the producers were mulling over a camp approach, maybe even a couple of love songs from girl to gorilla—but both ladies turned *that* one down. Cher's attitude was: "You've only got one shot, and you better do a good job. I don't believe in *King Kong*." Although the actress who played the part, Jessica Lange, later went on to more serious roles and acclaim, that might not have been the way it would have worked out for Cher; actually it might only have cemented her image as a ditz and lowbrow talent. Six years later, in 1982, Cher expressed interest in *Tootsie*, as Dustin Hoffman's girl friend, but Lange made off with the part.

There were other disappointments. Stockard Channing had landed the role Cher coveted in Mike Nichols's production of *The Fortune* (1975). Cher would have found herself working with Jack Nicholson and her old bedmate Warren Beatty and had been positive she could handle the required black comedy intrinsic to the role. Since at that point she was far better known nationally than Stockard Channing, Nichols must have had what he felt were very good reasons for not using her. For one thing, he already had plenty of star power with the teaming of Nicholson and Beatty. For another, it was not until he saw Cher perform in *Jimmy Dean* that he felt she had any real talent for acting. He later made it up to her by casting her in *Silkwood*.

Over the years Cher continued as odd girl out on various roles she wanted. She wanted to be reteamed with Meryl Streep in *She-Devil*, but good sense, in that instance, prevailed. The part went, more appropriately, to Roseanne Barr as the ugly wife and mother who loses her husband to the more glamorous Streep. In retrospect, Cher saw that the picture would have lost its sense of balance with Streep and herself in the parts; Cher, the wife, would have come off as far more glamorous than Streep, the mistress, for even when deglamorized, as she was in *Silkwood*, Cher retains a certain air and her classic bone structure.

Cher, turned down at least as many pictures as she was turned down for. About 1983 she had been just about to step in front of the cameras for *Grandview U.S.A.*—a study of small-town inhabitants—when a little voice inside told her she'd be making a mistake. It was easy to see why she was cast; as an independent-minded young woman who takes over her father's demolition derby, she'd have been yet another tough but feminine rebel. (Like Rocky Dennis, the character even lived in a trailer.) But Cher didn't think it the right step to take, and the part went to Jamie Lee Curtis, who was fine in it. Cher's fans were therefore deprived of seeing her interact with male heartthrob Patrick Swayze (in his pre-*Dirty Dancing* days), not to mention handsome up-and-coming C. Thomas Howell. Given Cher's propensity for young male adorables, one can only imagine what might have occurred off the set between her and hunky Howell. Without Cher's publicity clout, *Grandview U.S.A.* didn't make much of an impression on anyone.

It would have been interesting to see her in the Theresa Russell part in the 1986 *Black Widow*, another picture she turned down. Cher would have been cast as a woman who marries rich men— one after another—and then kills them off. Debra Winger played the investigator who is determined to bring Russell to justice. Hints of a lesbian attraction were dropped in halfway through but never developed. Rather than be teamed with deep-voiced Winger, Cher might have been more effective playing Winger's investigator role and interacting with the sultry Russell. That way the picture would have raised a lot more eyebrows.

Then there was the screenplay written specifically for Cher,

Fatal Beauty. She would have played a tough narcissistic detective named Rizzoli who's out to get the creators and dealers of a new designer drug called Fatal Beauty. Cher was to have been reteamed with her *Mask* costar, Sam Elliott, who was to play a mobster's head of security who switches sides when he starts to fall for the detective.

Cher should have done *Fatal Beauty*; the part was tailor-made for her. The dialogue was sprinkled with lines that only she could have slapped down with her unique combination of directness, sexiness, and insolence. When one of her male associates asks the character if she was delayed because she picked up a sailor, Rizzoli replies, "Yeah, almost had him, too, but your mother beat me to him."

Later, when she's bending over, another guy asks her, "Ever get it doggie-style?"

"No, but tell me what it's like," she rejoinders.

But it was not to be. Cher eventually turned the project down, some say because she was not eager to spend a lot of time with Sam Elliott. She could not have helped noticing as well that the part of Rizzoli might have been interesting and amusing but was not especially three-dimensional. She could be brassy and sassy, look a guy over, and ask, "Does that come in adult size?" but in the end the role was all style over substance.

Whoopi Goldberg, who needed another picture quickly, was drafted to take Cher's place. Whoopi is a talented and delightful performer, but she's no substitute for Cher in that particular role. In scenes that would have required Cher to lay on the sex appeal and glamour, Whoopi has to make do by playing for laughs, spoofing her none too glamorous image. She and Elliott have no chemistry together, and his flirtation scene with her seems somewhat grotesque. She's still called Rizzoli, and Elliott makes references to her Italian ancestry with a straight face no less. (Cher at least looks Italian.) Critics trashed it utterly because of the violence and because they thought it a poor vehicle for Whoopi.

Other pictures that Cher turned down were: *Baby Boom*, which she just didn't think was right for her (Cher may well have been a devoted mother in real life, but no one wanted to see her carrying around a baby and dealing with diapers in the movies); *War of the Roses* (she and Michael Douglas might not have had the right chemistry. Also, Cher as an upper-class housewife? She may *be* rich, but she doesn't "smell" rich); *Midnight Run* (her part went to Charles Grodin, of all people) and, of all things, the Mary Magdalene role in Martin Scorsese's *The Last Temptation of Christ*, back when it was still known as *The Passion*. Cher might have been very interesting and appropriate as Mary, but it might have been difficult for her to handle the more "spiritual" aspects of the character in a convincing manner. Although Cher is not a practicing Catholic, she still may have thought Scorsese's picture was too much of a hot potato to be bothered with. And Scorsese had a reputation for being difficult. Once with Bogdanovich was enough.

Then there were the projects that didn't work out for one reason or another. In 1976 Cher had bought the rights to one of her favorite classic movies, *The Enchanted Cottage*, which had been made as a silent and then with Dorothy McGuire and Robert Young in 1945. She planned to executive produce the picture as well as star in it, but in the Robert Young part instead of Dorothy McGuire's. She would have been a singer in a band instead of a pilot.

Her idea was to make the film as a "movie with music segments, like Streisand's *A Star Is Born*" instead of as an old-fashioned musical. "It's the same idea as the old one, just modernized so that it fits into what would be really upsetting to them today." She hired the screenwriter of *Going Home* to work on a script in 1979 and was considering either Gary Busey or Jon Voight as her costar. Years went by, however, and the picture just never got made for the multitude of reasons so common in tinseltown.

Then there was *Road Show*. This was originally going to be her big follow-up picture to *Silkwood;* it would have costarred her with Timothy Hutton and big gun Jack Nicholson. Cher had even gone so far as to sign with director Martin Ritt, and the film was slated to shoot in the summer of 1983. Marilyn Beck, industry columnist, touted it at the time as Cher's "real-l-ly big-screen break." While the possibility remains that Cher might do this in the future, it just never came together in 1983. Background troubles, a change of personnel, and Cher's own desire to find herself a vehicle where she would be the sole star probably contributed to the deal falling through.

There was talk of Cher playing Morticia in a film based on *The Addams Family* TV series and the Charles Addams *New Yorker* cartoons that inspired the series. Years ago someone reviewing her club act wrote of Cher: "She looks like the malevolent miss in the Charles Addams cartoons, with a line of chatter to match." Cher would have been a natural for Morticia, but she ultimately decided against it; Anjelica Huston was signed.

Other aborted projects included *Going to the Chapel*, which she wanted to do with Richard Benjamin, who eventually directed her in *Mermaids*. When filming on the latter picture ran overtime, Cher had to cancel plans to do what sounds like an ill-advised adventure film, *Pincushion*, for John Carpenter. Cher should probably be glad she never got a chance to do it.

While some of the decisions Cher made in rejecting material made perfect sense (*King Kong*, for instance), others are less logical when one considers the film that Cher did elect to make and followed through on, after *Mask*. In *The Witches of Eastwick* she was not only one of a coven of three women performers but also part of an ensemble that included powerhouse actor Jack Nicholson. Of course, she wanted to work with Jack when she had lost out to Stockard Channing in *The Fortune*, but one wonders why she would have wanted to share female-lead billing with two other women, particularly women as attractive as Michelle Pfeiffer and Susan Sarandon. Maybe she thought it would be fun. *And* easy.

Of this picture Cher has said: "It was like filming a movie on Friday the thirteenth in the middle of a hurricane. But a movie doesn't have to run smoothly to be good."

Witches not only didn't run smoothly but wasn't very good.

The picture was based on the novel of the same title by John Updike. The source material was not considered very cinematic, lacking the strong narrative structure that is an essential for a film. The strongest elements were its expository exploration of East-wick and its townspeople, as well as literary prose that would not easily translate to the filmic medium. The original book had not been designed as a supernatural genre thriller, but there were early indications that the screenplay would "punch" things up and add room for nifty special effects work that had little to do with what Updike was saying.

The basic story was intriguing enough. Three middle-aged divorcées, who just happen to have special powers, enjoy getting together on a weekly basis to share and meditate on their unusual abilities. Into their midst comes a stranger from New York, the charismatic Daryl Van Horne (Nicholson), who is soon sexually involved with all three women at the same time.

There was much criticism of the casting of the "witches." It is true that Cher, Pfeiffer, and Sarandon were hardly anyone's idea of typical small-town middle-aged matrons who spend their nights with one another instead of a man (until Jack shows up). Much of the tone and substance of the book were altered by an approach that favored glitz and comedy over depth and meaning.

The director, George Miller (most famous for directing the *Mad Max* series), didn't even bother to finish reading the novel. He found it heavy going, saying at the time, "To be honest, if I'd read it first, I don't think I've have seen a film in it."

The first difficulty was that Miller didn't want Cher at all. Then he asked her to play Jane, the quiet cellist (the role Sarandon eventually played), instead of Alexandra, the more exotic sculptress. Cher refused to switch parts. Miller kept telling her, "I don't want 'Cher' to ruin my movie."

The next thing Cher knew, Miller was on a campaign to make her as un-Cher-like as was humanly possible. He suggested she have elocution lessons to improve her diction and alter her speech patterns. He wanted her to dye her hair and change her whole image. Since he couldn't get out of having her in his movie, he was determined to make her unrecognizable or, in his view, some other person more suited to the role. "He completely wanted to change the base of where I came from," Cher said.

Finally Cher laid down the law: "At the bottom of all this it's still going to be me, and if you don't like Cher, there's no way I can come out of my skin. I can't really change. This is it," she told him. "Take it or leave it."

Miller didn't really have enough clout to get rid of her. He was no Bogdanovich or Nichols—or even Altman—and he knew it. He did not enjoy the same measure of respect that her previous directors had. And of course, he did not have Cher's. She would go ahead and do the movie, but she wouldn't take any shit from him. Miller got even with her in other ways.

Cher never thought much of the script. She just wanted to work with Jack, get her scenes done, take the money—and avoid George Miller whenever possible.

Even before filming began, the picture was embroiled in controversy. Warner Brothers had chosen the bucolic little town of Little Compton, Rhode Island, to stand in for Eastwick; it had a 202-year-old church, picturesque views, and the sea right nearby and would be a perfect setting to play out the more diabolical situations in the story line. Most of the townspeople were eager to have the film company come in—it would bring six million to the state's economy, according to the Rhode Island Film Commission in Providence, and it would, of course, increase the coffers of local businesses—but a small but vocal group of residents threw in a monkey wrench.

The sexy parts of the novel were bad enough, but what really infuriated some local inhabitants was that a church choirmaster was characterized as the devil. "It is a dirty, dismal, and depraved book," screeched Alan Simpson, a former president of Vassar College. "It is unworthy of Mr. Updike, a trashy, sensational book that is all evil and no good. It is unseemly and not consistent with civic pride." His supporters were particularly upset that the film would include shots of the United Congregational Church, their pride and joy.

Although the town council (during riotous hearings) eventually voted three to one to approve the use of the town as a location for *Witches*, Warner Brothers had already started scouting other, more hospitable hamlets. (It finally chose Cohasset, Massachusetts.) The negative publicity was threatening to get out of hand. Who needed the extra hassle?

But the controversy still wasn't over. Now that the Christians were through shouting, it was time to hear from the pagans. Laurie Cabot, a fifty-three-year-old Salem resident and the head of the recently formed Witches League of Public Awareness, explained (to *The New York Times*, not the *National Enquirer*) that witches were not devil worshipers but "holistic observers of nature, healers, users of the psychic senses as a way of life." A former Nieman fellow at Harvard suggested that about a hundred thousand Americans were practicing witches in a "revival of pre-Christian, West European paganism."

Most of the hundred thousand, however, did not protest *The Witches of Eastwick*, which had less to do with real witchcraft and paganism than with different aspects of the relationships between men and women. Updike had, in fact, never intended his book to be seen as a serious study of witches.

Miller and his company, meanwhile, were too busy making the movie to worry about whatever protests it was engendering. Cher, in particular, wasn't having an easy time of it. For one thing, she expected those niceties that she felt that a star on her level in a major motion picture was entitled to. She soon found out: Make sure everything's in writing.

First, the dressing rooms were dumps, trailers that looked as if they'd been left over from the set of *Earthquake*, facilities that were *filthy*. The women had to go out and get their own wardrobe. Cher wound up lending Sarandon three of her own outfits just so she'd have something appropriate to wear. The clothes budget was a joke.

Worst of all was the attitude of the men in charge toward the actresses. Cher complained, "We were always referred to as the girls, and I don't want anybody calling me the girls in that way."

Cher also had trouble with producer Jon Peters. Peters, a former hairdresser, had once had a relationship (professional as well as personal) with the difficult Barbra Steisand and thought he could use the same approach on Cher. Although Peters was straight so far as was known, because of his past history as a hairdresser, he tended to overcompensate to an extreme, belittling the "girls" and taking "macho" Miller's side on all issues. Moreover, he dreamed up little inexplicable rules that made Cher nervous, then furious. Nobody was allowed to bring anybody on to the set ("as if any of us really wanted to *take* anybody to the fucking set!" Cher scoffed), yet Peters stormed through with Barbra Streisand and ten other people in tow while Cher was working on a very important scene.

Cher went to Peters for a showdown. She felt it was time to stand up for herself and the other women. Peters and Miller were treating them like shit, and enough was enough. If they were so "threatened" by her, then she'd show them just how threatening she could be.

Peters's reaction was basically "Can I buy you something?" Infuriatingly patronizing, he thought that he could dissipate Cher's anger and real concern over how she and her costars were being handled by buying her a present, maybe a dress or bracelet. "What do I look like?" Cher countered. "A showgirl and you're Flo Ziegfeld?" She couldn't believe her ears; nothing she said seemed to matter to, or even register on, him. She joked ruefully later that it would have had to have been one unbelievable fucking bracelet!

Part of Cher's problem, as she knew, was that on this particular set she didn't have her usual clout. Her part was a small one, almost a supporting role; the whole show was really Jack Nicholson's, George Miller's, and Jon Peters's. Unlike the women in the Updike novel, the women in the film were basically sexy window dressing, gal toys the men could leer about. Finally Cher and the other women appealed to Nicholson for help.

Nicholson was a guy who did things in his own way. He did not make a scene, raise his voice, or move very quickly, for that matter. Eventually he quietly told his producer and director that if the women continued to be treated like trash, they would not be able to give the kinds of star performances the film required. Perhaps, as the always shrewd and knowing and psychologically aware Nicholson knew, there was no point in arguing on any other level. Things improved—somewhat. Peters and Miller weren't taking any chances of something screwing up their movie.

George Miller later claimed that he was having his own troubles with Peters and his coproducer, Peter Guber. At first he had intended the film to be a collaborative effort—he had been open to suggestions, willing to listen—but when the producers started interfering to an incredible degree, he began, he said, to realize just why so many of the Hollywood directors he'd met were "autocratic and guarded!" and that this attitude was in the best interests of overall efficiency. An Australian director had warned Miller that in Hollywood people mistook politeness for weakness, and Miller's trouble was that he was "too polite." His solution? "Eventually I had to become noncommunicative and willful. I cut myself off completely."

Overall, Cher and George Miller got off a lot better than Susan Sarandon. In one scene the script called for her to be levitated out of, and over, a swimming pool. Susan was a little nervous but figured these were professionals who knew what they were doing. She was standing in the water waiting to be lifted upward when she started to tingle and her hair began to feel peculiar. "Guys, something's wrong!" she called out. But they told her nothing was wrong; it was probably just her imagination. When she continued to complain, they finally came over and discovered that the wires were *hot*. She could have been electrocuted.

Cher and Susan had become good friends (which they remain to this day), and although by no stretch of the imagination could it be called a happy set, the actors on it all got along quite well.

That went for off the set, too. Cher, Jack, Michelle, and Susan all took some time off to drive into Boston to see *Aliens* at the Cinema 17 complex, where the passersby were amazed at all the celebrities in their midst. *Aliens* was scary, sure, but nothing, it turned out, was more horrible than making *The Witches of Eastwick*. Cher was beginning to wish she had never signed up for it. Working with Nicholson, however, was a compensating factor; she greatly admired him and continued to be grateful for his going to bat for her and the other actresses.

Rob Bottin, a man who excelled in special makeup effects, was brought in to add some special effects dazzle to the film's conclusion. A cast of a Jack Nicholson look-alike's head was made, modified, and used to create a sort of puppet Jack, who expands to giant size during his climactic battle with the women. Early plans to transform Cher into an obese witch by using a special "fat" makeup were scrapped.

The film had its premiere in Cohasset to raise funds for the high school's field improvements. Several hundred extras, including townspeople, were invited to attend. *The Witches of Eastwick* became Warners' biggest opening film of 1987 and, according to *Variety*, was the only one of fourteen megabudgeted movies (twenty-four million dollars or more) that did well at the box office that year. The picture, however, was to weather distinctly mixed critical reactions.

The Detroit *Free Press* didn't mince any words: "If you go in expecting a faithful adaptation of Updike's original material, you're in for a big surprise. [Screenwriter Michael] Cristofer and Miller do away with Updike's random malevolence and emotional violence for a sunnier and simple-minded approach. But Cristofer shows no grasp of the material, and lacks interest in following Updike's story. This reeks of a high-minded hack trying to turn a harsh, dissociative piece of fiction into a comic fight between men and women. Miller's weakness is a short attention span that veers away from the narrative."

Film Journal opined: "Those who came expecting a film equivalent of Updike's literate, upscale prose will be appalled. All of the gray areas that gave the novel a certain complexity—and produced in the reader a certain complicity with its scheming witches—have been erased in favor of a simple 'Pandora's Box' fable."

The performances in the film are excellent, but Cher found herself—along with the other women—outclassed by Nicholson, at least as far as most critics were concerned. "Nicholson's cool, malignant prowess so overpowers Cher as an actress that she's basically reduced to standing on the set watching [him] give his performance," declared the Detroit *Free Press* critic. "Cher has one good early scene opposite Nicholson, but not much more to do," another pundit declared.

Nicholson's performance—a variation on his work in *The Shining* (as is his Joker in *Batman*)—was actually overpraised. By this point in his career (1987) Nicholson had become a caricature of himself: the same nasal whine, clenched lips, laconic shtickful stock of familiar mannerisms. Nicholson takes exciting and energetic roles, but to the discerning viewer he's a boring actor. He has seemed to walk through his roles in recent years, relying lazily on leavings of his technique from the past and just "being himself" along path-of-least-resistance lines. Considering his enormous fees, he certainly gets a lot for giving very little.

The whole picture, in summation, was fundamentally built around Nicholson. True, Cher had fulfilled her dream of appearing with him, but given the overall results, she must have wondered if it was worth it.

The Witches of Eastwick did nothing for her career other than keep her on view in a film that was to prove inexplicably popular.

After *Witches*, *Suspect* must have seemed like a piece of cake, or at least an improvement.

Cher later claimed that the film held meaning for her, that it illuminated the problem of homelessness in America. (If it did so, it was only by accident.) As she put it, "Kathleen and the homeless man, they're the same kind of character, people who are caught in the human condition doing the best they can."

Cher was admittedly somewhat nervous about playing Kathleen Riley. She could identify with working-class women in spite of her life-style; she felt that she understood them. But Kathleen was well educated; she used ten-cent words all the time. Cher was afraid that it might be a mistake for a minimally educated person like herself to play a woman who has been to law school.

To help ease her apprehension and prepare for the role, she went to meet women in the public defender's office. Perhaps she could find some common ground, she felt, some little thing to catch on to and use judiciously in her performance. First she took note of the physical things and adapted her walk, how she held herself, for the movie so that she would approximate the movements of these women. Then she learned that these people had absolutely no time for social or private lives. The men in the office had wives and girl friends, but the women were single and alone. "Their work is their life," Cher told a reporter at the time, implying that that was something she had in common with these women.

She felt this lack of a private life was a key to the whole movie. Everyone was homeless. Not just the homeless person whom Kathleen defends from murder charge but Kathleen herself. (Actually the movie did not seem to have anything so "profound" on its mind.) Cher practiced intensively, saying all the complicated legalese so that it would sound authentic when she did her scenes. She felt that the words had to come out as if she used them all the time.

Cher conceived a great admiration and respect for the women she met in the public defender's office, saying: "It's the women who don't get any applause who are really the heroines of my life because it's *easy* to do what *I* do!" She also became good friends with Mitch Snyder, the noted advocate activist for the homeless who tragically ended his life a few years later.

Dennis Quaid was cast as the juror with whom Kathleen— foolishly, inexplicably—enters into a relationship that starts out professionally and then takes a turn in a romantic direction. It begins when he approaches Kathleen with some information on the case. She risks disbarment by even talking to him. From there on the picture piles up one unbelievable sequence after another.

Quaid was making a string of hits and near-miss pictures during this period. The cocky, saucy actor wasn't a youngster, but he was good-looking. He could tell that Cher got nervous every time a kissing scene came up. He deliberately screwed up takes so that they would have to play it over and over. Dennis was having his own brand of fun. Cher feigned annoyance but secretly enjoyed it as much as, if not more than, he did. She confessed to finding him "adorable" with "a nice manly quality," but nothing very heavy ever developed between them. Perhaps at thirty-three Quaid was a little too "old" for her. She was forty-one then, and it was twenty-two-year-old Rob Camilletti time in her life. But as one on-set wag put it, "But Dennis *at twenty-two* would have been master of all he surveyed in the Cher scheme of things; too bad he showed up eleven years too late!"

Peter Yates, the director, liked working with Cher. He called her a perfectionist, meaning it as a sincere compliment, and said he admired the fact that when she blew a scene, she never did any buck passing. Other actors were wont to blame the lighting, their costumes, anything and everything, he remembered, but Cher would just scream at herself: "Come on, Cher! What the hell do you think you're doing!"

Yates had made a splash years before with his film *Bullitt*. He had followed it up with such tepid suspense films as *Eyewitness*. He was okay at choreographing car chases and certain other action scenes, but he lacked the ability to craft tight suspense sequences or add depth to his narrative. *Suspect* turned out to be one of his worst-received pictures.

Liam Neeson played the homeless mute who is accused of murder. Public defender Cher can't understand why the judge in the case is being so obstructive and difficult—*and* why does he seem to have it in for her personally? (Guess who the real murderer is. And if you can't figure it out, turn in your Agatha Christie merit badge.) Cher's dallying with a *juror* on the case, Dennis Quaid, is never even remotely plausible, and it also doesn't make sense that Quaid, a self-centered lobbyist if ever there were one, would risk his own life to try to track down clues. Nothing in the picture, on balance, makes a lick of sense.

There is some on-screen chemistry between Cher and Quaid, but not enough to make up for the film's many deficiencies. Quaid sort of shoves his way through the film with a lot of his standard insolence and sex appeal, but Cher tends to be perfunctory, running strictly on charisma. And no matter what she has said to the contrary then and since, this cannot have been a film she had her heart in.

The picture got almost completely negative reviews. Dave Kehr in the Chicago *Tribune* wrote: "The undisguised phoniness of the story wouldn't much matter if it gave Cher an occasion to show the spunk and wit of her Witches of Eastwick role or Quaid the opportunity to flash his indolent Big Easy smile. But Yates wants to use the flimsy material to attack the callousness and corruption of the criminal justice system, which is like challenging Arnold Schwarzenegger with a wet newspaper."

Janet Maslin in *The New York Times* commented on Cher's "crisply compelling performance," while *Newsday* asked, "What to say about Cher's performance? Well, she manages (despite her character's 18-hour workday, despite being mugged twice in one day, despite being caught in a severe thunderstorm) to remain as unruffled as a Vogue cover, an incongruity that won't bother a single fan."

Pauline Kael, the *New Yorker* critic, was unimpressed with Cher, nailing down the discrepancy between her image and her role:

There has probably been no piece of casting this year more ineffably Hollywood than Cher as a busy, weary public defender in "Suspect"—Cher as a dedicated drudge. Cher being Cher, when she represents a man accused of murder, in a Washington, D.C., courtroom . . . she wears a black leather jacket, and her long, thick hair is loose on her shoulders. She's all wrong for this

241

public defender: her hooded, introspective face doesn't give you enough—she needs a role that lets her use her body. With the camera on her steadily here, you might be watching a still picture. After a while, you get the feeling that if she showed some expression, she'd wrinkle or crack. I heard someone whispering, "She isn't the undead—she's the unold."

Even Cher didn't like herself in this movie: "It was disappointing. In my effort to be really real, I was really boring. I wasn't embarrassed, but I wanted it to be more."

Finally Cher made a smart career decision.

"*Moonstruck* was too silly," she told Jay Gissen, "too much fun to be work. It was like getting paid lots of money to have a good time with a bunch of people you wouldn't have minded spending time with anyway."

Cher has said that she was almost afraid to do *Moonstruck*; paradoxically that was ultimately what helped her make her decision. She was used to taking chances. "I thought it might be bad for my career. . . . I thought it was so weird that no one would go to see it." But she admired the script tremendously and thought that if the picture turned out as well as she thought it would, it would be a work of art, something she'd always be proud of having been a part of.

Moonstruck was originally written for actress Sally Field by playwright John Patrick Shanley, whose plays include *Danny and the Deep Blue Sea*. Field, one of the few people who had actually seen a Shanley play, liked his work and asked him to lunch. She asked him to write something for her. Shanley agreed but refused to accept any advance payment. While virtually all professional screenwriters are paid for their work whether a script is eventually made into a film or not, Shanley has his own way of doing things: "If you own the material, you're in a much stronger position to negotiate. They *have* to deal with you." Or anyway your agent. Of course, writing his screenplays on speculation as he does, with no money up front, Shanley has to hope that someone will like —and like very much—his final product.

Sally liked his script—at that time it was called *The Bride and the Wolf*—but she couldn't get anyone to make it with her as the star. Shanley's agent turned it over to director Norman Jewison, who didn't care for the title (it sounded like a horror film) but thought the script had definite possibilities. Jewison bought the script and turned it over to MGM production chief Alan Ladd, Jr., suggesting that Cher would be perfect for the lead. Luckily she was available. Jewison announced himself happy to direct it.

Shanley was delighted to have Cher play the part. "She's a handful, that Cher," he said in one interview. "There is absolutely no b.s. about her. She is exotic, sort of like an Arabian princess. There's nobody else like her." And despite other people's feelings to the contrary, he added, "She's not a pain in the ass."

As Jewison saw it, *Moonstruck* was "an operatic, multigenerational romantic comedy, the central theme of which was betrayal." The main character, Loretta (played by Cher) is engaged to one man (Danny Aiello) but falls in love with his brother (Nicolas Cage). Loretta's father, Cosmo (Vincent Gardenia), is stepping out on Loretta's mother, Rose (Olympia Dukakis), with his mistress, Mona (Anita Gillette). Even Rose is developing a crush on handsome Professor Perry (John Mahoney). "All of this seems to be out of the characters' control," explained Jewison. "They're all affected by *la luna*; there's a full moon over Manhattan and Brooklyn. And I think the moon affects humans to a greater extent than most of us recognize."

Cher was at first somewhat afraid that audiences would not accept her as a comparatively dowdy Loretta. Loretta is thirty-seven (four years younger than Cher at the time), widowed, and living with her parents. She is employed in the "glamorous" job of free-lance bookkeeper. She is getting older, reaching the end of her child-bearing years, and figures a marriage to Johnny Cammareri (Aiello) will at least provide children and a certain measure of companionship and support, if not passion. In short, she is not in love with this guy. It is her misfortune—or luck, depending on how you look at it—finally to find the passion every woman secretly hopes for when she meet's Johnny's brother, Ronald.

Cher insisted on having Nicolas Cage play the part of Ronald. He first came to her attention when he appeared in *Peggy Sue Got Married* with Kathleen Turner. "Anybody who's got those kind of balls is absolutely the person to do this," she said, adding, "Nicky never plays it safe. You could play a role five different ways, and he'll go to the one where you've got the most to lose." The trouble was that no one else wanted Cage in the picture. Cher had to fight to get him, recalling later, "I was really a bitch."

She got the performance she expected from Cage, but she really couldn't say, in retrospect, that she enjoyed working with him all that much: "He works alone; he *acts* alone, and you kind of act alone with him." She found Cage a far cry from Eric Stoltz and Meryl Streep, whom she always cited as her favorite coactors up to that time. Cage was appropriately intense but distant. Cher had to build herself up to his level; he wouldn't help her or do it for her. He didn't *share* with her, she found, and that was something she wasn't used to. Also, he wasn't much fun on the set; he was always in the "mood."

Cher didn't particularly enjoy doing the love scenes: "The truth is, I don't enjoy kissing people I don't know." While she and Cage looked extremely passionate on-screen, Cher was actually concentrating on the choreography, the physical movements she had to make, and the comic effects some were supposed to produce. Nothing physical ever developed between Cher and Cage off the set. Cage was too absorbed in perfecting his characterization of the one-handed baker, his anger, and assorted neuroses.

To prepare for her role as a Brooklyn widow, Cher went to the same woman who had coached Anjelica Huston on her dialect in *Prizzi's Honor*. This was Julie Bovasso, who plays the aunt in *Moonstruck*. Then she asked the help of her boyfriend, Rob Camilletti. Although he grew up in Queens, not Brooklyn (the two boroughs have their own distinctive accents), and had no particularly Italianate flavor to his speech, he did come from an Italian-American family and could tell Cher when she was going wrong.

Julie Bovasso has said, "Cher was a very apt student, picked up the accent well; she was very dedicated and applied herself with an intensity that is pure Cher. I greatly respected and admired her in *Moonstruck*, and she certainly deserved her award Oscar night!"

While studying the accent, Cher also observed the other Italian-Americans in the cast. She took note of how everything came across slightly larger than life: big laughs, big gestures, loud yelling and a wonderful overall exuberance. These observations gave her the cue for such scenes as when she slaps Cage and hollers at him: "Snap out of it!"

Cher got along well with director Jewison—a veteran of such films as *In the Heat of the Night*, *The Landlord*, and *Fiddler on the Roof*—although she admitted finding him rather crotchety. She warned him that she was difficult. "What's that supposed to mean?" he shot back. She confessed that she didn't know; it was just her reputation. She clarified—and helped Jewison relax—by saying she was difficult only when people around her were stupid or wouldn't allow her to make suggestions on how to interpret her character. Jewison said he understood, gave her the requisite leeway, and all went fine, except for a few minor incidents.

One afternoon early in the filming Jewison found it necessary to do a number of retakes. Nobody had had any lunch, and it was getting later and later. When Cher asked him when they were going to be able to get something to eat, he snapped at her in an authoritative manner that nobody would eat until they got the scene right. Cher immediately turned to her co-workers and boomed out in her loud, Italian-influenced voice: "Did I just hear that? You're not going to let us have lunch?" Jewison was embarrassed by her action but gratified that she said it right in front of him instead of sneaking around whispering her discontent to the others. In any case Jewison had no real complaints. He had wanted Cher to play the part because of her honest quality, her lack of pretension, and her direct manner, which she was certainly proving, on camera and off.

He was also impressed with Cher's ability to improvise. One afternoon they were shooting in a butcher shop on Ninth Avenue when Cher suddenly began interacting, unscripted, with people in the shop and on the street. Of course, Jewison had to admit that New Yorkers were natural thespians, which made it easier for her. "Everyone's an actor in New York," Cher said later. "These are the kinds of things that a city like this offers that you just can't get anywhere else." Most of the film was actually shot in Toronto.

By the time they got to film the final scene, everyone was in a bad mood for one reason or another. Norman turned cranky and stomped off the set. Nicolas Cage was in a foul mood and started throwing furniture and cups of coffee. Cher rationalized that making movies was not about being nice or rational; the tensions were high; steam had to be let off one way or another. "Art is about stirring things up," Cher told an interviewer, with more discernment than she may have realized. Once everyone had gotten it out of his or her system, tempers cooled, and the cameras began rolling again for the last shots. The "heightened reality" created by all that anger and tension was sucked back, somehow, into the actors' spirits and used effectively in their performances, making for a better picture.

Moonstruck was a very odd movie for the 1980's, very contemporary in some respects, but still on the old-fashioned side, like a romantic or screwball comedy of the forties. It succeeds in milking good-natured humor out of situations that in real life would not be all that funny (for instance, Johnny's fiancée is stolen away from him by his own brother while he's off in Italy visiting their dying mother). The screenplay by Shanley, when all is said and done, is never especially believable, but its charming and entertaining qualities made it a hit with most audiences and critics.

Cher got excellent notices. "It is Cher that most filmgoers will be going to see," wrote one critic, "and her performance will not disappoint. Her capacity as an actress to grow and change with the parts she plays is astounding. And only Cher could look every bit as beautiful in Loretta's supposedly unglamorous 'before' scenes as she does 'after,' when she's all made over and decked out for her big opera date."

This time Pauline Kael of the *New Yorker* was won over by Cher, calling her "devastatingly funny and sinuous and beautiful." Most people agreed. Cher won the Best Actress Oscar for her performance in *Moonstruck*. That spring of 1988, age almost forty-two, she had finally attained the pinnacle of her long-standing hopes and dreams. She had *arrived*, in spades. Never again would she have to worry about not being taken seriously.

What next? Where did one go from such heights? Cher decided to take a little time off from moviemaking and cut a new album. She mulled over different projects, cuddled and cooed contentedly with Rob Camilletti, and basically relaxed, enjoying her money, her apartment, her estate and savoring her satisfaction with recent events.

During this time, many people noticed a change in Cher. It seemed as if she was afraid the award would jinx her. She became more demanding and temperamental. Her dressmakers began to complain that she was turning into a prima donna, that she would scream and throw things at them if she felt things weren't exactly right. She flirted with taking on a number of major roles—for instance Kathleen Turner's part in *The War of the Roses*—and then would bow out at the last minute because she could not get assurances of total control. Her experiences on the set of *Mermaids* were testament to her nervousness about the follow-up to *Moonstruck*.

Quite a bit of time went by while she hesitated about the next film project. It was well into 1989 before she finally decided on *Mermaids*. The film was not released until December 1990.

In *Mermaids* Cher plays Mrs. Flax, a single mother of two young girls, fifteen-year-old Charlotte (Winona Ryder) and nine-year-old Kate (Christina Ricci). Mrs. Flax keeps moving her children around to accommodate her frequent love affairs. Unlike Loretta in *Moonstruck*, she won't settle for just security; she's determined to pursue her romantic ideal. That ideal is probably *not* her latest suitor, Lou Landsky, who owns a shoe store and is played by portly, balding Bob Hoskins (*Who Framed Roger Rabbit*). The kids want their mother to settle down; Mrs. Flax is not sure at all *that's* the way she wants to go.

The first thirty pages of June Roberts's screenplay (based on a novel by Patty Dunn) sold Cher on the part. She found herself reminded of her own youth growing up with mother Georgia Holt. "My mother *was* Mrs. Flax," Cher says, referring to Georgia's provocative dress, frequent suitors, and other points of similarity. What particularly rang a bell for Cher was the way her mother kept moving her and Georgeanne from place to place all the time, just as Mrs. Flax does to Kate and Charlotte in the movie.

Faced with this, Georgia insists that the moves at that time were absolute necessities, honest, recurring attempts to improve the family's living conditions and nothing more than that. Comparing herself with the character of Mrs. Flax, sixty-three-year-old Georgia told *Vanity Fair*: "I also don't remember being, you know, a sex machine." She insists she only tried to *look* that way to get the attention of producers and other men in a position to help her professionally.

Cher says she also liked the script because it reminded her of *Moonstruck*, calling it "a sweet look at people who are totally out of their minds and doing the best job that they can, but they're just cracked."

Originally the basic story was to center on the character of daughter Charlotte, but when Cher signed on, the focus shifted to at least a fifty-fifty sharing, so that Cher's role was slightly enlarged from what was supposed to be only a supporting stint. Cher's coming into the project—it was said *Mermaids* would never have been made without her cooperation—engendered a lot of eventual changes, particularly in regard to personnel.

The first casualty was director Lasse Hallström. He started tinkering with the script, adding sequences of grim melodrama, such as the death of the younger child by drowning. Cher didn't think audiences would sit still for that. (Again Cher was no film historian. In 1952 another comedy-drama entitled *The Marrying Kind*, directed by George Cukor, had the couple's young son drown midway through the picture, and the result was one of the most powerful and moving sequences ever recorded on film.)

Cher had had a big hit with *Moonstruck*, a comedy-drama that placed the emphasis squarely on the comedy. She believed that kind of sitcomlike material was more guaranteed to please an audience, and the more pleased it was with the film, she reasoned, the more it'd like her performance. The emphasis in *Mermaids* had to be on the comedy; that was the irrevocable dictum from on high. Hallström was fired.

The second casualty was actress Emily Lloyd, who had been signed to play the older daughter, Charlotte, and who sued the production when she was dismissed. There are some who say that although Lloyd would have worked out perfectly fine in the movie, Cher had her own reasons for wanting to replace her with Winona Ryder. Ryder had appeared in a movie called *Heathers* and precious little else and was hardly better known than Lloyd. At her audition Ryder didn't even have to do any line readings; she just sat and chatted while Cher sized her up. Not only did she get the part, but Cher insisted she move into the same Boston apartment building where she was staying during shooting, instead of remaining at the Cambridge Hotel, where the crew had settled in.

Cher and Winona became close friends, socializing and spending a lot of time together, with Cher evolving into the role of mother and sister in real life as well as on-camera. Ryder was eighteen. Cher felt there was so much she could teach her, prepare her for. For Winona, it was strange to be playing Charlotte; her character was going through so much that she herself was experiencing. In some ways it gave her an advantage in playing the part, but it also intensified her own feelings as she emerged from adolescence into womanhood. Cher did her best to help the younger woman sort out her feelings.

For about a month during production Cher was out sick, and this gave the producers a hiatus in which to find someone to take over Hallström's directorial reins. Their choice fell upon Frank Oz. When Cher heard, she wasn't wild about the idea; wasn't this the guy who had something to do with muppets? (He had directed *The Muppets Take Manhattan* in 1984.) *Mermaids* wasn't a film about marionettes, Cher said; it was a movie about people. Cher found it hard to take Oz as director seriously. Finally Oz flew to Los Angeles to put his case to Cher, convince her he could do the job. But her mind was not easily changed. She finally agreed to go with him on a trial basis because Orion Pictures insisted.

Eventually Cher got her own way. Oz, it appeared, didn't understand what the picture was all about either. He, too, was treating it as if it were "Chekhov," laying stress on the tragic aspects as against the comedic ones. Another problem: Oz worked much too slowly; the film was threatening to go badly over schedule. Everyone but Cher liked Frank Oz personally, but the situation on the set was becoming intolerable.

Cher repeated that she had not wanted Oz on the movie. She had no faith in the Muppet man. Jewison may have been a grouch on her last film, but at least he was a *controllable* grouch. After dozens of pictures Jewison had acquired a reputation as a director who had virtually no personal style or vision; he just came in and got through the picture in a simple, workmanlike manner without any claim to artistry or imaginative furbelows. Oz, true, had more imagination than Jewison; he did have a "vision" of what he wanted the film to be. But Cher felt he was taking the movie too far from *Moonstruck* territory; she wanted *Mermaids* to be a "feel-good" movie. She didn't want "art." (She may have been right in her instincts, however; the script for *Mermaids* was no world beater.)

Oz became the second director to leave the picture, a development engineered by Cher. He went reluctantly, but he found that no one respected or even understood what he had tried to do, and Cher had turned everyone against him.

Cher's position was that she had had no choice; the production was like a sinking ship that she had to save. But she was utterly miserable. "Winona and I cried every night and every day," she told *Premiere*. "It was just the worst experience of my life."

She thought her acting in the picture bad, and Oz was assigned some of the blame for *that*, too. Winona was biting her nails, nervous and miserable, and as for Bob Hoskins, he tried to stay out of everybody's way; he wanted peace, just wanted to do his work and get out.

Hoskins and Cher got along fairly well. She gave him an ego lift when she told him that she helped him get the part because she wanted "a real man—the sort of thing with warts and hairs"—not a pretty boy. Hoskins found her unpredictable, however; during one sequence Cher snapped at him out of the blue: "You've got one line of dialogue, and I've got three pages, and you're giving me shit!" Then she followed this up with a taut smile, as if to say: Don't mind me. It was a good part for Hoskins, and he minded his P's and Q's as much as Cher's varying moods would allow. Soon there were rumors that Hoskins and Cher were having an affair; the tabloids denied it was so, only according the rumors added publicity.

But Cher had other things on her mind besides "real man" Hoskins's sexy warts and hairs. There was the matter of Mr. Director number three for *Mermaids*, and Cher sifted and winnowed, seething all the while, until she got the man she wanted: Richard Benjamin. Having been an actor himself, Benjamin had an intuitive understanding of how to direct actors, humoring and soothing them while keeping them firmly reined, a neat balancing act if it could be brought off. Cher had always hoped to work with Richard, ever since the *Going to the Chapel* project had fizzled; now he was hers, and everyone settled down to a satisfactory windup on a picture that had dragged on for months.

Meanwhile, Cher and Winona became closer and closer, "like a couple of college roommates," as one friend put it. Cher constantly nagged at Winona to stop biting her nails. Once Winona took Cher to the movies—*Sex, Lies and Videotape*—in Cambridge without realizing that it was homecoming weekend at Harvard. There went Cher's hopes of keeping a relatively low profile. Winona jokingly suggested that they go to a beer party at a frat house afterward. (Undoubtedly Cher would have been the hit of *that* evening, with few of the Harvard lads even noticing sweet but low-key Winona; it might have occasioned a break in the budding relationship of *Mermaids's* coactors.)

Cher became increasingly worried about Winona's health; the teenager was driving herself too hard. What with revolving-door directors, a part to learn and master, and this wondrous but frightening proximity to Cher, Ryder threatened to become a prime basket case before shooting ended—if and when it ever did. (Later Winona Ryder had to drop out of her next assignment, *The Godfather III*, because of "exhaustion.")

Cher also developed a fondness for little Christina Ricci, who played the younger daughter and who occasionally flubbed her lines in a coltishly endearing fashion. Cher seemed almost manically intent that she, Winona, and Christina should have relationships offscreen that were similar to those in the movie. Cher had her two "daughters" over for dinner and a sleepover even before filming began so they could "get used to each other" and do some "female bonding." It was as if Cher sought to compensate in a private context for all the revolving-door fuss and feathers of the usual production day, to which she had made her own contribution. Winona remembered that she could have done without the insubstantial "health food" she was served at her "dinners with Cher."

Filming proceeded more smoothly with Benjamin, but he, too, had to weather some "incidents." One day he made the mistake of asking Cher to give him "more, *more!*" during a hospital sequence calling for her to wax teary and emotional. He went on a retake jag ("Does he think he's Willie Wyler?' one crew member asked), and this got Cher strung out and on edge. She finally screeched at Benjamin and stopped work, going to her dressing room while he was still giving her instructions.

The following day they were doing a sequence at a swimming pool when Benjamin slipped and hit his head on some bleachers, falling unconscious. He briefly revived. "Who are you?" he asked Cher, then passed out again a moment later. Cher was horrified. He was bleeding profusely and looked "like one of the living dead," as a crew member put it. An ambulance was called, and

Cher rode with Director III, holding his hand as he was rushed to the hospital. To bring him out of his gloom and fright, Cher asked him if he remembered what they had done yesterday "Remember?" She joshed him. "We were doing a hospital scene and I was a cunt!" Benjamin laughed; that was the start of his recovery. (He needed, on that occasion, twenty-two stitches for a head wound and also sported a black eye and a chipped elbow, denying to all comers any rumors that Cher had given them to him.)

What with all the delays, changes, hirings and firings, and assorted exhibitions of destructive temperament, *Mermaids* was consuming months and running up frightening costs, and Cher was as sick of the picture as anyone and wanted it over with. She missed her family and was afraid the company would still be filming at Christmastime; that would have been intolerable for her. She was lucky. The production moved to Baltimore for a few days, then wrapped everything up by December 21, 1989. The studio took forever to set a release date for the troubled picture (which finally opened one full year after the end of production). Cher was apprehensive about the delay; for a while she feared that the disgusted and drained Orion executives would simply shelve it. It had been three years since her last picture. Even an Oscar-winning superstar couldn't stay off the screen too long without putting her career in jeopardy.

The critical reaction to *Mermaids* was mixed. *The New York Times* called it "a smooth, unexceptional entertainment about coming of age in a world where truly bad things happen only on television." *Variety* felt the film was "caught between worlds, oscillating between broad comic strokes and tired familial melodrama." Most felt Winona Ryder was the true star—and strength—of the film, although Cher's performance—"cheeky, broad, comically self-assured," according to the *Times*—dominated the picture.

Mary Hart in her CBS special *Power in the Public Eye* theorized that Cher was one of the few people in Hollywood to have real power not just because she was a star but because she had control behind the scenes (as witness all that had happened during the trouble-racked *Mermaids* shooting). Cher, however, scoffed at the notion. "I can't imagine it's true," she told Hart. "I don't know if it's that women are just different, but I never think about [power]; all I know is that I can control what's happening to me, and since I don't control what's happening to anyone else, I don't think of myself as being powerful. I just don't see myself as being able to be victimized."

If money equals power, Cher is powerful. She now heads her own production company, Isis, and a business empire and is the highest-paid performer in Las Vegas. (In five years, however, Isis has not produced a single film.) Cher's price for a movie has gone up from $500,000 for *Mask* in 1985 to $1.4 million for the 1987 *Moonstruck*, and after she won the Oscar, her asking price went to $4 million. Even before that she was "bankable." MGM/UA had agreed to finance the $11 million production of *Moonstruck* only if she agreed to appear in it.

Cher's films, even more significantly in producer thinking, all have made money: *Suspect*, $18.7 million; *Moonstruck*, $59 million; *The Witches of Eastwick*, $67.3 million.

In spite of all this, Cher thinks she will not be a movie star for much longer. "There are already parts I can't do," she insists forlornly. "I'm just too old for them." Nor does she, even now, think of herself as a "serious" actress. She told one reporter, "I'm deadly serious about my work, but I'm not gonna become Anne Bancroft or Meryl Streep and have all the burden that being a 'serious actress' entails." Part of the problem is that she really doesn't like making movies and has compared the experience with "swallowing razor blades." She told an interviewer, "It's very tiring and tedious and it's like working in a factory with small parts. You have to have so much concentration it's just really not much fun." Yes, she said, it was always great to have a hit movie, of course, but she preferred being on the road on a concert tour to working on a movie. She also remains highly critical of her acting, saying she finds it difficult to watch herself on film, that it makes her want to, you guessed it, "throw up!"

Given her basic attitude, Cher at forty-four may not make many more movies. If she does, there are several possibilities coming up. *Road Show* continues to appear on her list of possible future projects, this time with Sean Connery as her costar. The picture is about a cattle drive—Cher on the range?—but, says producer Donna Dubrow, "has a romantic comedy slant—like *The African Queen.*" Dubrow's husband, John McTiernan, who weathered *Die Hard* with Bruce Willis, would, she says, direct— this, along with all else, contingent on Cher's caprice.

Then she might get to work on projects that for some time have interested her, such as *Forever Sad the Heart*, *Rain or Shine*, and *Real Confessions*. The last is projected as a comedy about 1950's-era housewives, with Cher and Jessica Lange costarring. The first two were nonfiction books that Cher developed into scripts. *Rain or Shine* is a period piece—1930's—about the relationship between the "Howard Cosell of the rodeo circuit" and his wife. *Forever Sad the Heart* is about a nurse in Vietnam; this might be promising for Cher now that *China Beach*—also about Vietnam nurses—has been a minor hit on TV.

If Cher chooses wisely—very wisely—she could remain a movie star straight through her forties and on into the 1990's, right up to 2000.

And maybe even after.

She might become—who knows?—the world's first bankable sixty-year-old actress. If anyone can pull it off, Cher can.

TEN

PUBLIC SPECTACLE

*You know, if you were blond and blue-eyed, you'd probably be
a housewife in Van Nuys right now instead of where you are.*
—GEORGIA HOLT to her daughter CHER

No matter how much Cher
may protest that she hates to be bothered, values her privacy, or
"wants to be alone," it is no secret that she *loves* attention. Part
of it is a shrewd realization that people who get noticed sell more
records and movie tickets; part of it is a desire to be the center of
the media universe. She doesn't like lies being told about her—
who does?—but she loves the idea that people are talking. The
worst thing you can do to someone like Cher is to ignore her.

The evidence: her outrageous stage shows, which draw more
talk the wilder they get; her incredible outfits, which have been
raising eyebrows—and temperatures—for years; the impossible-
to-miss tattoos on her body—if you can't see them easily (like the
one on her arm), she makes sure to *show* them to you (like the
one on her butt) in her videos. Cher has been making a public
spectacle of herself for decades, and her fans love it as much as
she does.

"I have the most opposite personalities that could possibly
live in one body," claims Cher. "I'm obsessed with how I look,

for instance. Then, sometimes, I couldn't care less. I don't wear makeup. I walk around the house like a bum."

Privately Cher may not care how she looks at times, but publicly she is very much concerned about her appearance. Her appearance, her image are part of what makes her appealing and popular. In some ways Cher *is* image.

Cher is about five feet seven and one-half inches tall, weighs approximately 105 pounds, and has black hair and brown eyes. Twenty-five years have gone by since she and Sonny had a hit with "I Got You, Babe," but you wouldn't know it to look at her. Makeup and good lighting may account for some of the visual discrepancy, but mostly it's because Cher takes good care of herself. She hates smoking, deals with stress by going to the gym, and rarely indulges in anything more than a couple of glasses of wine with dinner. "I don't understand why the government lets people smoke," she says. "It's *terrible*. It's killing us. Smoking, sugar, and all that shit that no one cares about." *Cher* cares—about her body and what she eats.

Her good looks, of course, were helped by terrific bone structure, great eyes, and a winning smile, all of which helped her become a model. This came about when she ran into fashion maven Diana Vreeland at a ritzy party for Jacqueline Kennedy back in the sixties.

Vreeland was positively smitten with Cher's whole look, the shape of the head, the tall, slender body, and arranged a photo session with famed photographer Richard Avedon. Vreeland was editing *Vogue* at the time and ran a layout of twenty Avedon photographs of Cher. This was the beginning of Cher's love affair with glamour; the ugly duckling had been transformed into a swan by makeup, lighting, and Avedon's genius. In the photo layout was a new Cher that even she had never suspected existed. But the foundation had always been there.

Over the years Cher has done a great many fashion layouts, picture spreads, and magazine covers, including ones for *Vogue* and *Vanity Fair*. Once Avedon did a series in which she modeled new outfits in the tradition of the twenties to the seventies. Another spread—in which she wore Indian clothes—was killed because activists thought the feature was making fun of Native Americans.

In the November 1990 issue of *Vanity Fair* she appeared on the cover in a Giorgio Armani camisole—a kind of beaded, metallic outfit—and wore a magnificent mammoth necklace, an Australian crystal lace bib, with matching earrings. Inside, she modeled a feather dress with fishnet stockings, a fishnet and lace bodysuit with an Egyptian type of hairstyle that made her look like a latter-day Nefertiti, and a highly sexy crinoline bustier dress that looked like the fashion offspring of a sheer evening gown and a black leather motorcycle halter.

Cher is a fabulous-looking model but not a truly "beautiful" woman. Hers is a kind of aesthetic beauty that inspires admiration, as opposed to the kind of classic beauty of which "the poets sing" and which needs no added glamour or artifice. Although she is certainly found attractive by men, women are more likely to appreciate those certain qualities brought out by a professional photographer. Men are less interested in "bone structure" than women are. It is her sassiness and sexuality that appeal to males.

Cher uses much less makeup now than she used to. "A face is not a canvas that you have to apply colors and designs to; that took me awhile to find out." She's happier with her face than she used to be and wants it to show through. Although she has said that long hair looks a little desperate past the age of thirty, she herself rarely wears it *that* short and looks just fine.

One major element in the Cher mystique is her clothing, which she admits projects an image of wildness and promiscuity that is not the real Cher. "I just want to go out and have a good time. It doesn't mean I'm looking to fuck somebody. I just want to feel really sexy and appealing." She has a hundred pairs of shoes and a hundred pairs of pants but usually just wears Levi 501s. She asked the company that makes them if she could be its spokesperson, but it apparently bought into her "wild lady" image and turned her down.

The man who designs most of her clothes is Bob Mackie,

who said, "The old Hollywood stars had a look, and they had it forever. Marlene Dietrich or Lana Turner or Greta Garbo wouldn't look like any actress who was out for the evening. Cher is also very consistent over the years. You laugh or applaud or think it's shocking, but it's always just for fun."

Susan Brenna in *Newsday* agreed that Cher's relationship to clothing made her a "Hollywood throwback. Katharine Hepburn made a reputation in pants; Jean Harlow, in slinky satin and marabou mules. Cher, too, has a look, and it has nothing to do with fashion trends. No one but Cher was wearing pink-and-red-feathered floor-length Indian headdresses in 1973, and no one but she exercises in 1988 in torn mesh and a fright wig."

Cher's most sensational—or horrifying—outfit was the one she wore to the 1986 Oscars, either to "conceal her wounds," as one writer put it, for not getting a nomination for *Mask* or just as a way of spitting in the eye of the Academy, which stuffily frowned on such outré costuming. The infamous outfit was described thusly by columnist Suzy: "A little scrap of something in black wool jersey, heavily embroidered in gun-metal beads across her bosom, a bare midriff, skin-tight black stretch pants also heavily hung with gun-metal beads, a loincloth that sort of falls over the pants, black suede boots to her knees, and on the head a giant Mohawk headpiece dripping more beads. It'll either bring rain or set the wigwam on fire."

Bob Mackie designed the dress, which caused scandalous outcries from the more prim and proper observers of the Oscar telecast. How dare anyone come dressed in an outfit like that? So tasteless, so vulgar. Yet Cher was aware that the Oscar ceremonies themselves were all glitz and glamour, in many ways shallow and phony; an Oscar was not a Nobel Peace Prize after all. Her costume fitted right in with the general proceedings, even if a lot of people tsk-tsked. They didn't understand that incredible clothes were as integral to the Cher image as they were to Liberace's. She wasn't doing anything different from what she usually did: She was being Cher. Her fans and most industry observers would frankly have been disappointed if she had shown up in anything *ordinary*.

On the other hand, many of her fans were extremely disappointed in the outfit she wore for television appearances in late 1990: It was mostly beige—a blouse, a coat, and a hat with a flower and a kind of ribbon, along with dungarees that were artfully torn at the knees. This is what she wore for the MTV awards and (slightly varied) on an environmental special. It wasn't nearly shocking or scandalous enough to suit most people.

Cher is also a fan of chain mail couture, which is designed for her by Michael Schmidt, who stays with her while he is in Los Angeles. When Schmidt's bike was stolen in New York one afternoon, "Page Six" of the *Post* suggested he create a metallic bustier that his next bicycle could wear for protection.

Not all of Cher's "clothing" comes off when she goes to bed at night, for her tattoos are as much a part of her look as anything she wears. She gets most of them done at an all-female tattoo parlor, Red Devil, in Los Angeles on La Brea. The count is up to six: an odd splintered diamond-type design in red and green on her lower arm; a chrysanthemum on her ankle; a tiger lily on her right side, just below the waist; and the most controversial ones: a blue-black orchid right above her pubis and flowers and a butterfly on her behind. The sixth and latest tattoo looks like a map of Florida from a distance but is actually a coiling necklace with an ankh, a cross, and heart charms hanging from it. This one is on her left arm.

The tattoo on her behind was the first one she got and has become her least favorite. She got it in 1972 as a symbolic gesture to celebrate her independence from Sonny. She now thinks the tattoo is "pretty stupid." Most people would agree.

Cher admits the tattooing may seem crazy, but it's part of what makes her unique. She simply loves to get a new tattoo. "You either love them or are really disgusted by them, and I can understand both things, but this is my life, and I have to do what I want." She does say that she thinks women who go for piercing—noses, nipples, lips—are going to extremes.

Some believe that Cher herself has gone to extremes when it comes to fooling around with Mother Nature. She has had quite a bit of cosmetic surgery done, though not as much as people have accused her of.

Cher was always dissatisfied with her nose. Back in 1971 Earl Wilson asked her, "How do you feel about remarks that you have a Barbra Streisand nose?" She replied: "My nose is not one of my favorite things, and *her* nose is not one of my favorite things either."

It wasn't until she saw herself in *Mask*, however, that she decided to get a nose job—for professional reasons, she says. She had never thought her nose looked that big when she was on TV, and apparently it didn't bother her when she saw *Jimmy Dean* or *Silkwood*. But in *Mask* she was on-camera for most of the film's running time; she had time to study herself and didn't like what she saw.

She also got braces for her teeth. She didn't like the way they photographed; it was as if they disappeared when she turned a certain way. According to her, the cameraman had to use a special light just for her teeth. That problem had to be fixed also.

She also admits to having had her breasts worked on, but only once—not half a dozen times, as some tabloids have reported. She also had a chemical peel done on her face, but this was not to remove some scars, as some suggested, but because she had a bad allergic reaction to the makeup when she did *Silkwood*.

She initiated a lawsuit against *Paris Match* and *Bunte* for saying she had surgery she swears never happened. *Match* infuriated her by suggesting she had spent forty thousand dollars to get her body to look the way it did in the Jack La Lanne commercials. "I don't want women to think I'm full of shit," she said. "I don't want women to suddenly stop working out and say, 'Fine, if I only had forty thousand dollars, I'd be in great shape!'"

Cher has never had her stomach tightened or her backside lifted. "You'd find scars," she says. She also did not have any chin or cheek implants or ribs removed. Cher was particularly furious at the latter accusation. She was listening to a talk show when a woman said that *she* was thinking of getting some ribs removed because Cher had done it. Cher knew she was considered a "healthy" spokesperson, that a lot of women looked to her for direction, and the thought of some of them having unnecessary surgery performed because they thought she had had it done was frightening. Cher called the show and warned the woman not to believe everything she read.

Still, inveterate Cher watchers insist that Cher has had extensive cosmetic surgery and point to successive photos of the star over time as proof positive. In fact, the rumor mill on this subject has reached such ridiculous proportions that some people are claiming Cher recently had an operation to tighten her vagina and reshape her labia. So outrageous an idea hardly need be commented upon!

Nevertheless, Cher sees nothing wrong in getting surgery to improve oneself. "I think this way about it: It's my body, and if I want to do it like Michael Jackson, I will." (She does think that Jackson has gone a little too far: "He was a lot cuter before.")

In late 1990 columnist Liz Smith wrote that "some people have noted that Cher's mouth has taken on a new lushness. (A different lipstick?) One wag put it this way: 'She's working her way through collagen.' " Whatever the case, her lips seem fuller and brighter and more luscious than ever before.

Dental surgery Cher definitely *has* had. She got a bad toothache while doing her concert tour in April 1990 and rushed to a dentist in a suburb of Atlanta. When he got her call, the dentist assumed it was an April Fool's gag. It turned out she needed root canal work. It is safe to say that it was not one of her most pleasant experiences.

But the dental work was nothing compared with another health problem that not only had her taking off work while filming *Mermaids* but has been causing her problems for quite a while— and attracting attention. People wondered why she didn't seem quite herself at the Oscar telecast and why she was reporting frequent bouts with a "flulike illness" that had her bedridden for weeks at a time. She had learned she had the Epstein-Barr virus as far back as 1986, but the illness didn't start to hit her hard until three years later.

"I was so sick I thought I was going to die," she told Kevin Sessums in *Vanity Fair*. Finally a doctor told her the best thing for her to do was to take time off, stay in bed, and give her body a chance to recover. After that she was able to return to work and resume her busy schedule. She also came down with a case of chicken pox during the summer of 1989, which certainly didn't help matters.

Perhaps Cher should have gone public about the Epstein–Barr virus much sooner than she did to keep the rumors from flying. True, any mention of unusual "viruses" got people to thinking about AIDS, but it was just for that reason that Cher might have chosen to clear up any misconceptions. One tabloid got the ailment right (Epstein–Barr) but claimed that Cher had conquered the illness by using mind-over-matter techniques perfected by the Egyptians. This was written off as ridiculous, justifiably. Still, no matter what Cher said, the tabloids would distort it.

Meanwhile, Cher did her best to stay in shape. She thinks "subtle muscles" are attractive and works out on machines and occasionally runs, although she admits she's having an easier time aging than most because of heredity. In a 1985 interview she claimed that her seventy-one-year-old grandmother had gone to the gym four times a week.

The owners of the Jack La Lanne health club chain chose her for spokesperson after Joan Rivers, their first choice, turned them down. Cher's career wasn't going so great then, and she needed the money, which was terrific, at least six figures. She was happy when people credited her for their having joined the club and started taking care of their bodies. In the commercials Cher displayed her fine figure and a lot of "attitude" as well. It was as if she were saying, "You wanna look like this? Fat chance—unless you come in and do what I do!"

She wrote and produced many of the commercials, came up with the actual concept, and was extremely annoyed when the chain brought in actress Heather Locklear (of *Dynasty*) to finish what she started. (Cher was still doing print ads for Jack La Lanne, wearing her intense "I dare you" expression, as late as fall 1990.) She told Eugenie Ross-Leming and David Standish in *Playboy* that she felt *invaded* by the replacement. "I didn't write that commercial from my life experience to have some blonde bimbo of 25 stick her tongue out at the end of it. It *meant* something to me to talk about how I've arrived at this place after everything I've been through at the age of 42!"

Cher does a two-hour workout daily, starting with stretching to music. Her personal trainer runs her through routines with dumbbells, weights, and on the treadmill, rower, and vertical bench. (Granted not every working mother can spare two hours a day to work on her figure.)

In spite of all this attention she gives to herself, Cher thinks the whole obsession with looks thing can be overdone. While she thinks it's important to work out and take care of yourself, she also believes that a constant emphasis on looks can be pretty empty. "I *don't* want to spend my whole life with the beautiful people." Cher is much too down-to-earth for that. Sometimes she wants to feel free to look like a slob.

Not that a slob would necessarily fit right in with the decor of the various homes that Cher occupies on either coast and that are also part of her image. She recently planned to sell her triplex co-op loft in the East Village in New York City (the Silk Building) to rap music impresario Russell Simmons (no relation to Gene). The place was decorated with Aztec art, which Simmons will replace with African work more to his liking. Apparently Cher had trouble finding a buyer because few of them liked her taste in decor. Although reportedly worth $3 million, the apartment was offered to Simmons at somewhere over $1.6 million.

Cher's Benedict Canyon house was sold to Eddie Murphy in 1988 for $6.5 million after being on the market for quite a few years. This was a deal apart from her negotiations, off and on, for her famous Egyptian-style estate in Beverly Hills (four acres, fourteen thousand square feet), which Eugenie Ross-Leming described as "not impressive in Ptolemaic terms, but if you're saying anything less than an anointed descendant of Ra, the feeling of being in the Valley of the Kings can be heady; doors slide open silently at one's arrival, almost as if by themselves."

Cher also owns a condo in Malibu on the water's edge. It is an extremely attractive gray and white house with a large patio, a private pool, and an unobstructed view of the ocean. She is currently having new dwellings in Manhattan and in Beverly Hills built to her specifications.

The houses, the surgery, the tattoos—all are part of the image. In late 1988 Cher decided that the way she smelled was important, too—to the public, that is. She came out with her own brand of perfume, Uninhibited.

The perfume actually originated with Michael Stern, head of Parfums Stern. He was reading a magazine article about Cher when it hit him that she would be a good bet to enter the marketplace that already was offering Elizabeth Taylor's Passion. He did more research on Cher, discovered that many women liked and admired her, and got in touch with her. The inspiration for the perfume itself was the combination Cher already wore: Charles of the Ritz and a vanilla-based fragrance. The new perfume's ingredients included sandalwood, lily, peony, lilac, carnation, vanilla, dried fruit, and musk. Some names considered and dropped in favor of Uninhibited were Dare and Facets. The perfume sold for $175 an ounce. Initial sales were excellent, with Macy's reporting a record-breaking first week. The tag line for the commercial was "bottled but not contained."

Cher went on a personal appearance tour in department stores to hawk the new product. In Chicago she told a group of fans: "If you guys like it, wear it. And if you don't, buy somebody else's." Fans came in droves, some traveling long distances, to see Cher, talk with her, and get her to sign autographs; a few even bought the perfume (The eau de toilette, which cost only thirty dollars, had more buyers.) "I don't think of perfume as a luxury," said Cher. "When I get up in the morning, I spray it all over myself in a figure-eight design so that whenever I move, the scent moves with me, making a statement."

A Halloween party celebrating the perfume was thrown by Steve Rubell and Ian Schrager, famous for Studio 51. Guests included a million press people and Eric Stoltz, Sly Stallone, Gloria Steinem, and Rob Camilletti. According to *Village Voice* columnist Michael Musto, Cher was "costumed less Uninhibitedly than one would hope, but ready to party down with an encompassing combination of gaudiness and taste, as she is now all things to all people."

Musto described the party thusly: "Everywhere you looked there was somebody, something. Various performances surreally transpired without any announcement or applause: there was dancing macaroni, an alien ballet, a Kabuki-style magician with hoops and lots of pancake. On the sides of the room were living tableaux, like a little-people brunch group, and a couple sitting with their heads popping through a table. Sometimes you couldn't tell if the displays were hired help, costumed partiers or just regular people in their everyday garb. The Liz Taylor clone stuffing food to beat the band is still confounding many." To Musto, Cher was "a true star! As a drunk was being thrown out of the party, she ran after him to get him back in!"

The perfume itself didn't thrill everyone. "This should be packaged with a clothespin for the nose," wrote one publication. "It's so strong it would cover Right Guard after a workout. A powdery, woody, dirty scent—not for a lady in pearls who likes a clean fragrance. It's Cher in black leather." Generally it was considered far inferior to, and a lot less classy than, Liz Taylor's Passion or even Joan Collins's (now virtually extinct) Spectacular.

Although Uninhibited earned around fifteen million dollars in 1988, problems erupted when Cher and her backers disagreed on marketing strategy—with the result that sales plummeted. Cher bought back the rights to her name in late 1990 and decided to look for a new firm to distribute the product because she thought she owed it to her fans. At this point the success of the second coming of Uninhibited—or whatever it may eventually be called—depends a lot on what's happening with Cher when the perfume is newly distributed, according to marketing experts.

Uninhibited rode the crest of a *Moonstruck* Oscar, a new album, and a hot romance. Similar circumstances will perhaps have to be in motion for a revival of the scent to be successful.

It is true that the respective fragrances of such as Joan Collins, Sophia Loren, and Dionne Warwick failed because the women did not remain in the public eye.

If that's the case, Cher has nothing to worry about.

She's one lady who's never had trouble staying in the public eye.

Never is Cher's image more solidified and personified than in her stage shows, which are guaranteed to receive lots of media attention. Cher thinks that taking her act out on the road is a lot more fun than making a movie. "The actual work of it is more uplifting," she told Mary Hart. "You can see the joy you bring at that moment." She enjoyed seeing America, she added, but had to admit that at forty-four she was feeling a little too old to be on the road.

Cher is an incredibly successful stage performer as far as finances go. In 1988 *Variety* reported that she was by then believed to have "become one of the highest-paid attractions in the Jersey Casino Spectrum" with a salary that was on the level of Frank Sinatra's. She was already the top earner in Las Vegas. In the summer of 1989 she got the biggest ticket price in Atlantic City history—two hundred dollars a seat. In spite of the high price the concerts were sold out. (Some tickets went for thirty-five dollars.)

While it costs Cher about ten thousand dollars to put up the crew for each stop on a tour, that's chicken feed for her; she brings in more than a million dollars a week for her show. Her earnings as a concert performer are simply spectacular.

For her 1989–90 tour, which was an outgrowth of her successful *Heart of Stone* album, Cher took along a band that included her son, Elijah Blue Allman, on rhythm guitar. Her backup vocalists included, ironically, Darlene Love, for whom Cher sang backup years before when Darlene was making records with Phil Spector in the sixties. Reportedly Cher's entire crew for the show consisted of no fewer than eighty-seven people, including a cook and personal trainer. Cher travels in a four-hundred-thousand-dollar custom-made bus that is equipped with video monitors and sound equipment, as well as carpets, couches, and silk wallpaper. Two buses travel behind her and carry her dancers and musicians. "The shows are much less work than the preparation," she says.

The tour went all across the country and into Canada. In Manitoba Jets hockey players in the audience gave her an honorary jersey. She was en route to Canada in a twin-engine plane when the pilot had to return to Newark Airport because he thought an engine was overheating. It turned out to be a malfunctioning indicator, but Cher was shaken. She hated flying, to begin with. Her sister and her future husband and Cher's manager, Bill Sammeth, were also in the plane. After landing, Cher rushed to Richie Sambora's home to steady her nerves.

The show itself—"The Cher Extravaganza"—was Cher at her most pyrotechnic and outrageous. In earlier years Cher had used drag queens dressed as Diana Ross and Bette Midler. This time she hired a guy to dress up as herself, wearing the infamous 1986 Academy Award outfit. Cher then stepped out onstage in jeans and a T-shirt. "The impersonator, doing an impeccable impression and dressed to kill, looks more like Cher than Cher," wrote Bob Harrington in the New York *Post*. "But it's the real article, without the glitz, that's got the glamour. She's incandescent, vibrant and compelling, even competing with what was virtually an identical twin."

The show functioned as a sort of minihistory of Cher. Video montages showed her on her TV show, performing old numbers, and emoting in her recent movies. Cher was criticized for appearing onstage live for only about forty-five minutes out of a sixty-five-minute set, the rest of the time devoted to the clips. The video angle came full circle when her concert at Jones Beach was taped for a segment of *Prime Time Live*, with the whole show held up so that she could sing "If I Could Turn Back Time" directly on the program. According to *Newsday*, this made for "a perfect media moment. Even for Cher, a superstar created by television exposure and a mountain of press clippings, knocking off a TV appearance while raking in a cash gate rates as some kind of coup. . . . [S]he's not a bad singer, only hopelessly mediocre . . . the kind of camp celebrity who's beyond the bounds of mere talent."

Newsday continued: "Cher is indeed enjoyably sassy, and there's something genuinely admirable about her flip honesty and the fact that she has transformed herself from a pop cartoon into a genuine Hollywood star. The puzzling question is that, having come so far, why does she so willfully wallow in a past she has so successfully transcended? Cher would do better to leave the scrapbook at home."

Cher's outfits included "a sheer lace body suit that shows virtually everything" and a "relatively demure red velvet mini-dress," according to *The New York Times*. "It's easy to tell which songs are the serious ones; in those, Cher doesn't reveal her navel." Songs included "We All Sleep Alone," "Bang, Bang," "Tougher Than the Rest" (Springsteen), "Many Rivers to Cross," "I'm No Angel," and "Take It to the Streets." "Her show is a kind of Las Vegas mystery play with a message: Trust yourself, don't give up on life or love, and eternal celebrity can be yours. 'There's a time for substance and all that,' she said, 'but it's not here and it's not now.' No one could argue with that."

In Atlantic City Cher's voice was a little raspier than usual one night. In typical Cher fashion she jokingly told the assemblage: "Tough shit. You came on a bad night."

Cher was criticized for never just pulling up a stool and getting personal, as one critic put it. The video montages and "leather and chains dancers doing some S&M road tour of *Cats*" all seemed excessive and unnecessary. But others loved it. Said one reviewer: "She's put together a show that can't be described any better than in the words she uses herself: it's like a trip to Disneyland on acid, and she's the E ticket ride." Cher on that occasion was cited for her showmanship and star quality and a voice that was in fine trim. Critical opinion seemed to be divided among those who loved her and the show, those who hated both, and those who loved Cher but wished the show had been better.

In spite of its brevity, most of her fans were as thrilled as ever, with many of them taking off from work or school and getting up at an obscene hour just to be sure of copping tickets. They were impressed with her boundless energy, audacity, and that camp, almost vulgar sense of glamour.

Cher tried a similar approach to her video for *Heart of Stone*, the miniautobiography, putting together clips of everything from her press conference after Rob Camilletti was arrested for allegedly trying to run down a *Star* photographer to baby pictures of Chastity and Elijah Blue. Also included were shots of her and Sonny and her and Gregg Allman in their happier days, as well as moments from the old TV variety shows. This would have been all right—to a degree—had Cher not decided to blend these personal clips with shots of Jimmy Swaggart in tears, Ronald Reagan looking dopey, cops beating sixties protesters, and footage from both Vietnam documentaries and the Tom Cruise feature movie *Born on the Fourth of July*.

"According to Cher's new video," wrote Jim Farber in the New York *Daily News*, "the greatest American tragedies of the last 20 years were Watergate, the Vietnam War and her marriage to Sonny Bono. The point of this clip is to picture the situations that, over the years, have made us all wish our hearts were made of stone. Of course some of you may think it's a tad offensive for Cher to equate her love blunders with our national tragedies. But then, Cher has a better understanding of these things than normal humans do. As one of the most esteemed publicity hounds of all time, she realizes that political events are no more significant to the general media than personal ones." He thought the video was terribly obvious, as if it were "closed-captioned for the thinking-impaired," and concluded: "Still, for sheer political horror, nothing can outdo the most amazing footage here, shot during the era that produced that classic LP *Allman and Woman*."

It is not generally known that Cher's experience with videos goes way back to before the days of MTV. She starred in one of the very first music videos back in 1980, when Casablanca wanted a short promotional film to illustrate her single "Hell on Wheels," from the bomb album *Prisoner*, to be shown on European television. Producer-director Roger Flint was given a great deal of creative leeway and told to be as "outrageous" as possible. "We wanted the film to be as 'hot' as the lyrics and sound. We came up with three different concepts," said Flint. Cher and her associates chose the concept that Flint liked the best but that was the hardest to execute.

The basic idea was to show Cher skating down a highway, smoke pouring out of the wheels. First she has an encounter with truckers in a big semi, who follow her as she leads them on seductively. Cher makes her way safely past a wooden barricade, but the truck smashes into it because the driver is so bewitched with her beauty. Cher then arrives at a truck stop full of all sorts of hunky guys—cops, cowboys, bikers, surfers—all of whom are hypnotized by her appearance. Also in the crowd at the truck stop were the two female impersonators (of Midler and Ross) that Cher was using in her stage act at the time. Everyone jumps into a car or truck and follows Cher on down the highway in a blaze of hot wheels and dust. Flint and crew were able to put it all together in about three weeks and greatly enjoyed working with Cher, who was apparently making music videos before they even had a name for them.

Her most controversial video is the one for *If I Could Turn Back Time*, filmed on a battleship, wherein Cher wears her "X-rated underwear," which shows off her rear-end tattoos, straddles a cannon suggestively, struts around the deck, flirting with the sailors (she steals one guy's cap at one point), and generally comporting herself in a manner that would make Miss Lace (Milton Caniff's famous cartoon gal who was "friends" with all the World War II servicemen) blush in embarrassment. Other rock performers were outraged with what MTV let Cher get away with.

Sam Kinison explained, "There's a double standard at MTV. Cher can walk around in *complete nudity*." Billy Idol was also upset with the way Madonna could do bondage scenes and appear with "more or less her bazooms hanging out." Robin Gibb of the Bee Gees felt that Cher and other rock performers, including his group, were trying not so much to push the grounds of good taste as to capture the attention of their fans. No one was deliberately trying to be controversial.

With Cher, though, you never can tell.

Cher was inadvertently embroiled with more controversy when Andrew Dice Clay ad-libbed "a Jack Spratt rhyme with an oral-anal twist," according to Bob Colacello, as he introduced Cher to the MTV awards audience and got banned from the channel for life. Tabloids have also tried to create a major feud between Cher and Madonna, with a *Star* poll of readers determining that the former was liked much more than her "younger competitor."

Madonna has based a lot of her image on Cher, and it is no secret that Cher is not too crazy about her. She says she understands where Madonna is coming from—she's undergoing many of the same things Cher had to go through in her struggle for stardom—but Cher finds Madonna rude and unpleasant. In any case, the women both are probably much too busy to devote that much time to their "feud." However, now that Cher has gone public with her feelings (in *Vanity Fair*), there's no telling what may transpire between these two.

Most will agree that in spite of similarities in their respective styles and images, Cher has it all over Madonna. Cher is better-looking. Cher has a better voice. And Cher is certainly a better actress (and more successful in films). Cher may be tacky and vulgar in her costuming at times, but she still looks, by and large, more wholesome and attractive than Madonna.

To her credit, Cher has used her high visibility for a number of causes and charities. These include the National Craniofacial Foundation, with which she became involved during the making of *Mask* and which helps disfigured children. She is also heavily affiliated with the Pediatric AIDS Foundation. "Children with AIDS aren't getting the same attention as adults," she told Liz

Smith as she was preparing for a fund-raising event with Alan Alda in Washington in 1989.

She even went so far as to "use" her sexy image to help save women's lives in 1987. An ad appeared in *People* magazine with a provocative picture of Cher and the headline I NEVER SHOWER ALONE. Once she had your attention, it turned out to be a public service announcement for the Coors High Priority Shower Card, which contained instructions on how to do a monthly self-examination for breast cancer.

Although Cher does have political convictions and has campaigned for, and openly supported, candidates such as Michael Dukakis, whose cousin Olympia Dukakis played Cher's mother in *Moonstruck*, and Jimmy Carter, she does not get as much press coverage for her politics as she does for her "carryings-on." Because of this, politicos have come to regard her endorsements as a mixed blessing. She does have strong beliefs, however, and has indicated that if the *Roe* v. *Wade* decision is overturned by the Supreme Court, she will be out there marching, picketing, and getting herself arrested, if necessary, along with tens of thousands of other women.

She does not consider herself an out-and-out feminist because as she admits, she doesn't quite know what a feminist is. "I like men a lot. I have a sense of humor about myself. I don't care if people pose nude for *Playboy*, so I don't know if I'm a feminist or what. I don't really want to be anything. I don't like labels, and I don't like labeling other people. I respect people for who they are, and I don't care if they're not like me."

She is friends with Gloria Steinem (one can't imagine that they're particularly close friends, however). Her oft-quoted comment to Gloria: "My friends think that you're a tight-ass and your friends think that I'm a bimbo, so by all rights we shouldn't have anything to do with each other!"

Another woman Cher greatly admires is Jane Fonda, who she thinks is a talented, profound, and dedicated person. "I don't think I could be as strong as she has been to do what you believe in even when it goes against everyone else's opinion," she told Mary

Hart. Cher, however, was always rather oblivious of the political scene in the sixties and seventies, and it probably did not register on her that no matter how well meaning "Hanoi Jane" may have been, she hurt, dismayed, and infuriated a great many Americans by her actions. Sonny has always been severely disapproving of Jane, possibly the real reason why Cher admires her so much.

Cher is concerned about the social problems in her country and has said that she'd like to divide her time between her career and working for a better America. She was highly impressed with Jimmy Carter, had dinner with him at the White House when he was in office, and was moved by Carter's commitment to helping the many homeless and hungry people in the United States as well as doing something about the growing rate of illiteracy.

At one point she even went so far as to volunteer at a women's shelter near her home but was told by those in charge that there was no volunteer program and there was nothing she could do.

Cher has supposedly been criticized for not doing her bit to promote the Armenian-American community when she has spoken out on so many other issues and even recorded a song about being a "half-breed" Indian when she's more Armenian than Cherokee. (She is a mixture of Armenian, Cherokee Indian, and French, with recurring reports [for those interested in such detail] that her mother is part English, Irish, and German as well.)

Although the Armenian-American story was printed in a respectable magazine, not a tabloid, the protesting organizations and individuals were not named, and neither were the sources. Cher once told an interviewer: "I don't know many Armenians"; possibly she does not perceive them as being particularly discriminated against in any case. It must also be remembered that her father was Armenian and her relationship with him was not good, to put it mildly, so there is no reason why Cher should go out of her way to label herself an Armenian or Armenian-American when she has no ties to the community (or to Armenia) and hates being labeled as *anything*.

Cher has said that she likes a good piece of gossip as well as the next person, but she finds it hard to keep a sense of humor about some of the things that have been printed about her. "Some stories can really hurt you," she has said, "because then people want to like you but they think you're so crazy that how could they possibly respect you?" She hates the idea that people think she's actually giving out interviews to some of these rags—"CHER'S EXCLUSIVE STORY!!!"—and that there's a danger people will get sick of her, along the lines of "I don't *care* about Cher's new boyfriend!"

On occasion the tabloids may start with a grain of truth and then "elaborate" on it. A story about Cher's getting a human ear in the mail from an obsessed fan probably had its origins in the case of Ralph Nau, who spent four years traveling twenty thousand miles to pursue three singers he particularly "admired": Olivia Newton-John, Sheena Easton, and Cher. Nau not only attended their concerts but entered private locations where he thought he might find them. Frustrated in his attempts to interact with these ladies and other celebrities, he eventually began sending them threats.

In 1984 Nau murdered his younger stepbrother with an ax but was freed on a technicality. In late 1989 a judge ruled that Nau be placed in an Illinois mental institution for up to sixty days because he posed a danger to others. At a hearing in which Nau hoped to prove he should not be institutionalized, a joint statement from Newton-John, Easton, and Cher was read. (The three women shared a security adviser, Gavin de Becker.)

When Cher gets really angry, she sues. In 1981 she did an interview with writer Fred Robbins for *US* magazine. She insisted it be redone because it focused on her past instead of new career objectives, and *US* wound up running an entirely different interview from the one it'd received from Robbins. Information from Robbin's interview allegedly wound up in *Forum* magazine, published by *Penthouse*'s Bob Guccione, and the supermarket tabloid the *Star*. Cher sued *Forum*, the *Star*, and Robbins for $100,000 in general damages and $5 million in punitive damages. In 1982 she won a $663,234 judgment against the *Star* and *Forum* for "misappropriation of her name and likeness for commercial purposes."

The *Star* had the damage award reversed. Its court papers read: "What is at issue here is an emotional celebrity's blatant attempt to muzzle the press by limiting the publications which can write about her career to those she favors."

Cher also sued the *National Enquirer* for fifteen million dollars in 1988, when it claimed she chewed out Eddie Murphy backstage at the Academy Awards because he accused the Academy of discriminating against blacks. Cher told columnist William Norwich that she not only did not see Murphy backstage but never even heard his remarks. Apparently the *Enquirer* even called for confirmation of the story and was told it never happened.

Cher started getting a "big black backlash." Bill Cosby even called her up to criticize her over what he'd read in the *Enquirer*. That proves that sometimes people do take the tabloids seriously. They figure where there's smoke there's fire, and the tabloids are *correct* often enough to create just enough doubt in a reader's mind about a given story's lack of credibility.

In some ways Cher asks for trouble. While making her personal tour for Uninhibited, Cher heard a woman in the crowd yell out that she was having trouble seeing her idol. "That's because of all the stupid press people," Cher replied. It was rather tactless remark to pass when the whole purpose of her appearance was to publicize her new perfume—with the help of the press, which had attended the event.

Columnist Chris Chase really let her have it: "We all know how Cher hates to be photographed. Or even noticed. But the darn old press won't leave her alone. When she goes to the Academy Awards and flashes her belly button, or appears on the Letterman show wearing tights so revealing we can see the tattoo on her tail, some moron from the press always violates her privacy by taking her picture or writing about her. . . . Cher, honey, if you don't want us 'stupid press people' trailing you, get a real job."

Fans and the media have put these people in their exalted positions in the first place, but once they *get* there, the celebrity message seems to be: "Get lost. I'll call you when I need you." Cher has rationalized that no one in show business ever really expects to be successful, and once he is, he doesn't expect to become really famous, and by that time it's too late to back out. "Many others have had a much more difficult time giving up their privacy than I have, but it's something you don't know about at first," she has said.

Cher became famous at an early age. She never really went through the years of starvation and struggle that so many artists (including far more talented people) have to go through—often without payoff. If she had, she might realize that an occasional sleazy or stupid tabloid story is a small price to pay for the power and privileges she enjoys that so many people covet but will never themselves possess.

Cher doesn't know why so many people admire her. She turned the tables on interviewer Jay Gissen and asked him: "How do we make the universal *yes* on Cher? How do we all get together and go: Robin Givens is a bitch? Where does all *that* come from?" She suspects people admire her because she achieved the impossible: going from national joke to Oscar-winning movie star. Perhaps that is why she won the People's Choice Award for Favorite All Around Female Entertainer.

She has won other "honors" over the years besides her Oscar and People's Choice Award. In 1985 she was chosen Woman of the Year at Harvard's Hasty Pudding Theatrical Awards, where she was given an oversize bra as well as the traditional pudding pot, which she said she'd make into an earring. At the ceremony she was teased about her one-word name, physique, and bizarre attire, then was paraded through Harvard Square with jugglers and cross-dressed actors in tow.

Some people have been Cher admirers and boosters for years, long before she became an "actress" of note. As Michael Musto put it, "I must admit I am getting a little tired of Cher's 'fame without achievement is hollow' shtick—I think she reached her pinnacle in '70s Bob Mackie ensembles with her real nose, vamping and wisecracking on TV, jumping so wholeheartedly onto the machine—that wasn't achievement?"

Women find much to admire in Cher, such as her "putting up with Sonny Bono, tumbling him over, and getting on with her life," or so says Carol Altomare, a working woman in New York. "I like the fact that . . . she's forty-plus but doesn't look it, and constantly flouts convention. Those wild outfits of hers give her a very dynamic and unique appearance—she really carries it off!"

Columnist Stephanie Brush understood Cher's appeal to women when she saw her telling off her son's junior high school principal in *Mask*: "I realized then that she performs the function for women moviegoers that Jack Nicholson has always fulfilled for men. Free of the burden of ever having been America's sweetheart, she is the one who represents us in our revenge fantasies, telling all the fatheads and bureaucrats and half-witted pencil-pushers exactly where they can go. You need to be more than beautiful to get away with this. You need to have been Cher for 40 years."

Yet there were indications that more people disliked Cher than liked her—at least before she won her Oscar. In 1987 her Q rating—determined by the private Long Island-based firm of Marketing Evaluations/TV Q—indicated that although she was well known, she was not well liked, with a figure that was "below the mean for actresses," according to *The New York Times*. Her popularity had been highest when she was on television in the seventies.

Yet it is just possible that Cher is one of those entertainers who even delight their "disapprovers." People may smack their lips over her private life—at least what they are told of it in the tabloids—but it won't necessarily keep them from going to see one of her movies. Such people who were asked about Cher for this book—nonfans, that is—thought that she was a good actress and admired certain of her films (*Moonstruck* was the one most often cited).

Although Cher makes less money than Madonna and Oprah

Winfrey, both of whom made the Forbes top ten list of entertainment money-makers in 1990, she is still considered to have
quite a lot of clout, making the *Ladies' Home Journal*'s list of the
fifty most powerful women in America that same year.

Cher doesn't like having to be a businessperson; it's too boring
and too tough. "People try to fuck you every time you turn
around. If you're a woman, I believe it's harder because women
aren't supposed to stand up for what they want. If you're nice,
they walk all over your ass, and if you stand up for what you
want, you're a bitch—there's no happy medium. Sometimes you
can go too far and be an unadulterated cunt."

Cher finds it hard being in a man's world "when you have
to go fight your battles and all the people you work with. . . . I
find myself now preferring to spend time with women when I
want to fool around and have fun." While she feels there's nothing
like a man for a romance, she seems to "have a lot more in common
with my girl friends."

Many feel that aspiring entertainers can learn much from
studying Cher. Says producer Curtis Roberts, who has socialized
with her and is a longtime Cher watcher: "Young hopefuls could
do well to observe and analyze her career to date, her standards
and ambition which have helped her to become a world-renowned
'class act' in all media."

Barbara Barondess MacLean, the actress-writer-designer who
made her mark for decades in a world of men, says Cher has done
much to reaffirm women's place in life and the world. "She is a
feminist in the best sense of that term; she has demonstrated that
a woman can live an independent, fulfilled life apart from men.
It is *good* for women uncertain of their destiny, their talents, and
their hopes to have Cher for a role model."

Now that Cher has conquered the worlds of TV, film, and
music, she's setting her sights on the world of publishing. Her
fitness book came out early in 1990, and she is said to be working
on her autobiography. (Sonny Bono is also due to come out with
his own "tell all" book, reportedly in fall 1991, as is Cher's mother,

Georgia Holt.) Sonny will apparently spill intimate personal details, but it all will probably be about his relationship with Cher; no one in 1991 would read a Sonny Bono book for any other reason.

Cher is living proof of her personal philosophy that your life is your own and you only get one chance. "This is not a dress rehearsal for your life; this is it," she has said. Some might construe Cher's doctrine as being one of selfishness, a spawn of the me generation: think of A Number One, ignore responsibilities. But that's not Cher's message at all. What she is saying is that a person can either choose to float along on the sea of life, dreaming of what might be but never getting there, or take command of his or her fate to bring about his or her desired life.

At one point Cher let somebody else, Sonny, do it for her, and she has always regretted it. Perhaps she believes that if she had acted on her own initiative, she might have become just as successful without the years of "slavery" and heartache that came with it. True, Cher has advantages (money, for one thing) that the average person does not have, but anyone can still try to make improvements within the boundaries and limitations that life may have imposed.

"You could be great," she admits. "You could be a lot better than me and not be successful. A lot of it is luck. It's not enough just to be good—which is kind of sad—but it's true." Nevertheless, if Cher hadn't taken the risk of failing—first on the Broadway stage, then in serious roles in pictures—today she might well be doing one unsold sitcom pilot after another instead of being one of the most bankable women movie stars in Hollywood.

Cher's tale of triumph, her show business victory, has to be taken in perspective, of course. She goes on about how she hated being poor, but she wasn't poor for very long. She had her first hit record with Sonny while she was still in her teens. She talks about her "difficult struggle," but things have come rather easily for her. She has been called a survivor and a heroine when actually she is neither. A survivor is someone who lives through a plane crash, and a heroine is someone like Maria Hernandez, who gave her life in the struggle to remove crack dealers from her Bushwick, Queens, neighborhood. Next to that, Cher can't hold a candle.

Still, she has come very far from the confused, angry child, dark of hair and swarthy of complexion, who was mad at world and mother because all the good things seemed to happen only to blond blue-eyed people, not to her. Her mother always told her that she might not be the best or prettiest, but she was *special*. And in spite of their frequent arguments, which rage unabated to this day, Cher has undoubtedly forgiven her mother much because of that—the sense of *specialness* that kept her going when many others would have simply succumbed and given up. In her case she reinvented herself; she became *Cher*.

Today Cher has an enviable life, a dream life. She is a fantasy princess living in fantasy palaces with fantasy men. She has reached the plateau that every artist aspires to: the freedom to do what they want, to have a career that is important, and to *make a living* at it besides. She has money, friends, romance, and fulfillment. This is why she is so endlessly fascinating to all those who, unlike her, lead lives of "quiet desperation."

Let's hope she's grateful.

FILMOGRAPHY

1967

Good Times. Producer, Lindsley Parsons. Director, William Friedkin. Screenplay, Tony Barrett, from a story by Nicholas Hyams. Sonny and Cher (themselves); George Sanders (Mr. Mordicus); Norman Alden (Warren); Lennie Weinrib (Garth); Edy Williams, China Lee, Diane Haggerty (Mordicus' Girls); Larry Duran (Smith); Peter Robbins (Brandon); Kelly Thordsen (Tough Hombre); Hank Warden (Roy); Phil Arnold (Solly). Columbia. 91 minutes.

1969

Chastity. Producer, Sonny Bono. Director, Alessio de Paolo. Screenplay and music, Sonny Bono. Camera, Ben Coleman. Editor, Hugo Grimaldi. Assistant director, William Lukather. Cher (Chastity); Barbara London (Diana Midnight); Stephen Whittaker

(Eddie); Tom Nolan (Tommy); Danny Zapien (Cab Driver); Elmer Valentine (First Truck Driver); Burke Rhind (Salesman); Richard Armstrong (Husband); Joe Light (Master of Ceremonies); Dolly Hunt (Church Lady); Jason Clarke (Second Truck Driver). American International Pictures. 81 minutes.

1982

Come Back to the Five and Dime, Jimmy Dean, Jimmy Dean. Executive Producer, Giraud Chester. Director, Robert Altman. Screenplay, Ed Graczyk, based on his play. Director of photography, Pierre Mignot. Editor, Jason Rosenfield. Sandy Dennis (Mona); Cher (Sissy); Karen Black (Joanne); Sudie Bond (Juanita); Kathy Bates (Stella Mae); Marta Heflin (Edna Louise); Mark Patton (Joe); Caroline Aaron (Martha); Ruth Miller (Clarissa); Gena Ramsel (Sue Ellen); Ann Risley (Phyllis Marie); Dianne Turley Travis (Alice Ann). A Sandcastle production released by Cinecom International Films. 109 minutes.

1983

Silkwood. Producers, Mike Nichols and Michael Hausman. Director, Mike Nichols. Screenwriters, Nora Ephron and Alice Arlen. Director of photography, Miroslav Ondricek. Editor, Sam O'Steen. Music, Georges Delerue. Meryl Streep (Karen Silkwood); Kurt Russell (Drew Stephens); Cher (Dolly Pelliker); Craig T. Nelson (Winston); Diana Scarwid (Angela); Fred Ward (Morgan); Ron Silver (Paul Stone); Charles Hallahan (Earl Lapin); Josef Summer (Max Richter); Sudie Bond (Thelma Rice); Henderson Forsythe (Quincy Bissell); E. Katherine Kerr (Gilda Schultz); Bruce McGill (Mace Hurley); David Strathairn (Wesley); J. C. Quinn (Curtis Schultz). ABC Pictures/Twentieth Century Fox. 131 minutes. Rated R.

1985

Mask. Producer, Martin Starger. Director, Peter Bogdanovich. Screenplay by Anna Hamilton Phelan, based on the true story of Rocky Dennis. Director of photography, Laszlo Kovacs. Editor Barbara Ford. Music, various composers. Makeup, Michael Westmore. Cher (Rusty Dennis); Sam Elliott (Gar); Eric Stoltz (Rocky Dennis); Estelle Getty (Evelyn); Richard Dysart (Abe); Laura Dern (Diana); Micole Mercurio (Babe); Harry Carey, Jr. (Red); Dennis Burkley (Dozer); Lawrence Monoson (Ben); Ben Piazza (Mr. Simms); Alexandra Powers (Lisa); L. Craig King (Eric); Kelly Minter (Lorrie); Les Dudek (Bone). Universal. 120 minutes. Rated PG-13.

1987

The Witches of Eastwick. Executive Producers, Rob Cohen, Don Devlin. Producers, Neil Canton, Peter Guber, Jon Peters. Director, George Miller. Screenplay, Michael Cristofer, based on the book by John Updike. Director of photography, Vilmos Zsigmond. Production designer, Polly Platt. Editors, Hubert C. de la Bouillerie, Richard Francis-Bruce. Music, John Williams. Costume designer, Aggie Guerard Rodgers. Jack Nicholson (Daryl Van Horne); Cher (Alexandra); Michelle Pfeiffer (Suki); Susan Sarandon (Jane); Veronica Cartwright (Felicia). Warner Brothers. 118 minutes. Rated R.

Suspect. Producer, Daniel A. Sherkow. Director, Peter Yates. Screenplay, Eric Roth. Photography, Billy Williams. Production designer, Stuart Wurtzel. Editor, Ray Lovejoy. Music, Michael Kamen. Cher (Kathleen Riley); Dennis Quaid (Eddie Sanger); Liam Neeson (Carl Wayne Anderson); John Mahoney (Judge Matthew Helms); Joe Mantegna (Charlie Stella); Philip Bosco (Paul Gray). Tri-Star Pictures. 118 minutes. Rated R.

★ ★ ★

Moonstruck. Producers, Patrick Palmer and Norman Jewison. Director, Norman Jewison. Screenplay, John Patrick Shanley. Photographer, David Watkin. Production designer, Philip Rosenberg. Editor, Lou Lombardo. Music, Dick Hyman. Cher (Loretta Castorini); Nicolas Cage (Ronny Cammareri); Vincent Gardenia (Cosmo Castorini); Olympia Dukakis (Rose Castorini); Danny Aiello (Johnny Cammareri); Rita Cappomaggi (Julie Bovasso); Anita Gillette (Mona); John Mahoney (Professor Perry). MGM/United Artists. 100 minutes. Rated PG.

1990

Mermaids. Director, Richard Benjamin. Screenplay, June Roberts, based on the novel by Patty Dunn. Cher (Mrs. Flax); Winona Ryder (Charlotte); Christina Ricci (Kate); Bob Hoskins (Lou Landsky). Orion.

SELECTIVE DISCOGRAPHY

1964: Assorted backup vocals for various artists on records produced by Phil Spector.

"Ringo, I Love You" (single), billed as Bonnie Jo Mason for Annette Records.

"The Letter" (single), recorded with Sonny Bono as Caesar and Cleo.

"Love Is Strange" (single), Caesar and Cleo.

"Yes, Sir, That's My baby" (single), all-star recording included Cher and many top acts billed as Hale and the Hushabyes.

"Baby, Don't Go" (single), Sonny and Cher on Reprise Records.

1965: "I Got You, Babe" (single), Sonny and Cher.
Look at Us (album) Sonny and Cher.
All I Really Want to Do (album), Cher.
"Dream Baby" (single), billed as Cherilyn.

"Where Do You Go?" (single), Cher.
"Laugh at Me" (single), Sonny Bono.

1966: "Bang, Bang (My Baby Shot Me Down)" (single), Cher.
Sonny Side of Cher (album), Cher.
Alfie sound track album (Cher sings theme song on album and in the film).

1967: "The Beat Goes On" (single), Sonny and Cher.
Good Times sound track album; single "Little Things," Sonny and Cher.
With Love (album); single "You'd Better Sit Down, Kids," Cher on Imperial Records.

1970: *3614 Jackson Highway* (album), Cher on Atco Records.

1971: "Gypsies, Tramps and Thieves" (single), Cher.
"All I Ever Need Is You" (single), Sonny and Cher.
Cher (album); single "The Way of Love," Cher.

1972; "A Cowboy's Work Is Never Done," Sonny and Cher.
Foxy Lady (album); singles "Living in a House Divided" and "Don't Hide Your Love," Cher.
Mama Was a Rock and Roll Singer (album), Sonny and Cher.
Bittersweet White Light (album), Cher.

1973: "Half-Breed" (single), Cher.

1974: *Dark Lady* (album); singles "Train of Thought" and "I Saw a Man (and He Danced with His Wife)," Cher.

1975: "A Woman's Story"/ "Be My Baby" (singles), Cher.

1976: "(A Love Like Yours) Don't Come Knocking Every Day"
(single), Cher and Harry Nilsson.
Stars (album), Cher.

1977: "You're Not Right for Me" (single), Sonny and Cher.
Two the Hard Way (album), Cher with Gregg Allman, billed
as Allman and Woman.
Cherished (album); singles "Pirate" and "War Paint, Soft
Feathers," Cher, on Warner Brothers.

1979: *Take Me Home* (album), Cher, on Casablanca.
Prisoner (album); single "Holdin' Out for Love," Cher.

1980: *Black Rose* (album), with Les Dudek and band, billed as Black
Rose.

1982: *I Paralyze* (album), Cher, on Columbia Records.

1987: *Cher* (album), Cher, for Geffen Records.

1989: *Heart of Stone* (album), Cher.

SELECTIVE BIBLIOGRAPHY

Allen, Jennifer. "Cher and Altman on Broadway." *New York* (February 1982).

Cameron, Julia. "Were the Critics Prepared to Hate 'Jimmy Dean'?" Los Angeles *Herald Examiner*, February 22, 1982.

Carlson, Peter. " 'Silkwood's' Real-Life Characters." *People* (February 20, 1984).

Chase, Donald. "Bewitched, Bothered and Betrayed." New York *Sunday News*, May 3, 1987.

Connelly, Christopher. "Uncommon Women." *Premiere* (November 1990).

Ebert, Roger. "Cher-ing Thoughts." New York *Post*, October 21, 1987.

Gissen, Jay. "Cher Struck." *Cable Guide* (March 1989).

Goodwin, Jan. "What's Next for Cher?" *Ladies' Home Journal* (September 1988).

Guthmann, Edward. "Cher Strikes Again." San Francisco *Chronicle*, January 17, 1988.

Heitland, Jon. *The Man from U.N.C.L.E. Book*. New York: St. Martin's Press, 1987.

Jerome, Jim. "Cher's Got Critics Raving." *People* (March 18, 1985).

Kearns, Michael. "Cher, an Actress, Y'Know?" *Drama-Logue* (January 20, 1983).

Leeds, Nina. "Cher Unmasked." *US* (April 8, 1985).

Munn, Michael. *The Hollywood Murder Casebook*. New York: St. Martin's Press, 1987.

Quirk, Lawrence J. *Fasten Your Seat Belts: The Passionate Life of Bette Davis*. New York: William Morrow, 1990.

Ross-Leming, Eugenie, and David Standish. Interview with Cher. *Playboy* (December 1988).

Schoell, William. "Suspect (review)." *Quirk's Reviews* (December 1987).

———. "Loverboy (review)." *Quirk's Reviews* (July 1989).

Sessums, Kevin. "Cher—Starred and Feathered." *Vanity Fair* (November 1990).

Silverman, Stephen M. " 'Moonstruck'—on Spec." New York *Post*, December 28, 1987.

———. "The 9 Faces of Cher: Part One." New York *Post*, May 28, 1985.

Stokes, Edward Geoffrey, and Ken Tucker. *Rock of Ages: The Rolling Stone History of Rock and Roll*. New York: Rolling Stone Press/Summit Books, 1986.

Taraborrelli, J. Randy. *Cher*. New York: St. Martin's Press, 1986.

Wallace, Carol. " 'I Know Nothing About Men.' " New York *Sunday News*, February 14, 1982.

Warhol, Andy. "Cher at the Pierre." *Interview* (September 1974).

———, and Bob Colacello. "Cher." *Interview* (March 1982).

Wolf, Jeanne. "The Many Faces of Cher." *Ladies' Home Journal* (August 1987).

Wolf, William. "Cher." *Moviegoer* (January 1984).

Worth, Fred L. *Rock Facts*. New York: Facts on File, 1985.

Index